READING
CAVELL'S
The World Viewed

Contemporary Film and Television Series

A complete listing of the books in this series can be found at the back of this volume.

General Editor
Barry Grant
Brock University

Advisory Editors
Patricia B. Erens
University of Hong Kong

Lucy Fischer
University of Pittsburgh

Peter Lehman
University of Arizona

Caren J. Deming
University of Arizona

Robert J. Burgoyne
Wayne State University

READING
CAVELL'S
The World Viewed

A Philosophical Perspective
on Film

William Rothman
and
Marian Keane

WAYNE STATE UNIVERSITY PRESS   DETROIT

04 03 02 01 00 5 4 3 2 1

Library of Congress Cataloging-in-Publication Data

Rothman, William.
Reading Cavell's The world viewed : a philosophical
perspective on film / William Rothman and Marian Keane.
        p.   cm. — (Contemporary film and television series)
Includes bibliographical references and index.
ISBN 0-8143-2895-4 (alk. paper) — ISBN 0-8143-2896-2 (pbk. : alk. paper)
1. Motion pictures—Philosophy.   2. Cavell, Stanley, 1926 – World viewed.   3. Cavell,
Stanley, 1926 – World viewed.   I. Keane, Marian.   II. Title.   III. Series.
PN1995 .R685 2000
791.43'01—dc21
00-008768

For
Kitty Morgan and Marie Flynn Keane

CONTENTS

Preface   9

List of Abbreviations   12

Introduction   13

Reading *The World Viewed*

I   The Preface: A METAPHYSICAL MEMOIR   35

II   Chapters 1–5:   WHAT IS FILM?   42

III   Chapters 6–9:   FILM'S ORIGINS AND HISTORY   87

IV   Chapters 10–11:   THE END OF THE MYTHS   127

V   Chapters 12–13:   THE WORLD AS A WHOLE   140

VI   Chapters 14–15:   AUTOMATISM   174

VII   Chapters 16–18:   FILM AND THEATRICALITY   196

VIII   Chapter 19:   "THE ACKNOWLEDGMENT OF SILENCE"   233

Appendix:
Cavell's Philosophical Procedures and *Must We Mean What We Say?*   261

Notes   279

Index   285

PREFACE

The pages that follow present a consecutive reading of *The World Viewed*, Stanley Cavell's second book, published in 1971, between *Must We Mean What We Say?* and *The Senses of Walden*.

The World Viewed has been available for thirty years. Indeed, it has been available for the exact period during which film study has taken shape as an academic field in America and throughout the world. By reading *The World Viewed* as we do, in a way that uncovers and acknowledges its philosophical aspirations and depth, we seek to demonstrate its relevance to issues (for example: what film is; film's origins and history; film's relation to other arts, and to modernism; the conditions of film theory and criticism) fundamental to the study of film since its inception. *The World Viewed*'s perspective on such issues diverges in virtually every respect from the theoretical positions that have gained most prominence in the field. Our most compelling reason for undertaking this book was our sense of the importance and uniqueness of the perspective on film that *The World Viewed* articulates. We hope that the implications and consequences of the differences between the perspective set out in *The World Viewed* and the claims derived from other theoretical frameworks will present themselves as sufficiently interesting and vital to warrant their serious consideration.

When we were writing this book, we thought of all the colleagues we have met at film study conferences over the years who sincerely seek to express their ideas about film, and who are dissatisfied by certain of the procedures or obligations of the prevailing film theories. We also had in mind those of Cavell's readers, in many fields, to whom his work on film remains more or less uncharted territory.[1] Our reading is at once a response to *The World Viewed*'s words, to its ideas and its poetry, and an investigation of its leading concepts and philosophical procedures. It is also an investigation of the ground of our conviction that *The World Viewed* even now, thirty years after its publication, is capable of inspiring and encouraging readers to think in radically different ways about film.

9

We suspect that it will surprise many of our readers that *The World Viewed* is as relevant as it is to current issues in film theory and, moreover, that it is relevant because of its richly philosophical perspective. But one feature of *The World Viewed* likely to surprise nearly every reader is its reliance on memory. *The World Viewed*'s reliance on memory underscores the fact that it was written in the days (remember them?) before VCRs, laser discs, and cable television, not to mention DVDs, enabled us to "quote" films as Cavell himself does in his later writings—with the kind of textual accuracy long available to the study of literature. It also underscores the fact, which we can now take for granted, that there exists a field of film study that, like all fields, defines itself through particular conventions, procedures, standards, and goals of scholarship.

We are well aware that no serious or ambitious book about film can be written from memory now. It is no doubt a good thing that film study has incorporated the kind of accuracy facilitated by ever-advancing technology. But this development has had, perhaps, a hidden cost. Serious writing about film is now able to be, and required to be, accurate in this way. *The World Viewed* is equally committed to being accurate, but differently accurate. Its challenge is to be accurate to its author's experience of the films he writes about. Cavell is unerringly precise in his characterizations of particular films, particular performances, particular moments, and his particular responses to them. At the same time, he connects films and ideas in unexpected and provocative ways. The freedom of thought that brings the pages of *The World Viewed* so vividly to life sometimes suggests to us that film study's transformation into a field may have blunted, or squelched, our sense of intellectual independence, our courage to think creatively about our own experience of film.

Before we began to write about *The World Viewed*, we taught the book in numerous film theory courses over the years. Teaching *The World Viewed*, we felt the need to develop pedagogical methods that encouraged students to be responsive to the book's claims and, in particular, its investigation of its author's subjectivity. Innovative strategies were called for in order to challenge students to reflect upon, and express, their own experience of film. Teaching *The World Viewed* revealed two procedures to be essential to following its thinking: paying close attention to the exact words on the book's pages, and checking Cavell's claims against our own experience of the films discussed in the book. These, we now can say with gratitude to all of our students, in Miami, Boulder, and Stockholm, form our essential procedures in the present volume. These procedures required us to read *The World Viewed* ever more systematically and closely. It emerged that the more closely we read *The World Viewed*, the more challenging we found the book. The results of our adventures to date in teaching and reading *The World Viewed* are the pages that follow.

Of all of *The World Viewed*'s claims, the one we perhaps wish most to share is this: that coming to know what films are—what film is—is inseparable from acquiring self-knowledge. *The World Viewed* envisions the acquisition of self-knowledge as a journey, not from place to place, but from one way of thinking, one form of life (as Wittgenstein would call it), to another. In Cavell's view, self-knowledge cannot be achieved apart from the acknowledgment of others. Yet we resist making ourselves intelligible to others. It requires that we take our thinking to task, ask why we think this and not that, discover why we are fixed on that interpretation, that view, that claim, as if our fixity on such matters reveals, to our surprise, not the validity of our theoretical positions, but our resistance to change, our resistance to becoming differently accurate, accurate to the specifics of our experience, hence to our specificity as unique selves.

The kind of understanding Cavell seeks by reading a film is not only an understanding about the film, but an understanding, we might say, with the film—an understanding that acknowledges the film's understanding of itself. We cannot understand a film's worth, its meaning, by applying a theory that dictates what we are to say, but only by entering into conversation with the film, as Cavell will put it in *Pursuits of Happiness*.

The *World Viewed* does not explicitly investigate, as *Pursuits of Happiness* and *Contesting Tears* do, what is meant by "reading"—the kind of understanding reading articulates—or by "conversation"—the nature of the relation to self and others conversation exemplifies. But *The World Viewed* provides a foundation for those later writings. It is *The World Viewed* that unguardedly proposes that when we speak or write about films we be responsive to what they have to say, and that we find words we can believe in, words accurate to our experience of them. Thirty years ago, such a proposal was radical. But here's the wonder: it may be even more radical today.

■ ■

We take pleasure in thanking the many people who read all or parts of the manuscript at various stages, and who generously shared their responses with us, enabling us to improve the book in innumerable ways. They include Stanley Bates, Gus Blaisdell, James Conant, Michael Fischer, Bruce Kawin, Gilberto Perez, and Charles Warren. For special encouragement and ongoing conversation, we thank Allan Casebier, Suranjan Ganguly, Tim Gould, Ira Jaffe, Jerry Kunkel, Michael Lydon, Ellen Mandel, Carla Marcantonio, Victor Perkins, Vlada Petric, Dorothy Slater-Brown, Kathleen Thomas Woodberry. We wish to thank Frank Tomasulo, who invited us to submit a version of Chapter 2 for publication in *The Journal of Film and Video*. For their support, we wish especially to thank Lesley Brill, who encouraged us to submit the manuscript to Wayne State University Press, and Arthur Evans, Director of the Press.

Finally, Bill Rothman would like to acknowledge Kitty Morgan, the love of his life, for her irreplaceable friendship and her good sense in choosing such a wonderful mother. And Marian Keane would like to thank her father, Austin Keane, for a lifetime of love, and to acknowledge her son, Jimmy Laff, whose skill on the computer saved many a lost file, and whose songs and smile have given her more joy than she can ever say.

ABBREVIATIONS

Works by Stanley Cavell are referenced throughout the book using the following abbreviations.

CH&U *Conditions Handsome and Unhandsome: The Constitution of Emersonian Perfectionism* (Chicago and London: The University of Chicago Press, 1990)

DK *Disowning Knowledge: In Six Plays of Shakespeare* (Cambridge: Cambridge University Press, 1987)

MWMWWS *Must We Mean What We Say?* (New York: Charles Scribner's Sons, 1969)

PH *Pursuits of Happiness: The Hollywood Comedy of Remarriage* (Cambridge: Harvard University Press, 1981)

PP *A Pitch of Philosophy: Autobiographical Exercises* (Cambridge, MA: Harvard University Press, 1994)

SSC "An Interview with Stanley Cavell," interview by James Conant, in *The Senses of Stanley Cavell*, Richard Fleming and Michael Payne, eds. (Lewisburg, Pa.: Bucknell University Press, 1989)

SW *The Senses of Walden: An Exploration of Thoreau's Masterpiece* (New York: Viking, 1972)

TNYUA *This New Yet Unapproachable America: Lectures after Emerson after Wittgenstein* (Albuquerque: Living Batch Press and Chicago: University of Chicago Press, 1989)

TOS *Themes Out of School: Effects and Causes* (San Francisco: North Point Press, 1984, reprinted, Chicago: University of Chicago Press, 1988)

WV *The World Viewed: Reflections on the Ontology of Film, Enlarged Edition* (Cambridge: Harvard University Press, 1979)

INTRODUCTION

Between World War II and the Cold War, there was an all-too-brief period when thoughtful people everywhere were joined in recognizing humanity's awesome responsibility for creating a new world order. American films like *The Best Years of Our Lives* and *It's a Wonderful Life* reflected this moment's humanistic spirit. In Japan, it was reflected in the great postwar films of directors like Yasujiro Ozu, Kenji Mizoguchi, and Akira Kurosawa. Perhaps most notably, the guarded optimism of this moment was expressed by the remarkable Italian films that comprised the so-called Neo-realist movement (Vittorio DeSica's *The Bicycle Thief*, Roberto Rossellini's *Rome: Open City*, and Luchino Visconti's *La terra trema*, for example), which so profoundly moved viewers—and inspired filmmakers—throughout the world.

Liberated France was flooded in the late forties with American movies that had not been available during the war. André Bazin, in his thoughtful and eloquent reviews and essays, articulated a realist alternative to the privileging of montage by Sergei Eisenstein and other Soviet filmmaker/theoreticians in the twenties. Bazin's guiding conviction was that by virtue of the privileged role reality plays in the film medium, cinema had a unique role to play in helping to create a more humane world order. He championed films he saw as committed to such a goal. Although there was an anthropological aspect to his writing, and despite his fondness for mathematical metaphors, Bazin's aspiration was not to posit a rational, scientific basis for film's power, but to acknowledge the medium's mysteries, which were rooted in mysteries intrinsic to reality itself.

In the fifties, the ambitious screening programs at the *Cinémathèque Française* presided over by the charismatic Henri Langlois enabled Parisians to immerse themselves, in a way never before possible, in the entire range of cinematic history. In the Paris of the fifties, many of the best young minds were steeped in the past and present achievements of the art of film. They felt, as Bazin did, that film had a political or moral mission. But they were also in love with movies, convinced that at their best they were of transcendent value in and of themselves. A new understanding and appreciation of film, a new film culture, was emerging.

The famous journal *Cahiers du cinéma* was a yardstick of the growth of this new film culture. The regular contributors to *Cahiers* were nurtured by Bazin, but their views differed in a number of respects from those of their mentor. For the likes of Francois Truffaut, Jean-Luc Godard, Eric Rohmer, Claude Chabrol, and Jacques Rivette, what was of greatest value about film was less the medium's unique relationship to reality than its possibilities for self-expression. Bazin never grasped what his younger proteges saw in the work of some of the "*auteurs*" they most admired (Hitchcock, for example). Nor did he share their burning desire to make films. In the pages of *Cahiers*, they were expressing exciting new ideas about film's aesthetic possibilities, ideas rooted in their understanding and appreciation of the history of the art of film. And, by the end of the fifties, the French film industry, struggling to stay afloat, was ready to provide these young critics/theorists with opportunities to make films of their own in which they could put their ideas into practice.

If the fifties represented a privileged moment in the emergence of film as a subject for serious criticism, this was in part because it represented a privileged period in the history of the art of film. Directors whose careers had begun in the forties, who openly declared themselves to be film artists—Ingmar Bergman, Federico Fellini, Michelangelo Antonioni, and Robert Bresson among them—were gaining international recognition. Hollywood *auteurs* of a new generation, such as Nicholas Ray and Vincente Minnelli, were striking out in new directions, exploiting the new technological possibilities such as wide screen. And the "old masters" like Jean Renoir, Carl Dreyer, Alfred Hitchcock, John Ford, and Howard Hawks (and Orson Welles, who straddled both generations) were still at the peak of their form.

A striking feature of *Cahiers*'s critical perspective was the conviction that the art of cinema was as much to be located inside as outside the commercial mainstream. There were popular films and genres that had never been taken seriously by intellectuals, yet were among the greatest achievements of the art of cinema, and great directors, authentic *auteurs* like Alfred Hitchcock, Howard Hawks, and John Ford, who had presided over their creation.

In the fifties and early sixties, the *Cahiers* critics were affirming that numerous popular movies—so familiar, so much a part of our lives as to be taken for granted—were profoundly meaningful works of art. And in order to back up their claims, the *Cahiers* critics strove to develop new critical terms—"mise-en-scène," for example—and new critical practices, such as shot-by-shot analysis, that might prove adequate to address the artistic significance of films that had always been regarded as mere "entertainments."

The other side of the fact (first pondered by art historian Erwin Panofsky) that film had remained popular rather than esoteric, avoiding the obscurity that was the fate of other arts in the modern period, is that the achievements of so many of film's greatest directors, who were able at will to tap into the powers of the medium, remained critically unacknowledged for so long. Unlike great jazz musicians, who were unrecognized by the culture at large but fully appreciated within their community of aficionados, many of the greatest filmmakers remained unknown even among their peers. The emergence of the new film culture exemplified by *Cahiers* meant that the absence of recognition, the unknownness that was the other side of the popularity of film, seemed to be coming to an end. Not coincidentally, this was happening at precisely the historical moment when filmmakers could no longer take for granted their ability to tap into the powers of the medium, the moment when the traditional genres were losing their hold over popular audiences.

That is, a new understanding and appreciation of the value of popular film emerged at the precise moment its traditions seemed to be breaking down. It was the moment film, its audience fragmenting, was ceding to television its position of dominance, the moment what could be called modernism was emerging in film—the "New Wave" films the *Cahiers* critics went on to make were catalysts in the emergence of a modernist cinema—as it had emerged so much earlier in arts such as painting, music, and poetry. The fifties represented at once a high water mark of the art of cinema and the moment it was for the first time possible to imagine that film as a *traditional* art was coming to an end. (After all, the great art of silent cinema became extinct at the very moment of its greatest flowering.)

A new film culture was emerging in America, too, especially in New York, which had succeeded Paris as the scene of the most important developments in modernist painting. Like Paris in the twenties, New York in the fifties was a center for an *avant-garde* cinema (the so-called New American Cinema) that identified itself with the *avant-garde* art world, not with popular movies. Jonas Mekas, who felt that film as an art owed nothing to Hollywood, was a leading critical voice of this movement. But Mekas shared the pages of *Film Culture* and *The Village Voice* with Andrew Sarris, who concurred with the *Cahiers* critics in regarding the best Hollywood films as the equal in artistic achievement to the most esteemed works of self-declared film artists.

In France, the new film culture was an intellectual and cultural movement, but not one driven to establish itself as an academic field. As late as the mid-sixties, film had not gained a foothold in American colleges and universities, either. But it was in America, not France, that film study first demanded recognition as a legitimate academic subject.

The immediate impetus for film's large-scale entrance into American colleges and universities was the political upheaval of the sixties. Pressures for including film in the curriculum came primarily from students. This reflected the fact that a new appreciation of film and its history had already come to exist among students. And it reflected the fact that young Americans felt that film, like rock music, was integral to their so-called counter-culture.

Film's entrance into the American academy was opposed by faculty members and administrators who argued that a mass medium like film lacked the artistic stature to make it a subject of study comparable to established arts such as music, painting, or literature. The advocates of film study, in turn, attacked the assumption that popular art was inferior to "high art." A half-century earlier, similar battle lines had been drawn over the worthiness of modern literature as a subject of study. The goal of those championing film's admission into the academy was not only to assure that films were studied, but studied in a way that took seriously their artistic achievements, their own ways of thinking about society, about human relationships, and about their condition as films.

The legitimacy of studying film sociologically (as an alleged cause of "juvenile delinquency," for example), or within a context of experimental psychology, was not at issue. Those were not the kinds of study film's advocates were struggling to establish. What they were championing, rather, was a study of film that undertook to acknowledge the value of film as a medium of artistic expression. In America in the late sixties and early seventies, the fledgling field of film study was struggling, against powerful forces inside and outside the university, to win recognition for film as a worthy subject of critical study, and at the same time to win recognition for the study of film as a legitimate intellectual discipline.

As the above account implies, when the case for the academic study of film was originally made to American university administrations and faculties, film study predominantly envisioned itself as a new field of criticism. The works to be studied were to encompass, but not be limited to, ordinary movies, in particular American movies of what the field has since come to call the classical period (the thirties and forties, especially). And the new field predicated its claim for legitimacy on the conviction that the artistic achievements of cinema, importantly but not exclusively the achievements of American classical cinema, called for serious critical acknowledgment, and on the corollary conviction that no existing academic field was capable of the kind of criticism film called for. The medium of film was different from every other medium. Film study could not validly begin by adopting preexisting theories, taking for granted their applicability to film, but only by reflecting philosophically on the testimony of movies themselves, the testimony of our experience of movies. Films called for the creation of new terms of criticism, new modes of critical thought capable of taking instruction from films' own ways of thinking.

From the beginnings of film history, it has remained a mystery what it is that actually takes place within and among silent viewers sitting in those darkened theaters. In the thirties and forties, film could be said to have been our culture's dominant medium of expression. And yet public discourse about film (no doubt this was true of private conversation as well) has virtually never probed in a serious way our experience of movies, never attempted to articulate what movies really mean to us, our understanding of what they have to say to us. Movies address matters of intimacy and do so in a language of indirectness and silence. If we are to understand film's historical importance, or its present impact upon society and upon our lives, we must bring this experience, this knowledge, to consciousness.

Movies exercise a hold on us, a hold that, drawing on our innermost desires and fears, we participate in creating. To know films objectively, we have to know the hold they have upon us. To know the hold films have on us, we have to know ourselves objectively. And to know ourselves objectively, we have to know the impact of films on our lives. No study of film can claim intellectual authority if it is not rooted in self-knowledge, our knowledge of our own subjectivity. In the serious study of film, in other words, criticism must work hand in hand with the perspective of self-reflection that only philosophy is capable of providing. To back up its declaration of independence as an intellectual discipline, the field of film study needs to found itself, intellectually, upon a philosophical investigation of the ontology of the medium, and the art, of film. Such is the challenge *The World Viewed* takes upon itself.

In pursuing its philosophical investigation of film, *The World Viewed* embraces Ludwig Wittgenstein's methodological principle that we can find out what kind of object a thing is by investigating expressions which show the kinds of things that can be said about it. In all of his writings, Cavell proceeds (like Wittgenstein, and like Cavell's own professor of philosophy, J. L. Austin) by appealing philosophically to what we ordinarily say and mean.

To ask someone who has mastered the language—oneself, for example—such questions as "What should we say if . . . ?" or "In what circumstances would we call . . . ?" is to ask that person to say something about himself or herself. To come to know, through such a procedure, how we use a familiar word is to recognize something about what we do and what, and how, we think. Hence Cavell's appeals to ordinary language (like Freud's procedures of free association, dream analysis, investigation of verbal and behavioral slips, noting and analyzing "transferred" feeling, and so on) are procedures for acquiring self-knowledge. They are appeals to facts—about language, the world, ourselves—so obvious we cannot simply fail to know them. When what we fail to know is so obvious we cannot simply fail to know it, our ignorance cannot be cured by additional information, or by defining words or introducing new ones; it is a refusal to know. Knowing things we can fail to know only by refusing to know them reveals a special region of the concept of knowledge, one which is not a function of certainty but of acknowledgment. In investigating the kind of knowledge of which self-knowledge is a paradigm, Cavell employs philosophical procedures that enable one to acquire self-knowledge. Without knowing oneself, one cannot know what self-knowledge is.

To think seriously about film, *The World Viewed* is capable of teaching us, we must forsake the wish—without denying the depth of its motivation—for a scientific methodology that would provide an unchallengeable place, a place outside our own experience, to stand. To embrace theory as a higher authority than our experience of movies, as the field of film study has done, is to divorce the study of film from the philosophical perspective of self-reflection apart from which we cannot know what movies mean, or what they really are. It is to compound, rather than undo, their unknownness, to reinforce the philistine attitude of superiority to movies, and to their audiences, that it was the field's original aspiration to transcend or overcome.

When *The World Viewed* was published in 1971, however, the emerging field, for understandable historical reasons, altogether missed, or failed to take to heart, the book's true significance. From its first large-scale entrance into American universities, film study had cast its lot with criticism, and academic criticism in America was in the throes of a theoretical revolution, as a succession of powerful new theoretical frameworks and methodologies arrived from France.

One decisive early moment in this development was the publication in the late sixties of Peter Wollen's *Signs and Meaning in the Cinema*, an attempt to apply the structuralism of the French anthropologist Claude Lévi-Strauss to the study of the work of cinematic "auteurs" such as John Ford or Howard Hawks, and to genres of popular film such as the Western. Another is the work of the French film theorist Christian Metz, who championed a semiology of cinema, a scientific study of cinema's systems of signs or "codes."

In the aftermath of the political events of May 1968 in Paris, there was a major shift in the new French thought. This shift was made available to English-speaking film students through a series of translations published in the British journal *Screen*. The most provocative and influential of these essays was the first to be translated: a reading of John Ford's *Young Mr. Lincoln* written collectively by the editorial staff of *Cahiers du cinéma*. The *Young Mr. Lincoln* essay was significant less for the details of its reading— often misreading—of this particular film than for its attempt, the first of many, to incorporate the poststructuralist theories—mutually incompatible, one might well have thought—of the psychoanalyst Jacques Lacan, the Marxist philosopher Louis Althusser, and the literary critic/semiologist Roland Barthes. With this essay, *Cahiers du cinéma* found itself recanting its earlier affirmation of popular cinema as an art. *Cahiers* was now condemning films like *Young Mr. Lincoln*, as it was condemning popular cinema as a whole, as a repressive ideological apparatus.

The proper task in studying a film like *Young Mr. Lincoln*, the *Cahiers* piece argued, is not to acknowledge the film's thinking, but to expose its ways of not thinking, its systematic ways of repressing thought. Film study's new goal was not to grasp the astonishing capacities for meaningfulness that movies have discovered within the singular conditions of their medium, but to expose the ways movies are determined by the "codes" of the "dominant ideology." And the *Cahiers* editors assumed, on theoretical grounds, that those codes, and that ideology, were already fully known.

19

This shift, from valuing films as meaningful works of art whose own ways of thinking are capable of teaching us how we are to think about them to repudiating films as pernicious ideological constructs whose solicitations are to be resisted, was not motivated by the *results* of criticism. The *Cahiers* editors simply took for granted that their newly adopted Althusserian and Lacanian theoretical framework authorized them to detach themselves from their own experience and provided them with scientific knowledge of the objects they were studying. The essay's "conclusions" were dictated from above, as it were, by the higher authority of the theoretical systems they were applying to the film. And their privileging of theory over criticism, their denial of critical acts rooted in empirical experience, their forgoing of the philosophical perspective of self-reflection that *The World Viewed* had shown to be necessary for securing film study's independence as an intellectual discipline, increasingly set the agenda, and the tone, for the field of film study in the seventies and eighties—as if by bowing down to a higher authority a field lacking an intellectual foundation of its own could vicariously acquire the authority, the intellectual stature, of a science.

When film study in America—following and leading parallel developments in the study of literature—turned to the new French thought, it was attempting to *receive* philosophy, unaware that it was also forgoing philosophy. In response to America's traumatic experience of the late sixties and early seventies, when America was torn, every American was torn—agonizingly, ecstatically—between thinking and avoiding thought, Americans were turning to Europe in quest of ways of thinking that were freer, truer to their experience, than the traditional ways of thinking that were tearing America apart. But Americans were also turning to Europe to find relief from thinking about their own troubling experience.

In an illuminating interview with the philosopher James Conant, Cavell observes that the ascension of French theory was to be welcomed, because academic criticism in America "had been terribly undertheorized, much too dismissive and afraid of philosophy" (*SSC*, 64). Nonetheless, the fact that America "had to receive philosophy into the study of literature . . . at the hands of the French," Cavell goes on, "strikes me as an irony and a pity, however understandable the historical forces at play." That is because "the price of this reception, in the context in which literary studies have shunned philosophy as practiced in America, is that what is called philosophy by departments of literature is not by American criteria simply to be called philosophy."

When Cavell says that literary studies "have shunned philosophy as practiced in America," he is straightforwardly stating a fact, as he is when he says that "what is called philosophy by departments of literature is not by American criteria simply to be called philosophy." Behind these facts stands a further fact: Between philosophy as practiced professionally in America and England (where so-called analytical philosophy prevails) and philosophy as practiced in Europe (where philosophy edges closer to literature than to science or mathematics) there is a history of mutual ignorance, incomprehension, and distrust.

At one level, all of Cavell's work is engaged in extending Wittgenstein's and Austin's efforts to transform analytical philosophy radically from within. As this suggests, Cavell's own professional training locates him on the English-speaking side of this continental divide. Recognizing that both traditions have equal claim to the mantle of philosophy, however, his writings aspire to overcome or transcend this rift within philosophy by making it a subject for philosophy. His aim is to bring the two traditions into closer alignment, or, rather, to achieve a perspective from which it becomes manifest how intimately they are aligned, as if they represent two halves of the same mind, not opposed positions to be reconciled. In this spirit, he repeatedly returns to the surprising affinities he finds between Wittgenstein and Martin Heidegger (the latter being, for Cavell, the modern philosopher who effects a critique and transformation of the Continental tradition comparable to Wittgenstein's critique and transformation of the Anglo-American tradition).

> One affinity is their constant questioning of their own procedures in philosophy. . . . Another is their concern for the ordinary. They come out on some opposite ends of the philosophical world about the importance of the ordinary, but . . . each . . . recognizes that to define our relation to the everyday is part of what philosophy is for. . . . That goes . . . with my finding in both of them responses to skepticism that other philosophers seem to me not to seek. (*SSC*, 53)

Between Wittgenstein and Heidegger Cavell also finds significant differences. The fact that his own professional training places him within the Anglo-American tradition does not mean, however, that he necessarily sides with Wittgenstein rather than Heidegger on matters that divide them. For example, the question of the beginning of philosophy is for Cavell, as for Wittgenstein, a question about the ways "philosophy directs itself, motivates itself, in every given instant in which it has its origination." However, Cavell also understands the beginning of philosophy, as Heidegger does, to be a historical event that is in principle datable, as are the beginning of skepticism, the emergence of the modern, and, for that matter, what he calls "the splitting of the philosophical spirit between the Anglo-American and the Continental traditions" itself (*SSC*, 51).

Cavell dates this last event to the nineteenth century. Yet he also finds this "splitting" to play itself out whenever he engages in philosophy. If Cavell's professional training places him on the Anglo-American side of the gulf between the two traditions, though, how can both halves of the "divided philosophical spirit" be internal to his own thinking? The solution to this conundrum, Cavell comes increasingly to recognize, resides in his inheritance of the American way of thinking founded by the writings of Ralph Waldo Emerson and Henry David Thoreau.

> In their attention to the intimacy of words with the world, and in their inheritance of the transcendental strain in philosophy, Emerson and Thoreau underlie—I have said they underwrite—the idea of ordinariness that surfaces in ordinary language philosophy. At the same time, Emerson underlies in a direct historical way exactly what seems to be the opposite force in contemporary philosophy, so-called Continental philosophy, because through Nietzsche, who loved Emerson's writing, Emerson is at play in the work of Heidegger. . . . I might take "Emerson" as a name for the fact about the splitting of the philosophical spirit that neither ordinary language philosophy nor Continental philosophy is prepared to acknowledge an apparently opposite form of thinking as an ancestor, much less as a common ancestor. (*SSC*, 52)

The fact that Emerson underwrites the new French thought, conjoined with the fact that the Continental and Anglo-American traditions both resist acknowledging their common ancestor and thus their kinship, intensifies the irony that Americans "had to receive philosophy into the study of literature . . . at the hands of the French." America turned to Europe to receive a philosophy that was American to begin with. And that philosophy, as received back in America, no longer recognizes its American roots. "The tradition of philosophy it neglects is exactly our own," Cavell puts it (*SSC*, 65), registering that it neglects the analytical tradition represented by American philosophy departments as well as Emerson's and Thoreau's own understanding and practice of philosophy (which American philosophy departments also neglect).

In *Conditions Handsome and Unhandsome: The Constitution of Emersonian Perfectionism*, Cavell remarks that despite the attention recently accorded Emerson, there remains resistance among philosophers to recognizing his *philosophical* achievement. And yet Emerson is a thinker, Cavell writes, with the accuracy and consequentiality one expects of a mind "worth following with that attention necessary to decipher one's own" (*CH&U*, 1).

Crucially, Cavell's wording implies that if we follow our own thinking with the attention necessary to follow Emerson's, we will know that our minds, too, are worth following that way. We will find ourselves thinking with the accuracy and consequentiality necessary to achieve the perspective of self-reflection only philosophy is capable of providing. Cavell's words intimate something else as well. Without following our own thinking, we cannot know the minds of others. And without following the thinking of others, we cannot know our own minds, cannot have conviction in our thoughts, cannot claim them as our own. That the achievement of selfhood requires the simultaneous acknowledgment of others is a guiding philosophical principle for Cavell. This principle is inextricably bound up with the fact that, as his writing continually brings home to us, deciphering our own minds can be singularly difficult, difficult in a singular way.

"An essential portion of the teaching of *Walden* is a full account of its all but inevitable neglect," Cavell writes early in *The Senses of Walden*, his third book, which he published immediately after *The World Viewed*.

> I assume that however else one understands Thoreau's topics and projects, it is as a writer that he is finally to be known. But the easier that has become to accept, the more difficult it becomes to understand why his words about writing in *Walden* are not . . . systematically used in making out what kind of book he had undertaken to write, and achieved. . . . My opening hypothesis is that this book is perfectly complete, that it means in every word it says, and that it is fully sensible of its mysteries and fully open to them. (*SW*, 4)

Our point of departure, in the present volume, is that *The World Viewed*, like Emerson's writing, has the "accuracy" and "consequentiality" one expects of a mind "worth following with that attention necessary to decipher one's own." And our opening hypothesis is that *The World Viewed*, like Thoreau's *Walden*, is fully sensible of its mysteries and fully open about them, that it means in every word it says, and that it is perfectly complete, hence that, if we aspire to make out what kind of book Cavell has undertaken to write and achieved, we had best make systematic use of the book's own words.

When *The World Viewed* was published in 1971, some film journals dismissed it on the erroneous ground that it advocated a realist theory derived from the writings of Bazin. Others, equally erroneously, took it to advocate a Clement Greenberg-derived formalism. However, the book's continuing reception by the field of film study, or, rather, its continuing non-reception, cannot be attributed to simple mistakes about its theoretical claims. If that were the only problem, correcting those mistakes would be all it would take for the field to accommodate the book's way of thinking. Nor can film study's neglect of the book be attributed to a deliberate effort to repress its thinking. It takes no effort to deny or avoid *The World Viewed*'s thinking. What takes effort is to follow the book's thinking, to read it in a way that acknowledges the kind of book it is.

It is commonly supposed within the field of film study that the writing of *The World Viewed* is vague and impressionistic. Those who make this charge have simply not known how to read the book. To read *The World Viewed* in a way that acknowledges its philosophical aspiration and achievement, it is necessary to free oneself from prejudicial theories as to how philosophical writing has to *look*—the theory that it must proceed systematically by formal arguments, for example, or must employ rhetorical strategies of poetic persuasion. In the Conant interview, Cavell observes that if you give up those traditional routes to conviction in philosophy (as both Wittgenstein and Heidegger felt it necessary to do) "then the question of what achieves philosophical conviction must at all times be on your mind" (*SSC*, 59). Cavell's answer is that conviction must be achieved by the writing itself, by "nothing other than this prose just here, as it's passing before our eyes."

The sense that the words on the page must achieve conviction on their own is one key to reading *The World Viewed*. This sense is conjoined with another, which Cavell wishes, as he puts it, to "radicalize": the sense "that philosophy is at all moments answerable to itself, that if there is any place at which the human spirit allows itself to be under its own question, it is in philosophy; that anything, indeed, that allows that questioning to happen *is* philosophy" (*SSC*, 66). It is because it is under its own question, answerable to itself, that philosophy is capable of providing a perspective that cannot be provided by any other discipline, "a perspective of self-reflection that the human being cannot avoid, or cannot escape without avoiding."

A further key to the writing of *The World Viewed* can be found in *Disowning Knowledge*, a volume of Cavell's readings of Shakespeare plays. Cavell observes that those readings work out his intuition that "Shakespeare's plays interpret and reinterpret the skeptical problematic—the question whether I know with certainty of the existence of the external world and of myself and others in it," hence that "the advent of skepticism as manifested in Descartes's *Meditations* is already in full existence in Shakespeare, from the time of the great tragedies in the first years of the seventeenth century" (*DK*, 3).

In calling his guiding idea an intuition, Cavell distinguishes it from a hypothesis. "Both intuitions and hypotheses require what may be called confirmation, but differently." A hypothesis requires evidence, and "must say what constitutes its evidence. (I know what it means to say that lighter objects fall to earth at the same rate as heavier objects . . .). An intuition, say that God is expressed in the world, does not require, or tolerate, evidence but rather, let us say, understanding of a particular sort" (*DK*, 3).

"Primary wisdom [is] intuition," Emerson writes, "whilst all later teachings are tuitions." Thus Emerson is called a philosopher of intuition, Cavell observes, adding that it is not typically noticed that Emerson is at the same time a teacher of what he calls "tuition": "I read him as teaching that the occurrence to us of intuition places a demand upon us, namely for tuition; call this wording, the willingness to subject oneself to words, to make oneself intelligible. (Tuition so conceived is what I understand criticism to be)" (*DI*, 4–5). It would not be incorrect to call Cavell, too, a philosopher of intuition, as long as it is noticed that he is at the same time a teacher of tuition.

Once an intuition occurs to Cavell—that Shakespeare's plays interpret what Cavell calls the "skeptical problematic," for example, or that there is a genre of Hollywood comedies in which the thrust of the plot is not to get a man and woman together but to get them together again—he takes it upon himself to find words he can trust to make his intuition, to make himself, intelligible. Cavell's writing, like Emerson's, always aims both to exemplify the importance of intuition and to teach tuition, the rigorous discipline of finding words to render one's intuition intelligible, to achieve a critical perspective that enables a certain kind of understanding to take place. From his earliest essays to his most recent work on autobiography, opera, and Hollywood melodrama, Cavell's writing aims, as he says, "to follow out in each case the complete tuition for a given intuition" (with an echo of Wittgenstein, he adds, "Tuition comes to an end somewhere" [*DK*, 5]).

If the potential value of *The World Viewed* to the serious study of film is a function of the fruitfulness of its intuitions, it is no less a function of the exemplary discipline by which its writing—word by word, sentence by sentence, paragraph by paragraph, chapter by chapter—"follows out in each case the complete tuition for a given intuition," so that "this prose just here, as it's passing before our eyes," is capable of achieving conviction.

The World Viewed incorporates insightful remarks—remarks that in each case follow out the complete tuition for the given intuition—about a diversity of matters pertaining to film's origins; its historical development; its characteristic forms and genres; the myths and the human types around which those genres revolve; the medium's ability, until recently, to stave off modernism, to continue to employ without self-consciousness traditional techniques that tap naturally into the medium's powers; and so on. In addressing such matters, *The World Viewed* incorporates equally insightful remarks about particular films, genres, stars, and cinematic techniques.

Almost invariably, Cavell's intuitions run counter to views generally accepted without question within the field of film study. Within film study, for example, it remains a widely held belief, rarely questioned, that "classical" movies systematically subordinate women and, more generally, that they are pernicious ideological representations to be decoded and resisted, not treated as if they are works of art capable of instructing us as to how to view them. Other such beliefs, widely held and rarely questioned within the field, are that the stars projected on the movie screen in classical movies are best thought of as "personas," discursive ideological constructs, not real people; that the world projected on the screen is itself an ideological construct, not real; and, indeed, that reality itself—the so-called real world—is such a construct, too. In providing meaningful alternatives to views that are so often accepted without question within the field of film study, *The World Viewed* is capable of challenging the field to question the unquestionable, to check its theories against the test of experience, thereby opening for exploration regions that have remained closed.

To be sure, there are a number of intuitions crucial to his later work that had not yet occurred to Cavell during the period he was writing *The World Viewed*. It had not yet fully dawned on him, for example, the extent to which his own way of thinking inherited Emerson's understanding and practice of philosophy. Hence nowhere in *The World Viewed*, or in *Must We Mean What We Say?* before it, does Cavell invoke Emerson's concept of intuition in characterizing his own philosophical method, as he does in the 1989 Conant interview.

Not coincidentally, during the period he was writing *The World Viewed*, it had not yet fully dawned on Cavell the extent to which the unique combination of popularity and artistic seriousness of American movies, especially of the thirties and forties, was a function of their inheritance of "focal concerns of American transcendentalism . . . , concerns for society, for human relationship generally," as Cavell puts it in his conversation with Conant.

> Emerson and Thoreau write comprehensively, brilliantly, with full literary and philosophical achievement, at a moment before the split between the traditions of philosophy is set. But if American movies for two decades

26

continued their concerns, then perhaps American movies of that period were accomplishing a feat of philosophical imagination that neither tradition of philosophy could accomplish on its own. (*SSC*, 68–69)

In *Pursuits of Happiness* and *Contesting Tears*, Cavell's intuition that Hollywood movies have inherited the philosophical concerns of American transcendentalism, conjoined with his intuition that he has inherited these concerns, too, leads to the astonishing further intuition that his own philosophical procedures are underwritten by the ways American movies think about society, human relationships, and their own condition as films. It is in the very movies that were for so many years a normal part of Cavell's week that Emerson's ways of thinking remained alive within American culture, available as an inheritance. Apart from the role Hollywood movies played in Cavell's education, it would not have been possible for a philosopher who received his professional training within an analytical tradition that had never acknowledged Emerson as a philosopher to have "inherited" Emerson's ways of thinking at all. Apart from the roles movies played in Cavell's education, it would not have been possible for him to have accomplished those "feats of philosophical imagination" called *The World Viewed*, *Pursuits of Happiness*, and *Contesting Tears*, or, for that matter, *Must We Mean What We Say?*, *The Claim of Reason*, and all the other books and essays that comprise this American philosopher's singularly ambitious body of work. But those intuitions await the significant heightening, and deepening, of Cavell's work that coincides with the publication, all in 1979, of his first essay on Emerson ("Thinking of Emerson"); his reading of *The Lady Eve*, which was to become a cornerstone of *Pursuits of Happiness*; and his monumental *The Claim of Reason*.

In "The Avoidance of Love: A Reading of *King Lear*," written on the eve of the theoretical revolution that was to transform academic criticism in America, Cavell observes that the success of the so-called New Criticism was "a function of the way it is *teachable*. You can train someone to read complex poems with sufficient complexity, there is always something to say about them" (cf. *MWMWWS*, 269). In the Conant interview, Cavell remarks that the theoretical systems which have revolutionized academic criticism in the intervening decades likewise possess the feature he calls "extreme teachability" (*SSC*, 66).

Philosophy, as Cavell practices it, is difficult in a way that precludes its being "extremely teachable." There is no *system* for training students to achieve a philosophical perspective of self-reflection, for there is no system for generating intuitions, for acquiring the requisite kind of understanding. Yet there are practical methods of teaching, and learning, the discipline of following out the complete tuition for any given intuition. In the chapters that follow, our method of teaching, and learning, this demanding discipline is to attend to the utterly specific words of *The World Viewed* ("to this prose just here, as it's passing before our eyes"). For the teaching, and learning, of this discipline is a central concern of all of Cavell's writing.

To achieve conviction in *The World Viewed*, one must follow its thinking. To do so, one must follow one's own thoughts as they are prompted by the words on the page (as those words follow Cavell's thoughts as they are prompted by the films in his experience). Without achieving a perspective of self-reflection, it is not possible to acknowledge *The World Viewed*'s achievement of such a perspective. (The achievement of selfhood requires the simultaneous acknowledgment of others, and vice versa.)

Thus throughout our reading, whenever a passage thwarts our comprehension we keep thinking the passage through until we arrive at an interpretation that sustains our conviction—until an intuition dawns on us, prompted by Cavell's words, as to what his words are saying in this context, what prompted the author of *The World Viewed* to use precisely these words on precisely this occasion, and what prompted us to resist this understanding until now. In striving to arrive at words of our own we can trust to express, with equal accuracy, our own understanding of the words Cavell has arrived at ("to follow out in each case the complete tuition for a given intuition"), we read *The World Viewed* in a way that quite literally follows Cavell's thinking with the attention necessary to decipher our own. And, at each point, our writing invites readers to check Cavell's words, and ours, against their own experience, their own understanding.

That the writing of *The World Viewed*, like Emerson's writing, possesses "accuracy" and "consequentiality" means that its thinking *is* worth following with the attention we devote to it. It also means that attending to the words of *The World Viewed* can be difficult. Yet apart from facing this difficulty, it is not possible to know what makes the book worth attending to in this way. Apart from reading *The World Viewed* in a way that is worthy of it, it is not possible to know the book's true worth. That is the intuition for which the present volume undertakes to follow out the complete tuition.[2]

In characterizing Emerson's thinking as "consequential," Cavell means both that it has consequences (its radicalness resides in its power to change our way of thinking, hence our world) and that it is consecutive, ordered (each thought has consequences for those that follow). To demonstrate that *The World Viewed*, too, possesses "consequentiality," we proceed by reading the book from beginning to end, addressing each chapter, at times each page, each line, in consecutive order. We also add an Appendix in which we collect, and ponder, some of the remarks about Cavell's understanding and practice of philosophy that are to be found in *Must We Mean What We Say?*.

Mostly for the sake of convenience, we divide *The World Viewed* into eight sections, giving each section a descriptive name that singles out a prevailing theme or topic:

- Section I (The Preface: A Metaphysical Memoir), writing upon the completion of the body of *The World Viewed*, sketches the circumstances, and stages, of the book's composition, and introduces themes that will be developed in the ensuing chapters.
- Section II (Chapters 1–5: What Is Film?), the most widely-read part of *The World Viewed*, directly addresses the question, What is film? Its aspiration is not to provide a definition or theory that purports to explain the ontology of film, but, rather, to provoke us to acknowledge how mysterious movies, and their importance, remain to us.
- Section III (Chapters 6–9: Film's Origins and History) takes up the obscurity of film's origins and history.
- Section IV (Chapters 10–11: The End of the Myths) reflects on the fact that the traditional media of movies are losing their power to compel conviction and that film has begun moving into the modernist environment inhabited for generations by the other major arts.
- Section V (Chapters 12–13: The World as a Whole) explores the implications of two recent developments in movie-making which acknowledge the *a priori* condition that film is photographic and that its subject is reality, that is, the world as a whole.
- Section VI (Chapters 15–15: Automatism) investigates the concept of automatism, a concept that, in Cavell's understanding, provides a key to thinking through film's relationship to still photography and to painting.
- Section VII (Chapters 16–18: Film and Theatricality) brings to a close *The World Viewed*'s ongoing reflections on the question of how film for so long avoided the fate of modernism, for so

long maintained its continuities of audiences and genres without assuming the serious burden of justifying its existence as an art.

- Section VIII (Chapter 19: The Acknowledgment of Silence) dwells on the themes of silence, isolation in fantasy, and the mysteries of human motion and separateness, and takes us back, or forward, to questions of origin.

In "More of *The World Viewed*," composed several years after the original publication of *The World Viewed* and included in the 1979 Enlarged Edition, Cavell explains that he is writing this lengthy addendum because so many friends have told him he has written "a difficult book, a sometimes incomprehensible book." He goes on: "I have no choice but to believe this, and, since I also continue to believe in the book, to attempt to account for its difficulty and do what I can to alleviate it, at least do what I can not to discourage a genuine desire to assess it sympathetically" (*WV*, 162).

It might be thought that by writing "More of *The World Viewed*" Cavell was acknowledging that, unlike Thoreau's *Walden*, his own little book about film had failed in its aspiration to be "perfectly complete." But "More of *The World Viewed*" does not deny that *The World Viewed* is complete, that it means every word that it says, that it is fully sensible of its mysteries and fully open to them. Then how does Cavell account for the fact that even readers who are able to overcome the difficulties attendant upon reading *Must We Say What We Mean?* evidently find *The World Viewed* unfathomable? What is the book's special difficulty?

In accounting for the vexing response to *The World Viewed*, Cavell writes, "I persist in the feeling asserted in the book's Preface, that its difficulty lies as much in the obscurity of its promptings as in its particular surfacings of expression" (*WV*, 162). In suggesting this, he is acknowledging that *The World Viewed* is "obscure in its promptings" in a way that *Must We Mean What We Say?* is not.

In *Must We Mean What We Say?*, the procedures of ordinary language philosophy assure that what prompts each assertion strikes the reader as anything but obscure. In the essays that comprise his first book, Cavell placed his hope for conviction from the reader in his ability to motivate "assertions, and objections to them, and to voice them in such a form and at such a time that the reader would have the impression that he was himself thinking them, had been about to have said them—not about to have said something generally along their lines, but as it were to find himself thinking those specific words just when and just as they were appearing to him" (*MWMWWS*, 16).

The World Viewed, too, contains textbook instances of the procedures of ordinary language philosophy. Cavell appeals philosophically to what we ordinarily say and mean, for example, when he makes claims like "You can always ask, pointing to an object in a photograph . . . what lies behind it" (*WV*, 2)—that is, when he invokes imaginary instances of language use in order to elucidate the grammar of particular concepts. He also employs procedures of ordinary language philosophy when he makes claims such as "It is . . . misleading to say, as Bazin does, that 'photography freed the plastic arts from their obsession with likeness,'" (*WV*, 21). What Cavell is claiming in this remark is that the circumstances in which Bazin says what he says do not ordinarily allow such a thing to be said; Cavell finds that in fact he would not say what Bazin is led by his theory to say in those circumstances, and he calls upon us to agree that we, too, would not say it. Likewise, Cavell proceeds from ordinary language when he makes claims such as "One could accordingly say that photography was never in competition with painting" (*WV*, 21). In this remark he is in effect *saying* "Photography was never in competition with painting" even as he is calling upon us to agree that these circumstances make this something we *can* say.

Indeed, every assertion Cavell makes in the course of the philosophical investigations that comprise *The World Viewed* proceeds from ordinary language, claims to exemplify something that we, too, would or could say if we were in the particular circumstances in which Cavell is saying it. Then again, insofar as the writing of *The World Viewed* is prompted by Cavell's memories of movies, we are not in his particular circumstances. Even when we have seen the same movies, his memories are not ours. They are private, particular to him, given to no one else. That is one reason Cavell's philosophical procedures often seem reversed in *The World Viewed*, or to have an effect opposite their effect in *Must We Mean What We Say?*

"Given the feeling that a certain obscurity of prompting is not external to what I wished most fervently to say about film," Cavell writes in "More of *The World Viewed*,"

> the commitments I set myself as I wrote were, first, to allow obscurities to express themselves as clearly and as fervently as I could say, and, second, to be guided by the need to organize and clarify just these obscurities and just this fervor in the progression of my book as a whole. . . . I felt called upon to voice my responses with their privacy, their argumentativeness, even their intellectual perverseness, on their face; often to avoid voicing a thought awaiting its voice, to refuse that thought, to break into the thought, as if our standing responses to film are themselves standing between us and the responses that film is made to elicit and to satisfy. (*WV*, 163)

In the course of our reading of *The World Viewed*, we will be able more fully to appreciate this characterization. But its aptness can already be glimpsed in the obscure, fervent paragraph that opens the Preface:

> Memories of movies are strand over strand with memories of my life. During the quarter of a century (roughly from 1935 to 1960) in which going to the movies was a normal part of my week, it would no more have occurred to me to write a study of movies than to write my autobiography. Having completed the pages that follow, I feel that I have been composing a kind of metaphysical memoir—not the story of a period of my life but an account of the conditions it has satisfied. (*WV*, xix)

Nothing about this "surfacing of expression" seems especially difficult—nothing, that is, apart from the obscurity of its promptings. As will become apparent when we arrive at the conclusion of *The World Viewed*'s final chapter, what prompts the book's first paragraph is the entirety of the book it opens, the book whose completion it announces, the book its author has made out of material he has woven, strand over strand, from memories of movies and memories of his life. Placed at the beginning of *The World Viewed*, not at the end, how can this paragraph not be obscure in its promptings?

What prompts this opening paragraph, what prompts its placement, also prompts the entire book that follows, the book's progression as a whole: the subject of *The World Viewed*, which is film. The obscure promptings of the paragraph cannot be separated from what *The World Viewed* is about, in other words. What *The World Viewed* is about is film, its singularly obscure subject. It is also about the singular obscurity of film as a subject. What prompts the writing of *The World Viewed*, the thinking *The World Viewed* is capable of prompting, what the book is about, cannot be separated from what its writing *is*, the material out of which it is made ("a certain obscurity of prompting is not external to what I wished most fervently to say about film"). In part, it is this fact about its writing, Cavell suggests in "More of *The World Viewed*," that accounts for the book's difficulty, its special challenge to the reader.

READING

THE WORLD VIEWED

I
■ ■ ■ ■

THE PREFACE:
A METAPHYSICAL MEMOIR

DURING THE PERIOD of his life in which going to the movies was a normal part of his week, Cavell observes in the opening paragraph of the Preface, "it would no more have occurred to me to write a study of movies than to write my autobiography." It is because the writing of *The World Viewed* is prompted by his memories that Cavell finds himself feeling, upon completing the body of the book, that the study of movies he has been composing is also a memoir. *The World Viewed* is not an autobiography; Cavell does not feel that by composing this book he has told the *story* of the period of his life in which he enjoyed what he calls a "natural relation" to movies, the period in which going to the movies was a normal part of his week. The memoir he feels he has composed is an account of the conditions that were satisfied by movies and moviegoing for all who enjoyed the relation to movies he enjoyed. It is a *metaphysical* memoir.

"A book thus philosophically motivated ought to account philosophically for the motive in writing it," Cavell goes on, initiating the Preface's second paragraph. "What broke my natural relation to movies? What was that relation, that its loss seemed to demand repairing, or commemorating, by taking thought? (*WV*, xix). He concludes that answering these questions is the business of *The World Viewed* as a whole.

The World Viewed is about movies. It is about memories of movies. It is about the "natural relation" to movies. It is about the conditions that relation satisfies. It is about the breaking of that relation. Thus it is also

35

about the motive of its writing, its own obscure promptings. Although the kinds of philosophical remarks about philosophy everywhere to be found in *Must We Mean What We Say?* are all but completely absent in *The World Viewed*, as we have said, it is a leading claim of Cavell's little book that serious thinking about film requires the perspective of self-reflection only philosophy is capable of providing.

What makes film a subject that calls for philosophy, what makes film a subject for philosophy, what these facts reveal about film and about philosophy, are questions at the heart of *The World Viewed*, for it is the loss of his "natural relation" to movies that prompted Cavell to begin thinking philosophically about film in the ways that led to the writing of this book. *The World Viewed* keeps faith with Wittgenstein's methodological principle that we can find out what kind of object anything is by investigating expressions which show the kind of thing said about it. One way *The World Viewed* keeps faith with this principle is by taking its own writing to be such an expression. *The World Viewed* is one kind of thing that can be said about film. By investigating, philosophically, the obscure promptings of this expression, the motivations of its own writing, *The World Viewed* enables us to know something about the kind of object film is, and something about what philosophy is, as well. As Cavell puts it in the elegant formulation that concludes the paragraph, "To account for the motive in writing this book may be the most accurate description of its motive" (xx).

■ ■

Observing that it is easier to tell the immediate history of the composition of *The World Viewed* than it is to describe the book's motive, Cavell devotes the remainder of the Preface to chronicling the events that led to the writing of the book.

In 1963, Cavell chose film as the topic of a seminar in aesthetics he was teaching at Harvard. (A chronicle of the events that led to the writing of the present volume might also begin with this Harvard seminar, whose roster of students included a young Bill Rothman, quietly eager but slightly subversive.) Film promised pedagogical advantages, he explains in *The World Viewed*'s Preface. "Everybody would have had memorable experiences of movies, conversation naturally developed around them, and the absence of an established canon of criticism would mean that we would be forced back upon a faithfulness to nothing but our experience and a wish to communicate it" (xx).

36

The seminar was to proceed by forgoing or deferring theory and even criticism, and, in the absence of prejudicial theories, by finding words, faithful to the participants' experience of movies they cared about, which could provide starting points for a philosophical investigation of movies and their importance. As he explains in *The World Viewed*, however, "the seminar was a failure. Or, rather, what was learned was important enough, but it came from our failures" (xx).

Cavell began the seminar, whose business was to reflect on the experience of particular films, with the belief that it would be less difficult with movies than with other works of art to find words to communicate one's experience. The seminar's participants—he does not exclude himself—found it unexpectedly difficult even to describe movies accurately, however. A frequent reaction was to start "getting technical."

> Words flowed about everything from low-angle shots to filters to timings and numbers of set-ups to deep focus and fast cutting, etc., etc. But all this in turn lost its sense. On the one hand, the amount and kind of technical information that could be regarded as relevant is more than any of us knew; on the other hand, the only technical matters we found ourselves invoking, so far as they were relevant to the *experience* of particular films, which was our only business, are in front of your eyes. You can see where a shot begins and ends and whether it's long, middle or close; you know whether the camera is moving back or forth, or sideways, whether a figure brings himself into the field of the camera or the camera turns to get him; you may not know how Hitchcock gets the stairwell to distort that particular way in *Vertigo*, but you can see that he got it. Then what is the reality behind the idea that there is always a technical something you don't know that would provide the key to the experience? (*WV*, xxii)

After the semester was over, Cavell began to work out "bits of the questions" that the seminar, and its failure, had "started" in him. In the course of the next three or four years, however, he was immersed in writing the last several of the essays that comprise *Must We Mean What We Say?*

> The writing I was doing dealt mainly with problems in the philosophy of art, with the philosophical problem of other minds, and with the experience of two plays. Questions about movies kept coming to the surface, but on the whole I kept them aside. In an essay on *King Lear* . . . I managed to suppress them entirely; but months of immersion in the idea of theater—especially in ideas of an audience, of the actor, and of the theater's enclosed and total world—had their effect, and as soon as that essay was done I found I wanted to extend its thoughts to the work of film. (*WV*, xxii)

If the philosophical concerns of *Must We Mean What We Say?* are part of *The World Viewed*'s obscure promptings, it is no less the case, this passage suggests, that the questions about film the failed seminar "started" in him are part of what prompted Cavell to immerse himself in the first place in the philosophical problems addressed by the later essays of *Must We Mean What We Say?*, which were written subsequent to the seminar. *The World Viewed* extends to movies the thoughts about theater, for example, worked out in "Ending the Waiting Game" and "The Avoidance of Love." But those essays are also prompted by questions about film that are "pushed aside," "submerged," even "entirely suppressed" within the essays themselves. *Must We Mean What We Say?*'s thoughts about philosophy, which go without saying in *The World Viewed*, are part of the obscure promptings of Cavell's book about film. And the questions about movies *The World Viewed* undertakes to answer, which go without asking in *Must We Mean What We Say?*, are part of what prompts the later essays in Cavell's first book.

In *The World Viewed*, as we have suggested, the obscurity of its promptings is part of what the book is about; the book is about its own writing no less than it is about film, and this fact is inseparable from the book's difficulty. *Must We Mean What We Say?* is not in the same way about its own writing. It does not strike the reader as difficult in the same way, because what prompts its writing seems anything but obscure. And yet those essays, for all their clarity, push aside, submerge, even entirely suppress, the obscure questions about film that are part of what prompts their writing. They also push aside, submerge, even entirely suppress, the question of their own promptings. This means that the difficulty internal to the writing of *The World Viewed* is internal to the writing of *Must We Mean What We Say?*, too. In thinking about the closed and total world of theater, for example, or, for that matter, the procedures of ordinary language philosophy, Cavell feels free to push aside, submerge, even entirely suppress, this difficulty; in thinking about movies, he feels he must address it. What this fact reveals about movies and their importance to us, and about philosophy, and about the singular affinity between film and philosophy, is part of what *The World Viewed* is about.

■ ■

Between the seminar's disheartening failure to find words that were faithful to the participants' experience of movies they cared about, which could be the starting point of a philosophical investigation of movies and their importance, and the time he completed *Must We Mean What We Say?* and turned his attention to composing the book that was to become *The World*

Viewed, Cavell tells us, "several intellectual discoveries . . . better prepared me to say what I wanted" (*WV*, xxii).

The last such discovery is the volume of essays by André Bazin published in English under the title *What Is Cinema?* Early in 1968, Cavell read these essays, and this provided—in ways made quite clear by the references to Bazin in the body of *The World Viewed*—what Cavell calls "the final, or immediate, stimulus to consecutive writing" (*WV*, xxiii). Cavell also cites Rousseau's *Letter to d'Alembert*, which he read for the first time during this period.

> Rousseau's obsession with *seeing* (it is all about "spectacle")—with our going to the theater in order to be seen and not to be seen, with our use of tears there to excuse our blindness and coldness to the same situations in the world outside, with his vision that true spectacles in the good city will permit us to let ourselves be seen without shame—guided and confirmed my sense of the level at which viewing, in an audience and out, needs to be followed. (*WV*, xxii)

In *The World Viewed*, Cavell's thinking about viewing is indeed "guided and confirmed" by Rousseau's ideas about spectacle, and, more specifically, Rousseau's conviction that there is a *moral* dimension to seeing and being seen. "The accuracies in what is often taken as Rousseau's paranoia helped me to overcome a certain level of distrust I had developed about movies and about my interest in them—as though I had, in thinking about movies, forgotten what there is to distrust in the use of any art" (*WV*, xxii).

Early in the first chapter of *The World Viewed*, for example, Cavell invokes Tolstoy's dismissal of most great art, and confesses that he sometimes feels that our own lives may confirm radical criticisms of our culture such as Tolstoy's. When Cavell goes on to confess that his experience of going to new movies has come to be associated with anxiety, he places the distrust he had developed about movies and about his interest in movies—a distrust no doubt exacerbated by his seminar's failure to find words that could be trusted even to describe movies accurately—within a context that acknowledges "what there is to distrust in the use of any art." Doing so does, indeed, help Cavell to overcome his distrust of movies (and of his interest in movies).

To say what he has it at heart to say in *The World Viewed*, Cavell finds it necessary to acknowledge and thereby overcome the distrust he has developed about movies (and about his interest in movies). By reminding him of what there is to distrust in the use of any art, Rousseau's *Letter to d'Alembert* provides moral support, as it were. Rousseau's distrust of theater is not mere paranoia; it is accurate as to what there is about theater to distrust. The distrust of movies (and of his interest in movies) Cavell has come to develop is not paranoia, either. *The World Viewed* treats this distrust as a datum pertinent to investigating his "natural relation" to movies and what caused that relation, after a quarter of a century, to break. To say what he has it at heart to say, Cavell finds that he also has to acknowledge, and thereby overcome, a distrust he has developed about ordinary language, a doubt that we have words available to us, words we can believe in, which are capable of accounting for our experience of movies we care about. For helping him to treat this doubt—in part a legacy of his failed seminar on movies—not as paranoia but as a datum for philosophical investigation, Cavell credits Heidegger's *Being and Time*, a work he began studying during this period.

Mindful of the magnitude of the rift between Continental philosophy and Anglo-American philosophical analysis, and aware that his own professional training locates him on the English-speaking side of the continental divide between these philosophical traditions, Cavell does not make it his business in *The World Viewed* to explore the affinities and differences between Heidegger's philosophical project and his own. But he does specify some of *Being and Time*'s methods and concepts which helped prepare him to say what he wanted about film: Heidegger's "concept of world," his "way of limiting knowing as our access to the world," and his "philosophical confidence in his native tongue, and his suspiciousness of it" (*WV*, xxiii).

The composition of *The World Viewed*, as Cavell goes on to relate it, took place in two stages. When he had drafted what was to become the first five chapters, he had enough faith in what he had written to accept an invitation to give a public reading of this material, in May 1968, at the University of Illinois.

"Having got this far with the work," Cavell writes, "I had some words I could believe in to account for my experience of film" (*WV*, xxiii). He thus had already achieved his original aspiration in writing about movies. However, he remained quite unaware of the overall form his book was to take, or of the procedures he was to find himself following in bringing its writing to a conclusion. His feeling at that point was that he should now proceed systematically, should "find a way to view and review a good number at least of American talkies, and then test the words against them." That proved impossible—not just practically, but because his "thoughts would not form around any such procedure" (*WV*, xxiii).

I was seeing fewer movies than ever before and wanting to see fewer, and at the same time memories of old movies, and of the friends I had seen them with, kept on asserting themselves. Those facts underlay my desire to come to terms with movies, and I knew that no words of mine about film would be worth writing or reading unless they could first see that desire through. Therefore I am often referring to films I have seen only once, some as long as thirty years ago. In a few instances I have seen a film three times, but in no case enough times to feel I possess it the way it deserves and I would like: completely and wordlessly. . . . I mention this as a warning . . . that this is not a history of any stretch of the movies; as an apology for the off memories that may crop up; and as a confession that a few faulty memories will not themselves shake my confidence in what I've said, since I am as interested in how a memory went wrong as to why the memories that are right occur when they do. (*WV*, xxiv)

Cavell began the second stage of the writing of *The World Viewed* during a sabbatical he spent at the Humanities Center at Wesleyan University. As it turned out, the topic he then took up (in Chapter 6) is the obscurity of film's history and origins, the medium's own obscure promptings. The writing of *The World Viewed* did not become more systematic, as he had expected it would (and as he had assumed it *should*) after completing the first five chapters. On the contrary, the writing became more fervent, more subjective, more private, more absorbed with its own obscure promptings, as well as film's.

When Cavell confesses that "a few faulty memories will not themselves shake my confidence in what I've said," there is a fierceness in his tone. It has been a struggle to find these words he trusts to communicate the experiences he remembers, and he is prepared to defend them should they be attacked. And yet, Cavell also confesses, he has not seen any film he writes about "enough times to feel I possess it the way it deserves and I would like: completely and wordlessly." If he had already possessed these films completely, why would he need the words of *The World Viewed*, or any words, to account for them? Nor do the words of *The World Viewed* enable him to possess these films completely. In these words he trusts to communicate his experience, in any words he might have chosen, the films he remembers are lost, as well as found. *The World Viewed* must find a way to acknowledge this, if its words are to sustain Cavell's conviction, and ours.

II

■■■■

CHAPTERS 1–5:
WHAT IS FILM?

Chapter 1: "An Autobiography of Companions"

The opening chapter of *The World Viewed* begins with the question of why movies are important. It ends with the question "What is film?" For Cavell, these questions are not separable. This fact about film, or our concept of film, reflects a fact about art, or our concept of art: What art is cannot be separated from what makes art important. This is the thrust of the chapter's long and complex first paragraph, which begins:

> When Tolstoy asked, 'What is art?' his answer was to dismiss most of the great art of the past. There's the unflinchingness of genius for you. And . . . what reason is there to care about any radical criticism of one's culture— about, say, the fact that Plato and Rousseau wished to dismiss poetry and theater from their republics; or that Matthew Arnold thought poetry had lost its voice; or that Hegel and Marx thought philosophy had come to an end, or ought to; or that Wagner and Walt Whitman and Thoreau and Nietzsche thought that man and his society would have to be transformed before the thing they had it at heart to say could be understood? (*WV*, 3)

Cavell's question "What reason is there to care about any radical criticism of one's culture?" invokes the radical cultural critics he cites, Tolstoy among them. It also invokes the possibility that the book Cavell has begun will turn out to be a work of radical cultural criticism in the tradition of Tolstoy's *What Is Art?* (Then, if Cavell succeeds in saying what he has it at heart to say, what reason will there be to care? Will we and our society have to be transformed before this writing can be understood?)

As the paragraph continues ("The trouble is, we are sometimes unsure whether we have survived these prophecies or whether our lives now are realizing their worst fears" [3]), Cavell's prose slips into the first person plural. He is making a confession: Sometimes, but not always, his own life strikes him as confirming Tolstoy's judgment that our culture must be radically transformed because it denies the importance of art. By undertaking to speak for the reader as well as for himself, Cavell is calling upon us to acknowledge that we, too, sometimes feel this way, that whether or not we ought to care about radical criticisms of our culture, we do care, at least at times. "Tolstoy knew [art's] saving importance," Cavell writes, implying that he knows art's "saving importance," too (4). The knowledge of art's "saving importance" is the bedrock that grounds what he has it at heart to say in *The World Viewed*. And the reader to whom, and for whom, he is speaking is a reader who knows art's "saving importance," too.

In investigating the importance of movies, the first piece of evidence Cavell considers is that it can be taken for granted that movies *are* important.

> Music, painting, sculpture, poetry—as they are now sought by artists of major ambition, artists devoted to the making of objects meant as the live history of their art—are not *generally* important, except pretty much for the men and women devoted to creating them. For them, the arts are of *such* importance, and that importance raises such questions, that no one free of the questions is free to share their arts with them. These artists have virtually no audience any longer, except in isolated and intermittent cases. (4)

Movies are different. They are important for almost everyone. "[T]hose who care about no (other) art and those who live on the promise of art, those whose pride is education and those whose pride is power or practicality—all care about movies, await them, respond to them, remember them, talk about them, hate some of them, are grateful for some of them" (4–5).

Cavell pairs this point with a second: Film "seems naturally to exist in a state in which its highest and its most ordinary instances attract the same audience" (5). Indeed, in the case of movies "it is generally true that you do not really like the highest instances unless you also like typical ones. You don't even know what the highest are instances of unless you know the typical as well" (6). He demonstrates both points by compiling a list of glorious movie moments—some from films of recognizably "high" ambition, others from typical instances of familiar genres—that anyone ought to be able to appreciate. Anyone ought to be able to rise

> to the occasion of recognition at the end of *City Lights*, to the eloquence of Garbo's moods, to the intelligence and manliness of Olivier's *Richard the Third*, to the power of justice in Henry Fonda's young Lincoln, to Carole Lombard's wit, to Emil Jannings' despair, to Marilyn Monroe's doomed magnetism, to Kim Stanley's sense of worthlessness, to the mutual pleasure and trust William Powell and Myrna Loy give one another, to Groucho's full and calm acceptance of Harpo's raging urgencies, to the heartbreaking hesitations at the center of an Astaire routine. (5)

And the "highest sensibility must thrill," Cavell's passage goes on, at the

> knowledge with which Fonda interrupts the mythical question—"Say, what's your name, stranger?"—looking around straight into Walter Brennan's eyes, dropping it as he walks out, "Earp. Wyatt Earp"; and hate and fear Basil Rathbone's courtly villainies or Richard Widmark's psychotic killers or Lee Marvin's Liberty Valance, at once completely gratified and perfectly freed of guilt at their lucid and baroque defeats; and participate in the satisfaction of one of Kirk Douglas's or Burt Lancaster's rages. Merely to think of the way Bette Davis makes her entrance in *Jezebel*—bursting into view on a rearing horse, her elegant riding habit amplifying the dash with which she dismounts, then jamming the point of her whip back into the side folds of her skirt to free her boot for the step into the house where she knows she is awaited with dazzled disapproval—merely to think of the way, in *Now, Voyager,* her restoration to sanity is signaled by an opening shot on her sheer-stockinged ankles and legs, released from the thick, shapeless, dark cotton wrappings and health shoes into which her wicked mother had charmed her—these moments provide us with a fair semblance of ecstasy. (5)

The fact that there is such a continuity between ordinary and extraordinary movies, hence that there is a "necessary region of indiscriminateness" in the acceptance of movies, is defining for film, in Cavell's view. He treats it as a datum in investigating what film is. And because to accept something as an instance of a particular art is to accept it as an instance of art, as "carrying the intentions and consequences of art," as he puts it in *Must We Mean What We Say?*, Cavell understands this fact to be defining for art, as well.

The idea that in the case of movies there is a necessary region of indiscriminateness leads Cavell into an extended digression—roughly half the length of the chapter—about "three separable nightmares" this condition creates (6).

(1) One is that of the movie reviewer who must cover every opening. James Agee's gift for "finding and describing *something* to like, in no matter what yards of junk," established the significant fact about movies and their

importance that, in Cavell's words, "there is always something to find . . . , often enough to justify a hundred minutes of speculative solitude." This is a fact whose significance is highlighted by the *auteur* theory. "It was a clarifying shock to realize that films were directed," Cavell writes. "I certainly felt rebuked for my backwardness in having grown to fatherhood without really knowing where movies came from. . . . I must have had an idea that they sprang full grown from iron-gated sunglassed heads of studios" (7). Once he got over feeling rebuked, he was led to pose a quintessentially Cavellian question: "How could anyone not have known what the *auteur* theory forces us to know?"

The *auteur* emphasis forces us to recognize a fact about movies whose very obviousness allowed it to remain unnoticed, but it turns us away from recognizing another aesthetic proposition even more unnoticeable in its obviousness—that a movie comes from other movies. Film, like every art, has an internal history, its own traditions within which directors work out their individuality.

(2) A second nightmare is for the writer who takes indiscriminate attention to movies "as a manifestation of bad taste and of a corrupt industry and society," rather than as a datum in understanding our appetite for film. With a nod to *Dr. Strangelove*, Cavell remarks that some people have "stopped worrying and started loving the unminding devotions of the eye and ear, claiming them as a natural reaction to the demise of the printed word" (8). His tone is derisive because he detests the casual assumption that movies and books are natural enemies. "No doubt it is true that more people than ever do not read. In my experience it is also true that more people read, and read better. . . . Some among the people I know who like movies best are among the best readers I know" (8). This fact motivates another quintessentially Cavellian question: "The question for me—and it prompts and pervades the occasions I have found to speak concretely about particular films—is why the standards . . . we take for granted (or criticize) when we give or are given readings of books are ignored or unavailable when we give or are given readings of movies" (8–9).

In *The World Viewed*, Cavell finds numerous occasions to "speak concretely about particular films." These are at least in part "prompted" and "pervaded" by the question—another legacy of his failed seminar on movies—of why the standards we apply in speaking about books are ignored or unavailable when speaking about movies. A central goal of *The World Viewed*, indeed, is to arrive at a clearer understanding of the standards that *are* appropriate, given what film is, when we undertake to attach words we believe in to films we care about.

(3) A third nightmare is for those "trying to awaken both from empty indiscriminateness and from futile discrimination" (9). "A standing discovery of the *auteur* theory," Cavell writes, "was of the need for a canon of movies to which any remarks about 'the movie' should hold themselves answerable"; without this, "the natural circle of theory and evidence will not inscribe the knowledge we want" (9).

The World Viewed is not in the business of establishing a canon, Cavell notes, but "since I am bent on going ahead anyway, I will take what bearings I have, trying at each point to meld the ways of thinking that have invited my conviction with the experiences of films that I have cared about" (9). In going ahead, Cavell also notes, his "way of studying films has been mostly through remembering them, like dreams. Unlike dreams, there are other equally essential ways of getting to movies, like reading their scripts and learning their outer history and viewing them again and counting and timing their shots" (12).

In the chapters that follow, Cavell relies primarily on memory, forgoing other ways of "getting to" movies, because he takes it to be his business to "think out the causes" of his "consciousness of film as it stands," to bring his experience of movies and moviegoing to an explicit self-consciousness (12).

An advantage in proceeding from memory is that what he has to remember will be recalled by others. Thus he will be keeping faith with the experiences of movies he cares about, experiences whose nature is to be lined with fragments of conversations and responses of companions. "[T]he audience of a book is essentially solitary, one soul at a time; the audience of music and theater is essentially larger than your immediate acquaintance—a gathering of the city; the crowd at a movie comprises various pools of companions, or scattered souls with someone missing" (10).

What movies are cannot be separated from what makes them important. And what makes movies important cannot be separated from the importance of the events of companionship or lack of companionship associated with our experience of movies. (Hence the chapter's title, "An Autobiography of Companions.")

"I don't care whether anyone quite knows the week of awe I spent at the age of twelve reading *Les Misérables*," Cavell writes; "there are always twelve-year-olds and there is always that book for them. But movies, unless they are masterpieces, are not there as they were. . . . If you see them now for the first time, you may be interested and moved, but you can't know what I know." Those hours and days at the movies, shared with those companions, are past. They "were momentous, but only for the moment," Cavell adds, sounding an elegiac tone, "unrecapturable fully except in memory and evocation; gone" (10).

In the two paragraphs that follow, Cavell confesses what he calls his "increasing difficulty over the past several years to get myself to go to new movies." "This has to do partly with an anxiousness in my response to new films I have seen (I don't at all mean I think they are bad), but equally with my anxiousness in what I feel to be new audiences for movies (not necessarily new people, but people with new reasons for being there), as though I cannot locate or remain together with my companions among them" (11).

Cavell treats his increasing reluctance to see new movies as another datum pertinent to his investigation of what has caused his natural relation to movies to break, the traumatic loss that motivates the writing of *The World Viewed* as a whole. This reluctance, he suggests, has partly to do with the fact that in his response to new movies there is now an element of anxiety, as if he is no longer quite sure what response is appropriate. (On the topic of new movies and his response to them, Cavell will have much to say in later chapters.)

But his reluctance also has to do with an anxiety he has come to associate with his relation to others in the movie theater. Because "movie showings have begun for the first time to be habitually attended by an audience, I mean by people who arrive and depart at the same time, as at a play," the ideas worked out in Rousseau's *Letter to d'Alembert*—ideas about our going to the theater in order to be seen and not to be seen— have come to apply to going to the movies, too. "When moviegoing was casual and we entered at no matter what point in the proceedings," Cavell writes, "we took our fantasies and companions and anonymity inside and left with them intact" (11). The old conditions of moviegoing enabled us to respond to movies in ways that reflected our innermost fantasies. Our companions were responding in ways that reflected their private fantasies, too. It did not matter that our responses to the film were not really shared. Going to the movies together was the bond that connected us. The privacy of our responses, like the privacy of our fantasies, was preserved.

Now that when we go to the movies we find ourselves in the presence of an audience, a claim is made upon us to forgo our privacy. But Cavell finds that now it matters to him that his responses are not really shared. If others do not share his responses, why should he forgo his privacy? In his anxiety, he feels that the other people are not in the theater for the same reasons he is. He feels he cannot share their reasons not because their responses to the film are so private, but because they do not seem to be responding to the film at all, at least not in ways that reflect their private fantasies. "At the same time that the mere fact of an audience makes this claim upon me to forgo my privacy, it feels as if the old casualness of moviegoing has been replaced by a casualness of movie-viewing, which I interpret as an inability to tolerate our own fantasies, let alone those of others—an attitude that equally I cannot share (11)."

This last remark reveals a Rousseau-like moral dimension to Cavell's increasing reluctance to go to new movies. Now, people are casual about the films they view, as if they had no real stake in them, as if their private fantasies were not really at stake, as if they had no real stake in their own fantasies, as if they really had no fantasies at all. Now that people gather at the movie theater to deny their private fantasies, not to acknowledge them, we are further than ever from realizing Rousseau's vision of true spectacles in the good city that will permit us to let ourselves be seen without shame.

The old conditions of moviegoing, which preserved privacy, allowed moviegoers to respond to films in ways that respected their private fantasies, and respected the fantasies of their companions, as well. If those conditions "harbored the value of illicitness that from the beginning was part of moviegoing," so be it. The new conditions do not "dispel illicitness or make it unnecessary; the audience is not a gathering of citizens for honest confession and acceptance of one another. The new need for the gathering is as mysterious as the old need for privacy; so the demand that I forgo privacy is as illicit as my requirement to preserve it" (12).

If the new conditions of moviegoing foster a "casualness of movie viewing," the old conditions fostered, or required, a certain indiscriminateness in accepting movies. In that respect, film can be contrasted with other contemporary arts, Cavell argues. In the case of literature, for example, there are obviously "a few instances of very great artists who are at the same time popular," but "people who read serious novels do not on the whole read potboilers." As for music, "People who attend to serious music do not attend to light dinner music, say, or movie music." Such people may well admire "Cole Porter, Rodgers and Hart, Jerome Kern, the Beatles, jazz. But then everyone should admire inspired inventiveness, true sentiment, rocking joy, passionate honesty, and the turning of captivity and grief into radiant shouts and virtuoso murmurs of community" (6).

The overriding point of this pair of quotes is that people who attend to serious music (who "live on its promise," in Cavell's charged phrase) attend to the Beatles, say, in the same way and for the same reasons other people do. They do not attend to the Beatles the same way or for the same reasons they attend to works they take to be "serious instances, as they now occur," of the art of music. The necessary indiscriminateness in accepting movies does have analogues in the past of established arts ("Anyone who is too selective about the classical composers whose music he likes doesn't really like music" [13]). But not only does such a requirement not apply to contemporary music or painting or theater, it negates their condition.

> [F]or it can be said that anyone who cultivates broadly the current instances of music or painting or theater does not appreciate, and does not know, the serious instances of those arts as they now occur. This condition of modernist art has been described by Michael Fried as one in which an art leaves no room, or holds no promise, for the minor artist. It is a situation in which the work of the major artist condemns the work of others to artistic nonexistence, and in which his own work is condemned to seriousness, to further radical success or to complete failure. (13)

Some readers will no doubt find terms like "major artist," "minor artist" and "artistic seriousness" rankling, for we are continually being told that art has moved beyond modernism, that modernism is a discredited ideology, that ours is a postmodern age. But does the theory that modernism has been discredited, however widely-held that theory may be, really allow us to rest assured that art no longer has, no longer can have, "saving importance"? On what ground could we possibly know this?

Bringing the chapter full circle by returning to Tolstoy's radical criticism of our culture, Cavell observes that the condition of serious art in today's world is "in one light, sadder, certainly crueler, than the one Tolstoy described." It was possible for Tolstoy to

> blame society and artists for their shortcomings, whereas if we seek to place blame, it will have to be upon the necessities of the separate arts themselves: upon music, for refusing tonality; upon sculpture, for no longer allowing a material to be sculpted; upon painting, for refusing not merely the presence of humanity in its content but evidence of the human hand in its making. Or we will have to blame reality for withdrawing itself from our powers. If this is cold, it is clarifying; for now blame can be squarely placed for an art's *de facto* exclusiveness. (13–14)

Those who accept it as a given that modernism has been discredited charge it with being exclusive, elitist. But modern art, as Cavell understands it, does not restrict its audience to an exclusive elite. "While the community of serious art is small, it is not exclusive—not the way an elite is exclusive. It is esoteric, but the secret is open to anyone" (14).

When Cavell sums up the condition of modern art by saying, "Art now exists in the condition of philosophy" (14), he is also summing up the condition of modern philosophy, as *Must We Mean What We Say?*

articulates it. Philosophy today exists in the condition of modern art; it leaves no room, holds no promise, for the minor philosopher, whose work is condemned to nonexistence—nonexistence *as* philosophy—by the work of the major philosopher. In turn, the major philosopher's work is "condemned to seriousness," to "further radical success or to complete failure" (13).

In so characterizing the condition of modern philosophy, Cavell is also declaring, or confessing, that this is the condition of his own writing. As a work of modern philosophy, *The World Viewed* is "condemned to seriousness," which means that unless it achieves "radical success" by establishing its validity as a new medium of philosophy, it fails completely. It also means that, although *The World Viewed* does not measure its success by the size of its readership, it is not elitist. The community of its readers may not be large, but it is not exclusive the way an elite is exclusive. *The World Viewed* is esoteric, but the secret is open to anyone.

The chapter's penultimate paragraph begins, "It is often said that film is *the* modern art, the one to which modern man naturally responds" (14). Cavell rejects this formulation, first, because it "assumes that other arts are *not* capable of eliciting the old values of art," and no one is in a position to make such an assumption. Second, the idea that film is *the* art to which modern human beings naturally respond "shows a poor view of what is 'natural,'" for if we are seriously to be called "modern," one fact about us is that what is natural to us "is not natural," that naturalness for us "has become a stupendous achievement" (14). Sounding a theme that will echo throughout *The World Viewed*, Cavell argues that if film is seriously to be thought of as an art at all, it needs to be explained how it can have avoided

> the fate of modernism, which in practice means how it can have maintained its continuities of audiences and genres, how it can have been taken seriously without having assumed the burden of seriousness. For the blatant fact about film is that, if it is art, it is the one live traditional art, the one that can take its tradition for granted. . . . The movie's ease within its assumptions and achievements—its conventions . . . remaining convincing and fertile without self-questioning—is central to its pleasure for us. (14–15)

Because film is important in ways only art can be important, film *is* seriously to be thought of as an art. Thus Cavell *is* led to ask how this art has been able for so long to avoid the fate of modernism, how film has been able to provide the pleasure it has been able to provide, a pleasure that cannot be separated from the reasons we care about movies, from what movies are, from their importance to us. This is a question about art (what is art? what is an art? what is a medium of art?) no less than it is a question about film (what is this particular art? what is this particular medium?). And it leads to another question. "The more we learn . . . of the corruptions and stupidities of the industry that formed to produce those objects, the more we are likely to wonder how the films we care about can ever have been made. . . . What is the power of film that it could survive (even profit artistically from) so much neglect and ignorant contempt by those in power over it?" (15).

And these two questions—How can film have for so long avoided the fate of modernism? How can the movies we care about have been made?—prompt Cavell to pose the question that will occupy the next four chapters: What is film?

■ ■

Because Gerald Mast and Marshall Cohen included Chapters 2 through 5 in their anthology *Film Theory and Criticism*, which has been used (in a succession of editions) for over twenty years as a textbook in innumerable college courses, this is by far the most widely-read section of *The World Viewed*. In our reading of these chapters, we will take special pains to address some common ways of misreading them. Before turning to Chapter 2, however, we will pause to consider a passage in "More of *The World Viewed*" in which Cavell qualifies his insistence that the importance of film lies in its condition as the last traditional art, the last to push itself to modernist self-questioning.

"One may share the sense of change in the art of movies over the past fifteen or twenty years," Cavell writes in "More of *The World Viewed*," and "even agree that this has something to do with the encroachment of modernist problems, but then account for this encroachment in at least two ways I have not considered: as a repetition, more or less farcical, of film's first and most serious modernist phase, expressed, say, in revolutionary Russia; or (non-exclusively) as the new emergence of experimental filmmaking" (216).

When *The World Viewed* was published, it was pointedly ignored, or attacked, by champions of the cinematic *avant-garde*, such as Annette Michelson, Rosalind Krauss, and their followers. They were convinced that it is the films by the likes of Eisenstein and Vertov, not the "illusionistic" narrative films of the "commercial" or "mainstream" or "industrial" cinema, which represent the authentic history of the art of film, and that it

51

is the experimental films of Stan Brakhage, Michael Snow, Andy Warhol, and other filmmakers of the so-called New American Cinema that are *the* serious films of the present. They interpreted *The World Viewed* as a broadside against the cinema they championed, one which only served to expose its author's ignorance of both the history and the present state of the art of cinema. Thus Krauss asserts, in a quite patronizing review in *Artforum*, that Cavell's book must seem an "extreme curiosity" to "those readers who are knowledgeable about Soviet films of the 1920s, who are aware of Eisenstein's excruciation about the ways in which the world is 'there' for film and his ambition to awaken the consciousness of his viewers by means of the variability of that 'thereness,' who are as well conversant with Vertov's films and the ways in which they both confront and account for their audiences."[3]

Krauss's point in calling attention to Cavell's ignorance, she insists, is not to imply that everyone who writes on film be first and foremost a historian of it, but to ask "whether one can construct an 'ontology of film' in which its conditions and limits are set out without knowing about (or 'acknowledging') the serious engagements with those conditions and those limits that have gone on in the past and are going on in the present."[4] Of course, Cavell's own answer to this question would be "no." Or, rather, he would be reluctant to answer Krauss's question without countering with a question of his own: On what grounds can one claim to be certain that the films he writes about in *The World Viewed* do not count among those "serious engagements"? In any case, Krauss's question is improperly formulated. It erroneously implies that the ontology of film is something that Cavell takes himself to be *constructing* in the pages of *The World Viewed*, as one might construct a *system* of thought. And it erroneously implies that it is the business of *The World Viewed* to "set out," to determine *a priori*, film's "conditions and limits."

It goes against everything Cavell stands for, everything he has written about the arts, to suppose that in *The World Viewed* he is using philosophy to settle by theoretical fiat issues about an art or its history that can only be settled by acts of criticism. As he points out in "More of *The World Viewed*," in *The World Viewed* his interest is not in adjudicating the issue of whether the films he values or the films Krauss values are the more serious engagements with the conditions of their medium. His interest is in emphasizing that the adjudication of such an issue "is a matter essentially and simultaneously of the value and understanding one places on the particular objects in question and of the value and understanding one places on the concept of modernism" (*WV*, 216).

52

Cavell uses the term "modernist," he reminds us, to "name the work of an artist whose discoveries and declarations of his medium are to be understood as embodying his effort to maintain the continuity of his art with the past of his art, and to invite and bear comparison with the achievements of his past" (216). Not only does he not use the term to cover "everything that may be thought of as advanced or *avant-garde* in art," his point in using it is in part to "break into" certain uses of

> the concept of the *avant-garde* at least three points: into its implication that advanced art looks away from the past toward the future; into its tendency toward promiscuous attention to any and all claims to advancement, together with a tendency to cede the concept of art altogether, at any rate, to cede the idea of the arts as radically distinguished from one another, which is the sensible significance of the "pure" in art; and into the military-political image prompting its title, which suggests that an art can advance, or survive, in some way other than through its faithfulness to itself, and in particular that what prompts this advance, or promotes this survival, is a synchronized or imminent social advance. (216–17)

Such considerations may provide grounds to regard Eisenstein's films, say, as *avant-garde* but not modernist, Cavell suggests, adding that "this in itself would not imply that his work is less good than any other." They may also provide grounds "on which to regard certain recent experiments in filmmaking as inheritors, or relatives, not of modernism in the other arts, but of (what I called) their modernizings" (217).

In invoking this latter possibility, Cavell is not demeaning the work of experimental filmmakers. When he says, "I do not know this work well or extensively enough for my judgments of it in individual cases to be much use," he is to be taken at his word. He is also to be taken at his word when he says that "if there is a genuine artistic movement in question, and if claims concerning the state of the arts of film are to be based upon it, then it is worth saying that the role of experimentalism in filmmaking is as specific to it as any other of its features," hence that "one cannot assess its significance apart from an assessment of the significance of film as such" (217). One feature in particular that begs for assessment is the fact that

> in the arts of the novel, of music, and of painting contemporary with the establishment of the art of film, the major experimentalists have generally proven to be the major artists of their period, i.e., their "experiments" have been central to the development of the art itself, not more or less peripheral attacks upon it. One can, of course, claim that this will prove to be true of the art of film as well, that the dominant position of movies with their famous directors and stars and their mass audiences will ultimately be shown to have been an aberration of the art from almost its beginning, caused and maintained

by historical, economic forces essentially external to its autonomous development. We should be able to convince ourselves of this about a century from
now. (218)

There is disdain in this last line, but it is not directed at experimental films.
Cavell's disdain is for the claim sometimes made on their behalf that it has
already been shown, on the basis of some theory, that the movies that
are strand over strand with his life have no value as works of art. No one
is now in a position to make such a claim, in his view. However, in the
meantime he is prepared to modify some of the assertions he has made
about film's relation to modernism by making it clear that there are other
ways of speaking about this relation that seem to him acceptable. He finds
himself prepared to say, for example, either that

> movies from their beginning have existed in a state of modernism, from the
> beginning have had to achieve their power by deliberate investigations of the
> powers of the medium; or else that movies from their beginning have existed
> in two states, one modern, one traditional, sometimes running parallel to
> and at varying distances from one another, sometimes crossing, sometimes
> interweaving; or else that the concept of modernism has no clear application
> to the art of film. (219)

Cavell does not feel that any of these alternative formulations weakens
The World Viewed's insistence that film is the last traditional art. On the
contrary, each would be a way of explaining that insistence. He also
continues to hold the view, which runs through *The World Viewed*, that
"pride of place within the canon of serious films will be found occupied
by those films that most clearly and most deeply discover the powers
of the medium itself" (219). Again, whether "pride of place" will go to
experimental films or to ordinary movies is a question to be settled by acts
of criticism, not by theoretical fiat.

Chapter 2: "Sights and Sounds"

The starting point of Chapter 2 is that movies have to do with the
projection of reality, of "live persons and real things in actual spaces,"
as Cavell puts it in "More of *The World Viewed*" (165–66). In arguing that
the unprecedented role reality plays in film must be his starting point
in reflecting on what film is, Cavell is aware he is bucking a "pervasive
intellectual fashion, apparently sanctioned by the history of epistemology
and the rise of modern science, according to which we never really, and
never really can, see reality as it is" (165). Cavell resists this fashionable

skepticism because of his conviction that "a general dismissal of reality depends upon theories (of knowledge, of science, of art, of reality, of realism) whose power to convince is hardly greater than reality's own" (165). (The Lacanian/Althusserian theoretical framework that for so long dominated academic film study in America, as well as semiology, deconstruction, and cultural theory, are instances of theories that dismiss reality in general as a mere ideological construct.)

The question of the role reality plays in film was in any case forced on him, Cavell testifies, by reading Panofsky and Bazin. Nonetheless, it is incorrect to think of Cavell as a Bazinian realist, as he has sometimes inappropriately been labeled. (It may well be incorrect to think of Bazin himself as the kind of realist he is often claimed to be, but that is another question.) In 1971, when *The World Viewed* was published, *Cahiers du cinéma*, once a bastion of Bazin-inspired film criticism, was advancing a systematic critique of the ideological underpinnings of realism. *The World Viewed*, too, articulates a powerful critique of realist theories of film.

While agreeing with Panofsky and Bazin that movies are committed to communicate only by way of what is real, Cavell rejects the "unabashed appeals" to nature and reality inherent in Panofsky's view that the medium of the movies is physical reality as such or Bazin's view that the cinema is of its essence a dramaturgy of Nature. "What Panofsky and Bazin have in mind," he suggests, is that "the basis of the medium of movies is photographic, and that a photograph is *of* reality" (16). But Panofsky and Bazin do not ask the question that guides the thinking of *The World Viewed*, or do not ask it in the same way: What *becomes* of reality when it is projected and screened? What *becomes* of objects and persons in the world when film displaces them from their "natural sequences and locales"?[5]

"On film reality is not merely described or merely represented," Cavell writes (*WV*, 166). Movies project and screen reality rather than describing it, as (some) novels do, or representing it as (some) paintings do. Insofar as movies represent reality, they do so *by way of* projections, not representations, of reality. The difference between projections and representations is one of the central themes of *The World Viewed*. Equally central is the difference between reality and projections of reality—what film's mode of displacing reality comes to, what film's transformations of reality make possible (and what they make necessary). These themes are linked, in turn, to yet another: the difference between film and painting— what their difference comes to, what it makes possible, and necessary, for each. In attempting to understand what film is, Cavell employs the procedures of ordinary language philosophy to work through ways film differs from other kinds of things, ways what we say about film differs from what we say about other kinds of things.

One way *The World Viewed* develops these themes is by reflecting on the historical fact that modernist painting came to forgo the representation of reality. Embracing Michael Fried's interpretation of the origins and history of modernist painting, Cavell argues that painting contemporary with the advent of motion pictures (in common with other representational arts, such as the novel) had been "withdrawing from the representation of reality as from a hopeless, but always unnecessary, task" (16).[6] According to *The World Viewed*, when painting withdrew from representing reality, photographic media like movies did not take up that task. Reality plays a central role in film, but its role is not that of being represented. Then again, reality continued to play a central role in painting, too, even when painting was forced to forgo representation and likeness.

One of *The World Viewed*'s guiding intuitions is that the role reality plays in movies cannot be accounted for without addressing the ontological differences between photography and painting. Another is that the differences between photography and painting cannot be accounted for without addressing the mysterious relationship between a photograph and the things (and/or persons) in that photograph.

In Chapter 2 of *The World Viewed*, Cavell takes an initial stab at characterizing this relationship: "A photograph does not present us with 'likenesses' of things; it presents us, we want to say, with the things themselves" (17). His Wittgensteinian or Austinian "we want to say" alerts us to his awareness that it sounds paradoxical, or even obviously false, to say that photographs present us not with likenesses of things but with the things themselves. But "Photographs do not present us with things themselves" sounds equally paradoxical or false. As always, Cavell's aim in appealing to what we ordinarily say and mean is not to convince readers without proof, but to call upon us to prove something to ourselves, to test something against ourselves.

In accordance with the principle that we can find out what kind of object anything is by investigating expressions which show the kind of thing said about it, the lesson Cavell draws from the fact that we do not know how to characterize the relationship between a photograph and the things and persons in that photograph is that we do not know how to place photographs ontologically. We are perplexed as to what they are.

Cavell specifies a source of our perplexity. "We might say that we

56

don't know how to think of the *connection* of a photograph and what it is a photograph of. The image is not a likeness; it is not exactly a replica, or a shadow, or an apparition either, though all these . . . share a striking feature with photographs—an aura or history of magic surrounding them" (18).

An audio recording is not ontologically unplaceable the way a photograph is. A recording (of a French horn, say) is a copy (in principle, an all but perfect copy) of something (the sound made by that horn). There is no comparable "something"—no thing separable in principle from the object in the photograph, the way the sound of a horn is separable from the horn itself—that a photograph is a copy of.

> We said that the record reproduces its sound, but we cannot say that a photograph reproduces a sight (or a look or an appearance). . . . What you see, when you sight something, is an object—anyway not the sight of an object. Nor will the epistemologist's "sense-data" or "surfaces" provide correct descriptions here. . . . If the sense-data of photographs were the same as the sense-data of the objects they contain, we couldn't tell a photograph of an object from the object itself. To say that a photograph is of the surfaces of objects suggests that it emphasizes texture. . . . I feel like saying: Objects are too *close* to their sights to give them up for reproducing; in order to reproduce the sights they (as it were) make, you have to reproduce *them*—make a mold, or take an impression. (19–20)

The implication of this painstaking passage is not that photographs reproduce the objects in them, but that photographs are not recordings. To speak of a photograph as if it were a recording, as Bazin does, is to forget how different these things are, to fail to acknowledge what each, in its difference, is, what makes each singular and special.

Cavell also finds himself unable to accept Bazin's suggestion that photographs are visual molds or impressions. To speak of photographs as molds is to forget how different photographs and molds are from each other. In particular it is to forget that "molds and impressions and imprints have clear procedures for getting *rid* of their originals, whereas in a photograph, the original is still as present as it ever was. Not present as it once was to the camera; but that is only a mold-machine, not the mold itself" (20). By speaking of them as molds, Bazin forgets what it is about photographs that we find so perplexing. When we forget this, we not only forget something about photographs, we also forget something about ourselves, something about our own experience that it is perplexing for us to think about, to try to place.

"A child," Cavell observes, "might be very puzzled by the remark, said of a photograph, 'That's your grandmother' " (18). The puzzled child does not yet know (as we might put it) what a photograph is, has not yet learned to say and mean the kinds of things we ordinarily say and mean about photographs. This object she is beholding is not her grandmother in the flesh. Then how can she point to it and say "That's my grandmother"? How can it be her grandmother—who is not now present—she is seeing? The child's puzzlement also reveals that if she does not (yet) know what kind of thing a photograph is, simply pointing to a photograph of her grandmother and saying "That's your grandmother" is unlikely to teach this to her.

Characteristically, Cavell's example, however casual it may appear, is a resonant one. To know that an object is a photograph is to know something about its origins. To know that it is a photograph of one's grandmother is to know something as well about one's own origins—about how one entered the picture, about how one enters into *this* picture. The scene of instruction Cavell invokes intimates a connection, explored within *The World Viewed* as a whole, between the way it is a mystery to us what photographs are, how they have entered the world, and the way it is a mystery to us what we are, how we have entered the world.

As Cavell notes, "children are very early *no longer* puzzled by such remarks, luckily" (18). Children quickly learn to say and mean the kinds of things we ordinarily say and mean about photographs. And, Cavell's "luckily" implies, they are fortunate to learn these ways of speaking. The fact that very soon children are no longer puzzled by remarks like "That's your grandmother" said in the presence of a photograph does not mean they have arrived at a solution to the puzzle the existence of photographs once posed to them. When we stop to think about it, the fact that when we look at photographs we see things that are not present remains as puzzling to us as it ever was. The fact that ordinarily we do not stop to think about photographs, that we forget our original puzzlement, is itself a puzzling fact (about photographs and about ourselves) that we do not ordinarily stop to think about.

"It may be felt that I make too great a mystery of these objects," Cavell writes. "My feeling is rather that we have forgotten how mysterious these things are, and in general how *different* things are from one another, as though we had forgotten how to value them" (19). When we forget how mysterious photographs are, how different they are from all other kinds of things, we forget something of value about photographs. When we forget this, we forget how mysterious we are (how different human beings are from other kinds of beings, how different we are from each other).

Sarah Shagan Rothman (Bill Rothman's grandmother);
Catherine O'Brien Keane (Marian Keane's grandmother).

We forget how to value our own lives, our own experience. We forget something of value about being human.

■ ■

To this point in Chapter 2, Cavell has not provided a definition of "photograph." Nor does the remainder of the chapter provide such a definition. Neither does the chapter go on to advance a *theory* to explain the ontology of the photographic image. Cavell does not attempt to counter Bazin's theory that photographs are recordings or molds, for example, with a comparable theory of his own. The claim made by Chapter 2 as a whole is that to advance such a theory—to theorize that photographs are, say, indexical signs, or ideological constructs, or media texts—is to attempt to explain away the mystery that when we look at a photograph we see things which are not present. In Cavell's view, theory is not to be used, as it so often is, to deny the puzzlement internal to our experience of photographs, the puzzlement internal to what, in our experience, we know photographs, and know ourselves, to be. To use theory that way is to escape only by avoiding the perspective of self-reflection that philosophy alone is capable of providing.

Because Cavell's claim is that it is mysterious to us what photographs are, it is no evidence against his position that it may be difficult or impossible to spell out a coherent realist theory of photography. Hence the objections Noel Carroll raises against Bazin in *Philosophical Problems of Classical Film Theory*, whether or not they fairly address Bazin's position, do not apply to Cavell's. Nonetheless, Carroll takes them to apply to *The World Viewed* as well: "Bazin believes," Carroll writes, that a "photographic image is always an image of . . . the objects, places, events, and persons that gave rise to it. A photographic image re-presents its model. . . . Bazin himself does not really supply an argument for this point. The leading contemporary Bazinian, Stanley Cavell, however, does. Cavell initiates his argument by asking what it is that films reproduce."[7]

As we have seen, however, Cavell does not initiate his argument in Chapter 2 by asking what films "reproduce" or "re-present." Acknowledging our impulse to say that a photograph presents us not with reproductions, likenesses of things, but with the things themselves, Cavell's question concerns what it is that a photograph of an object *presents*.

Perhaps it is inattentiveness to Cavell's words (to "this prose just here"), or perhaps it is a reluctance to tackle head-on the opinion common within film study that Cavell is a Bazin acolyte, that leads Carroll to assert that Cavell argues "that 'sights' are rather queer metaphysical entities that might better be banished from one's ontology in the name of parsimony. . . . But if it is not the sight or the appearance of the object that a photographic image represents, then it must be the object itself that is represented."[8]

Cavell's argument is not, as Carroll supposes, that objects do not have sights the way French horns have sounds, that for that reason a photograph of an object cannot represent the sight of that object, and that therefore it must be the object itself that the photograph represents. Cavell argues, rather, that a photograph does not bear the relationship to *anything* that a recording bears to the sound it reproduces. A photograph does not reproduce the sight or appearance of an object that is in it, but neither does it reproduce the object itself. Cavell's point is that there is no thing that a photograph reproduces, and he concludes from this that photographs are not copies or recordings at all. Nor do photographs represent ("*re*-present") the objects that appear in them, for the reason that in a photograph the original is still as present as it ever was.

When Cavell asserts that what makes photographs different from all other kinds of things in the world, what makes their singularity so singularly difficult to place, is the mysterious fact that when we look at a photograph we "see things that are not present," he anticipates an objection: "Someone will object: 'That is playing with words. We're not seeing something not present; we are looking at something perfectly present, namely, a *photograph*' " (19).

Carroll voices precisely the objection Cavell anticipates: "But why must we believe that something or anything is in fact re-presented via photographic representation? . . . What photography does is to *produce* a stand-in for its model."[9] Cavell's reply to his own imagined interlocutor is equally telling as a rejoinder to Carroll: "That is affirming something I have not denied. On the contrary, I am precisely describing, or wishing to describe, what it means to say that there is this photograph here" (19).

Cavell's point is that the relationship between an object or person in a photograph and the photograph itself is different from that object's or person's relationship with any other kind of thing in the world. Merely saying that a photograph "produces a stand-in for its model" does not illuminate the way photography's kind of stand-in is different from other kinds of stand-ins—from counterfeits, fakes, or straw men, for example, which are intended to be passed off for the real thing, or from proxies or agents, which are not.

Ordinarily, a stand-in takes the place of a different person or thing. There are criteria for distinguishing between the two, although in some cases it may require special expertise to apply those criteria. However, the person(s) and/or thing(s) the photograph is *of* and the person(s) and/or thing(s) *in* that photograph are not separate individuals. There can be no criteria for distinguishing them for the simple reason that they are one and the same. To speak of photographs as stand-ins, then, is not in itself to account for the singular relationship between a photograph and the person(s) and/or thing(s) in that photograph. It is to forget, once more, how different photographs are from other kinds of things.

Again, Chapter 2 in no way claims to explain away what we find perplexing in the relationship between photographs and the person(s) and/or thing(s) in them. The chapter only calls upon us to stop forgetting how mysterious it is to us that when we look at photographs we see persons and things that are not present.

■ ■

Although *The World Viewed* does not accept Bazin's suggestion that cameras are mold-machines, it does endorse his view that, as Cavell puts it, "Photographs are not *hand*-made; they are manufactured," that there is an "inescapable fact of mechanism or automatism in the making of these images" (20). The mystery of photographs is their capacity to allow persons and things in the world to present, to reveal, *themselves*.

In our experience of teaching *The World Viewed*, students frequently take umbrage at the idea that in photography the world itself plays such an active role. They take Cavell to be asserting that there is no art to photography. However, nothing could be further from his intention than to deny that photography can be an art. He is not denying that photographs can be composed like paintings, for example, or otherwise shaped or manipulated. His claim is that there is an inescapable element of mechanism or automatism in the making of photographs, not that there is *nothing but* mechanism or automatism in their making.

Although Cavell agrees that it is a significant fact about photographs that they are not handmade, he rejects what he takes to be Bazin's claim that the element of mechanism or automatism in the making of photographs enables them to satisfy "once and for all and in its very essence, our obsession with realism" (20). This claim is misleading because it denies photography the status of a medium. The fact that photography enables the world to present or reveal itself does not mean that there is no difference between a photograph and the thing or person in that photograph.

Then what does the fact of automatism in the making of photographs mean, what does it come to? "Getting to the right depth of this fact of automatism," this fact that film enables the world to present or reveal *itself*, is a task the remainder of Chapter 2 undertakes. Rather, these extraordinarily dense two-and-a-half pages *begin* to undertake this task. "Getting to the right depth of this fact of automatism" is a project that occupies the entirety of Chapters 2 through 5 and, indeed, the whole of *The World Viewed*. This must be so, given that the relationship of film and painting is a central concern of the book, and given Cavell's conviction that the concept of automatism is a key to thinking through that relationship.

As a first step in "getting to the right depth of this fact of automatism," Cavell argues that it is "misleading to say, as Bazin does, that 'photography has freed the plastic arts from their obsession with likeness,' for this makes it seem (and it does often look) as if photography and painting were in competition, or that painting had wanted something that photography broke in and satisfied" (21).

Bazin's formulation implies, in effect, that painting wished to be photography. But painting's aspiration was always to create *paintings*, and its obsession was not with likeness but with *reality*. The obsession with reality that led painting to create ever more perfect likenesses ultimately forced painting, in Manet, to forgo likeness "because the illusions it had learned to create did not provide the conviction in reality, the connection with reality, it craved" (21).

Photography did not free painting from likeness, nor from the idea that a painting had to be a picture (that is, *of* or *about* something else), "until long after the establishment of photography; and then not because it finally dawned on painters that paintings were not pictures, but because that was the way to maintain connection with (the history of) the art of painting, to maintain conviction in its powers to create paintings, meaningful objects in paint" (21).

Furthermore, painting's final denial of objective reference was not a complete yielding of connection with reality. On the contrary, it was precisely the craving for connection with reality that likenesses were no longer able to satisfy that motivated this denial. Objective reference no longer enabled painting to satisfy this craving, Cavell argues, because it no longer enabled painting to provide a convincing sense of *presentness*—our presentness to the world, the world's presentness to us.

The concept of presentness, crucial to *The World Viewed* as a whole, is taken up at length in the pivotal Chapter 15 ("Excursus: Some Modernist Painting"), which reflects on "the recent major painting which [Michael Fried] describes as objects of *presentness*," and on what such painting finds it necessary to do, and to be faithful to, in order to "maintain its conviction in its own power to establish connection with reality" (22). Suffice it to say here that Cavell does not give the word some special meaning, does not use it as a technical term. "Presentness," as it occurs in *The World Viewed*, is an ordinary noun like "whiteness" or "blackness," a noun formed from the word "present" in accordance with the familiar grammatical rules of the English language. What the word "presentness" means, what presentness is, hinges on what "present" means, on what the present is, on what we mean when we speak of the present, or speak of someone or something *as* present. ("Presentness" is *not* synonymous with "presence," as in Jacques Derrida's critique of "the metaphysics of presence.")[10]

That objective reference no longer enables painting to provide a sense of presentness reflects a fundamental change in human existence, in Cavell's view. At some point, "the unhinging of our consciousness from the world interposed our subjectivity between us and our presentness to the world." For modern human beings, "our subjectivity became what is present to us; individuality became isolation" (22).

The World Viewed returns again and again to this idea of the unhinging of our consciousness from the world. At one level, Cavell locates it at a particular historical moment (the Protestant Reformation, the theater of Shakespeare, the birth of modern philosophy in Descartes's experience of skeptical doubt). He also suggests that it can be located (as it were psychoanalytically) at a particular moment in the life of every modern human being; once having taken place, it is also repeated again and again in that individual's life.

The World Viewed understands the "unhinging of our consciousness from the world" to be a historical event and also a mythical event, like the Biblical fall from grace. Picture it as a spiritual and psychological and political cataclysm that presents us with a new fact (or is it a new consciousness of an old fact?) about ourselves, about our condition as human beings. We now feel isolated by our subjectivity. It is our subjectivity, not a world we objectively apprehend, that appears present to us. Nor do we objectively apprehend our own subjectivity; our subjectivity, too, appears present to us only subjectively, as if our consciousness has come unhinged from our subjectivity no less than from the world.

"So far as photography satisfied a wish," Cavell goes on, it satisfied "the human wish, intensifying in the West since the Reformation, to escape subjectivity and metaphysical isolation—a wish for the power to reach this world, having for so long tried, at last hopelessly, to manifest fidelity to another" (21).

It is crucial not to misconstrue this point, as Douglas Lackey does in his review of *The World Viewed* in *The Journal of Aesthetics and Art Criticism*. Misquoting Cavell as claiming that "Photography satisfied . . . the human wish to escape subjectivity and metaphysical isolation," Lackey understands Cavell to mean that photography *succeeded* in satisfying this human wish that painting had failed to satisfy.[11] This ignores Cavell's insistence that painting and photography were never in competition. It also fails to recognize that Cavell would find it as appropriate to say of modernist painting as of photography that "so far as it satisfied a wish" the wish it satisfied is the human wish to escape subjectivity and metaphysical isolation. Cavell's underlying point is that so far as photography and modernist painting succeeded in satisfying this wish, they satisfied it in fundamentally different ways.

The problem is that Lackey ignores Cavell's crucial "So far as . . . ," which pointedly leaves open the possibility that photography's satisfaction of this wish was less than complete. The thrust of *The World Viewed* as a whole is that although film appeared to have solved the problem of reality by "magically" neutralizing the need to represent it in order to connect with it, movies really "brought the problem of reality to some ultimate head," as "More of *The World Viewed*" puts it (*WV*, 195).

In Cavell's understanding, our wish to escape subjectivity cannot be separated from our wish to achieve selfhood. Selfhood cannot be achieved apart from reaching this world, apart from escaping the metaphysical isolation that has become our condition. Cavell's idea is that selfhood cannot be achieved apart from the acknowledgment of others (their acknowledgment of us, and ours of them). Hence he writes, "Apart from the wish for selfhood (hence the always simultaneous granting of otherness as well), I do not understand the value of art. Apart from this wish and its achievement, art is exhibition" (22).

Merely to represent (as expressionism does) our terror of ourselves in isolation, which is our *response* to this new fact of our condition, is to *exhibit* our isolation, to theatricalize our isolation and thereby seal our fate. Cavell argues that for modern human beings, for creatures like us who find our subjectivity interposed between our selves and the world, photography and modernist painting exemplify different routes to overcoming theatricality, to reaching this world and achieving selfhood.

Modernist painting accepts the recession of the world so as to maintain its conviction in its own power to establish connection with reality. It acknowledges "that endless presence of self" in order to permit us "presentness to ourselves, apart from which there is no hope for a world" (23).

"To speak of our subjectivity as the route back to our conviction in reality is to speak of romanticism," Cavell writes.

> Hence Kant, and Hegel; hence Blake secreting the world he believes in; hence Wordsworth competing with the history of poetry by writing out himself, writing himself back into the world. A century later Heidegger is investigating Being by investigating *Dasein* . . . and Wittgenstein investigates the world . . . by investigating what we say, what we are inclined to say, what our pictures of phenomena are, in order to wrest the world from our possessions so that we may possess it again. (22)

In passages like this, *The World Viewed* acknowledges its own roots within romanticism. Cavell, too, is a philosopher who investigates reality by investigating what we say, what our pictures of phenomena are. He is a philosopher who seeks by writing to restore himself to the world, who calls upon us to wrest the world from our possessions so we may possess it again. *The World Viewed* begins with its author's acknowledgment that what he calls his "natural relation" to movies has been broken. His book calls upon us to acknowledge that we, too, are no longer possessed by the world of movies the way we once were, that we no longer possess the world of movies the way we once did. In giving thought to our new sense that the world of movies has become lost to us, Cavell proceeds by investigating, philosophically, what we say, what we are inclined to say, about the phenomena of movies. By investigating "what our pictures are of movies," by investigating an experience of movies he calls upon us to acknowledge as ours as well, *The World Viewed* calls upon us to make our experience present to us. The goal is to wrest the world of movies "from our possessions so that we may possess it again"—not to enable us to restore the relation to movies that once came naturally to us, but to enable us to achieve a new relation to movies, to the world, to ourselves.

Movies are photographic. Photography's route to "reaching this world," as opposed to modernist painting's route, is by overcoming the endless presence of subjectivity.

> Photography maintains the presentness of the world by accepting our absence from it. The reality in a photograph is present to me while I am not present to it . . . (through no fault of my subjectivity). . . . Photography overcomes subjectivity in a way undreamed of by painting, a way that could not satisfy painting, one which does not so much defeat the act of painting as escape

it altogether: by *automatism*, by removing the human agent from the task of reproduction. (23)

With this idea that photography produces images of reality automatically, without subjectivity intervening, Cavell feels he is getting "to the right depth of this fact of automatism."

We are now prepared to say why Cavell believes it is misleading to claim that the inescapable element of mechanism or automatism in the making of these images enables photography to satisfy once and for all, and in its very essence, our obsession with realism. First, because our obsession was never with realism but with *reality* (with reaching this world, attaining selfhood). Second, because photographs are not more realistic than paintings. That photographic media communicate by way of what is real does not make them inherently realistic. Indeed, it makes no more sense to speak of photographs as realistic than to speak of reality as realistic. Realistic as opposed to what? Fantastic? What could be more fantastic than reality? Reality is real, not realistic. After all, as Cavell will go on to remind us, reality is precisely what it is that fantasy may be confused with. When objects and persons in the world are projected and screened, they are displaced from their natural sequences and locales. This displacement, which enables movies to depict the fantastic as readily as the natural (a point crucial to *The World Viewed* as a whole), itself acknowledges their physical reality. Only what exists in the world can be photographed, subjected to photography's way of displacing things and people. And what exists in the world already bears the stamp of our fantasies.

As we have seen, *The World Viewed* resists what Cavell calls the "pervasive intellectual fashion" that holds that we do not, cannot, really know reality. Cavell resists this skepticism on the ground that reality's powers of compelling conviction are at least as strong as that of any theory. If appeals to theory cannot ultimately defeat our conviction in reality, unabashed appeals to reality like Bazin's or Panofsky's cannot ultimately free us from skeptical doubt. Reality is precisely what fantasy can be confused with (and what can be confused with fantasy), and reality is precisely what it is whose existence human beings are capable of doubting (as Cavell puts it, the possibility of skepticism is internal to the conditions of human knowledge). There is no particular feature, or set of features, by which the world on film can be distinguished from reality. The objects and persons projected on the screen appear real for the simple reason that they are real. And yet these objects and persons do not really exist (now), are not (now) really in our presence.

67

The role reality plays in movies enables them to depict the fantastic as readily as the natural, and makes the world on film what in "More of *The World Viewed*" Cavell will call "a moving image of skepticism" (*WV,* 188). But for Cavell it is a fundamental principle that the possibility of skepticism is internal to the conditions of human knowledge. That we cannot know reality with absolute certainty is a fact about human knowledge, a fact about what knowledge, for human beings, *is*. It does not follow from this fact that we cannot really know the world, or ourselves in it.

Chapter 3: "Photograph and Screen"

Chapter 3 makes a number of points that further Cavell's philosophical investigation of what film is.

The first is that a photograph is *of* the world, the world as a whole. Pointing to an object in a photograph, Cavell notes, you can always ask what lies behind it. "This only accidentally makes sense when asked of an object in a painting. . . . When a photograph is cropped, the rest of the world is cut *out*. The implied presence of the rest of the world, and its explicit rejection, are as essential in the experience of a photograph as what it explicitly presents" (24). Because it is the field of a photograph, the moving picture screen has no border; it does not *have* a frame, it *is* a frame.

Douglas Lackey raises an objection. "If you have the usual still photograph, it does make sense to ask what lies in the space beyond the area represented in the photograph. But if you have a feature film that employs *sets*, then the question is out of place. You cannot ask what parts of Babylon lie beyond the part of Babylon you see in Griffith's *Intolerance*. What lies there is Los Angeles."[12]

The sets Griffith constructed for *Intolerance* are meant to convey the impression that what is revealed to the camera is located in Babylon, not Los Angeles. What lies within the frame is meant to lead us to think it appropriate to ask, "What parts of Babylon lie beyond the part of Babylon within the frame?" Whether or not we recognize that it is a studio set projected on the screen, not an ancient temple, and that it was located in the American Babylon, not the Biblical one, what we see on the screen is really in the world. It certainly makes sense to ask, at any given moment of *Intolerance*, what is in the region beyond the frame.

Cavell's claim is that "the whole history of movie production technology, with its special effects, back-projections, miniatures, false fronts, etc.," does not "show how unnecessary the fact of reality is." On the contrary, it shows "just how necessary it is, or how it is necessary," as he puts it in "More of *The World Viewed*." "For the point of all this elaboration of machinery is exactly that it shall serve for reality, from the camera's point of view" (*WV*, 197). The philosopher Alexander Sesonske formulates an objection akin to Lackey's: "What is 'the world' that Cavell says photographs, and therefore movies, are of? It is not clear. . . . That the events we see on the screen really occurred at some past time in this same actual world that we now share, as the events in old newsreels did? But . . . Spade and Archer never shared an office in San Francisco; Jules and Jim never shared a girl in prewar Paris."[13]

In "More of *The World Viewed*," Cavell paraphrases Sesonske's charge that *The World Viewed* neglects the fact that the events of most movies are fictional, and that they therefore

> *cannot* from the beginning be real or have happened, except perhaps by the purest or most miraculous of coincidences. . . . It may seem to follow that the issue of reality is settled, that movies are "something on their own"; the only things they *could* be recordings of—real events happening as they are transcribed on the screen—have simply never taken place. . . . Events in a movie are ones we can never be, or can never have been, present at apart from the movie itself. (183)

Cavell's response in "More of *The World Viewed*" to Sesonske's objection merits careful attention. First, he reiterates the reasons *The World Viewed* already spells out for insisting that movies are not recordings. He then argues,

> When someone says that we cannot have been present at the events projected on the screen apart from that projection itself, it does not follow that reality has played no essential role in the origin of that projection. All that follows is that any role reality has played is not that of having been recorded. But reality is not so much as a candidate for that role, because the projections we view on a screen are not in principle aurally or visually indistinguishable from the events of which they're projections—what could be more distinguishable? (183)

Having disarmed the objection, Cavell does not simply let it drop, but allows Sesonske's puzzlement to motivate a question of his own: What *is* reality's role in movies, if it is not that of being recorded? Finally, he notes that the entirety of *The World Viewed* gives "a series of answers to that question": "I describe the role of reality as one of being photographed, projected, screened, exhibited, and viewed. (These answers are the paths of my differences from Panofsky's and Bazin's emphasis on 'reality itself.') The significance I attach to these terms can be assessed . . . by nothing short of my book as a whole" (184).

By taking its motivation seriously, in other words, by undertaking to understand the view he is criticizing from the inside, Cavell turns what seems a devastating objection into a valuable piece of instruction as to how *The World Viewed* calls for being read.

■ ■

A second point, or set of points, made by Chapter 3 is that a moving picture's world is screened.

> The screen is not a support, not like a canvas; there is nothing to support, that way. It holds a projection, as light as light. A screen is a barrier. . . . It screens me from the world it holds—that is, makes me invisible. And it screens that world from me—that is, screens its existence from me. That the projected world does not exist (now) is its only difference from reality. (There is no feature, or set of features, in which it differs. Existence is not a predicate.) (24)

That the screen is the field of a photograph means it does not *have* a frame, it *is* a frame. "The frame is the whole field of the screen—as a frame of film is the whole field of a photograph, like the frame of a loom or a house. In this sense, the screen-frame is a mold, or form" (25). In a moving picture, "successive film frames are fit flush into the fixed screen frame"; the result is a "phenomenological frame that is indefinitely extendible and contractible."

Film quickly discovered that the screen-frame, constantly in flux, can be made "the image of perfect attention." Cavell writes, "Drawing the camera back, and panning it, are two ways of extending the frame; a close-up is of a part of the body, or of one object or small set of objects, supported by and reverberating the whole frame of nature" (25). Chapter 3 concludes with an eloquent passage that is supported by, and reverberates, the whole frame of *The World Viewed*:

> Early in its history, the cinema discovered the possibility of *calling* attention to persons and parts of persons and objects; but it is equally a possibility of the medium not to call attention to them but, rather, to let the world happen, to let its parts draw attention to themselves according to their natural weight. This possibility is less explored than its opposite. Dreyer, Flaherty, Vigo, Renoir, and Antonioni are masters of it. (25)

■ ■

Cavell's characterization of the movie screen as a barrier has two aspects. First, the projected world is separated from reality by the fact, and only by the fact, that it does not exist (now). Second, when we are viewing a movie, we are invisible to the projected world, absent from the world the movie screen frames.

1. The projected world does not differ from reality by being, for example, two- rather than three-dimensional. Although photographic images may be printed on two dimensional surfaces, photographs are of a world in three dimensions. Similarly, although the world framed by the movie screen is projected onto a two-dimensional screen, it is not a two-dimensional world. (As always in *The World Viewed*, Cavell is at pains to avoid underestimating the difference between painting and film. His point here, that film images are not flat the way paintings are, will be amplified in later chapters.)

When Cavell writes "There is no way the projected world differs from reality apart from the fact that it does not exist (now)," his parenthetical "now" may seem to suggest that in the past the projected world really existed (24). This line echoes the ending of Chapter 2—"The reality in a photograph is present to me while I am not present to it; and a world I know, and see, but to which I am nevertheless not present (through no fault of my subjectivity) is a world past" (23).

As will emerge, the temporality or tense of film is an important issue in *The World Viewed* as a whole. At this stage, it is useful to keep in mind that Cavell's understanding of film's temporality—the pastness (as opposed to presentness) of film's projected world—is tied to one of the book's most suggestive claims, which is that the mode of narrative of movies is closer to myth than to fiction.

In any case, as "More of *The World Viewed*" points out, *The World Viewed* does not imply that the projected world of a movie is *literally* the past. There was no time at which the world now framed by the screen was literally present. This follows from the fact, upon which *The World Viewed* insists, that reality's role in movies is not that of being recorded. The projected world, we might say, is the past *mythically*. (We are reminded of the passage in the foreword of *Must We Mean What We Say?* in which Cavell suggests that in a modernist situation "one's own practice and ambition can be identified only against the continuous experience of the past," adding that in this formulation "past" loses its temporal accent and means anything "not present," that within modernism "the past" does not refer simply to the historical past, but also to "one's own past, to what is past, or what has passed, within oneself" [*MWMWWS*, xix].)

2. The other aspect of Cavell's picture of the movie screen as a barrier is the fact—crucial to *The World Viewed* as a whole—that we are invisible to

71

the projected world, absent from the world the movie screen frames. The fact that the projected world is free from us—free from our subjectivity, from our presence, from the need to represent itself to us—cannot be separated from the fact that the projected world differs from the existing world only by not existing (now). As Cavell puts it in "More of *The World Viewed*," what "makes the physical medium of film unlike anything else on earth lies in the absence of what it causes to appear to us; that is to say, in the nature of our absence from it" (*WV*, 166).

Our absence from what appears projected before us is the other face of the absence of what these projections make present. The mode of absence of the world framed by the movie screen cannot be separated from the mode of our absence from the projected world. They are two faces of the same reality.

Chapter 4: "Audience, Actor and Star"

Seamlessly extending the reflections of Chapters 2 and 3, Chapter 4 begins with the assertion that "the depth of the automatism of photography is to be read not alone in its production of an image of reality, but in its mechanical defeat of our presence to that reality" (25).

Joel Snyder raises the objection that by focusing on the mechanical or automatic aspect of the production of photographic images, *The World Viewed* slights the role of developing and printing.[14] Although the human hand plays no active part in developing and printing, either, those processes do not seem automatic but rather mysterious, even magical, like alchemy. The science of chemistry identifies mechanisms on which developing and printing rely, but those mechanisms are theoretical abstractions; they are not comparable to tangible machines like cameras and projectors, whose work is as readily visualizable as the operation of a bicycle.

However, Cavell's passage claims only that there is an irreducible element of mechanism or automatism to photography, not that the production of photographic images (or the defeat of our presence to the reality in photographs) is nothing but mechanical or automatic. Far from denying that there is something unvisualizable, seemingly magical, about the production of photographic images (and the defeat of our presence to the reality in those images), Chapter 6 will go on to argue—and "More of *The World Viewed*" will reiterate—that (mythically, as it were) movies arise out of magic, from "below" the world.

Movies defeat our presence in a way impossible for theater, Cavell argues. "The audience in a theater can be defined as those to whom the actors are present while they are not present to the actors. But movies allow the audience to be mechanically absent" (25).

Sesonske points out that the first part of the above formulation is a misstatement, since in a theater the audience is present to the actors.[15] In "More of *The World Viewed*," Cavell acknowledges that his own formulation is, indeed, incorrect as it stands. It conflates two ideas. One is that the audience in a theater can be described "as those to whom the *characters* are present while they are not present to the characters" (*WV*, 179). (This is an idea *Must We Mean What We Say?* develops in the essays "Ending the Waiting Game" and "The Avoidance of Love.") The second is that viewers in a movie house, by contrast, can be described "as those present neither to the characters nor the actors."

In "The Avoidance of Love," Cavell observes that "practically, or conventionally, 'audience'—for theater in the period after Shakespeare through, say, the 19th century—means 'those present whom the actors ignore' " (*MWMWWS*, 337). We can at any moment rush onto the stage and confront the actors. But we do not. The fact that we remain "hidden and silent and fixed" needs accounting for (*MWMWWS*, 338). And different cases call for different accounts.

As *King Lear* runs its course, we do nothing. But we are not acknowledging the tragedy that is unfolding on stage if we explain our inaction by saying that we are distracted by the pleasures of witnessing this folly, or because of our knowledge of the conventions of theater, or because we think there will be some more appropriate time in which to act, or because we feel helpless to undo events of such proportion. We cannot acknowledge the tragedy of *King Lear* without acknowledging the awesome fact that we do nothing as the tragedy unfolds because there is nothing for us to do. No more than Lear can we "do and suffer what it is another's to do and suffer" (*MWMWWS*, 339).

In viewing a movie, however, "my helplessness is mechanically assured," as Cavell puts it in *The World Viewed*. Choosing his words to echo formulations in "The Avoidance of Love," he writes that the fact that we are invisible and inaudible to the actors and fixed in position "is not part of a convention I have to comply with; the proceedings do not have to make good the fact that I do nothing in the face of tragedy, or that I laugh at the follies of others. . . . I am present not at something happening, which I must confirm, but at something that has happened, which I absorb, like a memory" (26).

Cavell anticipates resistance to the claim that the difference between movie house and theater lies in a difference in our modes of absence. "But surely there is the obvious difference . . . that is not recorded by what has so far been said. . . . In a theater we are in the presence of an actor, in a movie house we are not. You have said that in both places the actor is in our presence and in neither are we in his, the difference lying in the mode of our absence. But . . . also . . . in a theater a real man is *there*, and in a movie no real man is there" (26).

Bazin counters this resistance by simply denying that the screen is incapable of putting us in the presence of the actor; it, as Cavell paraphrases Bazin, "relays his presence to us, as by mirrors" (26). Cavell argues that Bazin's claim "really fits the facts of live television, in which the thing we are presented with is happening simultaneously with its presentation." ("In live television," Cavell adds, "what is present to us while it is happening is not the world, but an event standing out from the world. Its point is not to reveal, but to cover (as with a gun), to keep something on view" (26).[16]

Incontestably, no live human being is up there on the movie screen. "But a human *something* is, and something unlike anything else we know," Cavell writes. "We can stick to our plain description of that human something as 'in our presence while we are not in his' (present *at* him, because looking at him, but not present *to* him) and still account for the difference between his live . . . and his photographed presence to us" (26–27).[17] But to account for this difference "we need to consider what is present or, rather, since the topic is the human being, *who* is present" (27).

Who is this "human something" present on the movie screen? "One's first impulse may be to say that in a play the character is present, whereas in a film the actor is" (27). One may also have the impulse to say that both are present in both. "But there is more to it, ontologically more," Cavell adds. In this context, he quotes what he rightly calls a "fine passage of Panofsky's":

> Othello or Nora are definite, substantial figures created by the playwright. They can be played well or badly, and they can be "interpreted" in one way or another; but they most definitely exist, no matter who plays them or even whether they are played at all. The character in a film, however, lives and dies with the actor. It is not the entity "Othello" interpreted by Robeson or the entity "Nora" interpreted by Duse, it is the entity "Greta Garbo" incarnate in a figure called Anna Christie. . . . (27)[18]

If in movies "the character lives and dies with the actor," Cavell argues, the actor also "lives and dies with the character" (28). There is only one entity on the screen, a "human something" not in principle separable from the being the performer is ("In a photograph, the original is still as present as it ever was"). And yet this "human something" cannot be

The entity Garbo incarnate in a figure called Marguerite (*Camille*).

separated from, has no existence apart from, the movies in which she or he is present.

On stage, by contrast, there are two beings, and the character's being "assaults the being of the actor; the actor survives only by yielding. The stage actor explores his potentialities and the possibilities of his role simultaneously. . . . An exemplary stage performance is one which, for a time, most fully creates a character. After Paul Scofield's performance in *King Lear*, we know who King Lear is, we have seen him in the flesh" (28).

In a similar vein: "A role in a play is like a position in a game, say, third base: various people can play it, but the great third baseman . . . has accepted and trained his skills and instincts most perfectly and matches them most intimately with his discoveries of the possibilities and necessities of third base. . . . The actor's role is his subject for study, and there is no end to it" (28).

The screen performer, however, "*is* the subject of study, and a study not his own. (That is what the content of a photograph is—its subject.)" In an exemplary screen performance, a star is born. "After *The Maltese Falcon*, we know a new star, only distantly a person. 'Bogart' *means* 'the figure created in a given set of films.' His presence in those films is who he is . . . in the sense that if those films did not exist, Bogart would not exist, the name 'Bogart' would not mean what it does" (28).

The Maltese Falcon gives birth to the star we call "Bogart." Surely, though, Bogart's performances in *Casablanca, To Have and Have Not,* and *The Big Sleep* are no less "exemplary." Every film in which Bogart is present, and not just the first one, participates in making Bogart who he is on the screen, participates in his creation *as* a figure capable of repeated incarnations. Bogart is born, or reborn, in every film that participates in his creation. In any case, as Cavell observes, these matters are complicated.

> A full development of all this would require us to place such facts as these: Humphrey Bogart was a man, and he appeared in movies both before and after the ones that created "Bogart." Some of them did not create a new star (say, the stable groom in *Dark Victory*), some of them defined stars— anyway meteors—that may be incompatible with Bogart (e.g., Duke Mantee and Fred C. Dobbs) but that are related to that figure and may enter into our later experience of it. And Humphrey Bogart was both an accomplished actor and a vivid subject for a camera. Some people are, just as some people are both good pitchers and good hitters; but there are so few that it is surprising that the word "actor" keeps on being used in place of the more beautiful and accurate word "star"; the stars are only to gaze at, after the fact, and their actions divine our projects. Finally, . . . the creation of a (screen) performer is also the creation of a character—not the kind of character an author creates, but the kind that certain real people are: a type. (28–29)

There is no need to go into these complications here (or others Cavell might have cited; for example, the fact that in *The Maltese Falcon* Bogart is also one of several incarnations of Sam Spade, the character Dashiell Hammett created in a series of literary narratives). Our consideration of Chapter 4 will close by addressing a possible way of misconstruing Cavell's argument, then by noting two points that will be useful as we proceed.

1. Viewing *The Blue Angel*, Douglas Lackey writes, we are "compelled to accept the existence of Emil Jannings, at some time and place," but our acceptance of Jannings's reality "is not relevant to the film, which does not contain Jannings but Professor Emmanuel Rath, the character that Jannings plays. Certainly *The Blue Angel* does not compel us to accept *Rath* as real, inhabiting a space and time continuous with our own."[19]

In fact, however, Jannings in *The Blue Angel* provides an excellent illustration of Cavell's point that in an exemplary screen performance character and performer are one entity, not two. *The Blue Angel* is among the films that participate in creating that particular "human something" we know as "Jannings." It is Jannings—a star with no existence apart from the films containing him—who is present whenever Professor Emmanuel Rath appears on screen. Jannings is related "only distantly" to the actor who plays him. But in *The Blue Angel* Professor Rath is not a character who is in principle different from the actor Emil Jannings.

Lackey takes Cavell to be claiming that movies "represent reality in such a way that we *must* accept their subjects as having a reality independently of the films in which they appear," as "inhabiting a space and time continuous with our own."[20] Hence he believes he can refute *The World Viewed* by showing that in *The Blue Angel* (a) our acceptance of Emil Jannings's independent reality is irrelevant to the film, and (b) the film does not make us accept its characters as inhabiting a space and time continuous with our own.

Cavell's claim, however, is that characters in movies have no existence apart from the "human somethings" present on the screen, hence from the particular stars who incarnate them. These stars, who have no existence apart from the persons they ("only distantly") are, also have no existence apart from the films in which they are present. And the space and time stars inhabit when projected on the screen are *not* continuous with our own. This follows from the Cavellian principle that the role reality plays in movies is not that of being recorded.

2. Cavell speaks of the screen performer as "the subject of study, and a study not his [or her] own." While this study is not the performer's own— he or she cannot claim exclusive possession of it—it does not follow that the performer plays no active part in the study. (That is why Cavell uses the words "subject of study," rather than "object of study.") Cavell argues, as well, that the stage actor must yield to the being of the character he studies. Then are viewers called upon to yield to the being of the movie star? (Is that what Cavell means when he says of the stars, "Their actions divine our projects"?) Again, Cavell's implication is that the human somethings present to us in movies are active subjects, not passive objects. The way movies present them *acknowledges* their subjectivity.

The idea that the human somethings movies present to us are not objects but subjects, that their active participation is essential to their presentation in movies, becomes increasingly prominent in Cavell's writing about film (cf. "What Becomes of Things on Film?" in *Themes Out of*

School), but already plays a crucial role in *The World Viewed*. It is one of Cavell's ideas, we might point out, that have the power to call radically into question views that often go unchallenged within film study, in this case the proposition that, in movies, the human subjects of the camera are merely objects of the camera's gaze.

3. Equally challenging to the field of film study is the idea Cavell formulates by saying that a star is "only distantly a person." What is most telling in this formulation is not its implication that there is a gap between person and star, but its insistence that what a star is, however distantly, is a person. The particular human something present in Bogart films is not a mere discursive construct—what might be called a "star image" or "persona"—but a person, however distant. However transformed or transfigured by the medium of film, Bogart cannot be separated from who Humphrey Bogart is. Bogart has Humphrey Bogart's body, his face, his voice. What *other* person could he possibly be?

As we noted, Cavell argues that Bogart has no existence apart from the films in which the human something Bogart is present. Bogart also does not exist apart from the person Humphrey Bogart, although that person does—did—have an existence apart from Bogart films. Humphrey Bogart and Bogart, the human being and the human something who is distantly that human being, have and have not separate beings, separate existences, separate identities.

Chapter 5: "Types; Cycles as Genres"

"Around this point," Chapter 5 begins, "our attention turns from the physical medium of cinema in general to the specific forms or genres the medium has taken in the course of its history" (29). (Note Cavell's Thoreau-like pun: Around this point in the book, there is a turning of our attention; and our attention literally turns around this point, that is, the last point made in Chapter 4, that "the creation of a screen performer is also the creation of a character—not the kind of character an author creates, but the kind that certain real people are: a type.") Indeed, the book's investigation of what film is now turns to the specific forms or genres that the medium, historically, has taken, and also to a philosophical investigation of the concepts "medium" and "genre."

Cavell notes, approvingly, that both Bazin and Panofsky "begin at the beginning, noting and approving that early movies adapt popular or folk arts and themes and performers and characters: farce, melodrama, circus, music hall, romance, etc." (29). However, they do not ask the question

78

Cavell now asks: "Why did such forms and themes and characters lend themselves to film?"

In an impressive passage Cavell quotes at length, Panofsky raises the question of the appropriateness of the original forms, but gives a misleading answer. Panofsky writes:

> The legitimate paths of evolution [for the film] were opened, not by running away from the folk art character of the primitive film but by developing it within the limits of its own possibilities. Those primordial archetypes of film production on the folk art level—success or retribution, sentiment, sensation, pornography, and crude humor—could burst forth into genuine history, tragedy and romance, crime and adventure, and comedy, as soon as it was realized that they could be transfigured . . . by the exploration of the unique and specific possibilities of the new medium.[21]

Panofsky maintains that it was the exploration of its own "unique and specific possibilities" that enabled the new medium to transfigure the primitive forms or genres that were its original sources. He defines film's unique and specific possibilities as "dynamization of space" (in a movie, things move) and "spatialization of time" (movies transport us instantly from anywhere to anywhere, and events happening at the same time can be viewed successively).[22]

Without denying that these are important properties of movies, Cavell denies that we have grounds for calling them film's "unique and specific possibilities." He is not simply denying that we can know these to be *the* possibilities unique and specific to the film medium. He is denying that we know what it means to define the possibilities of a medium *at all.*

The earliest films consisted of a single shot. Early on, films began to be made—newsreels, for example—that consisted of shots "just physically tacked on to another, cut and edited simply according to subject" (31). In principle, films could have continued to be made only in this way (as most home movies are). In films made this way, cutting and editing and taking shots at different distances and angles do not take on significance, as they do in the films we go to the movies to see. For dynamization of space and spatialization of time to become *aesthetic possibilities*, it must be realized what would give them significance—"for example, the narrative and physical rhythms of melodrama, farce, American comedy of the 1930s. It is not as if film-makers saw these possibilities and then looked for something to apply them to. It is truer to say that someone with the wish to make a movie saw that certain established forms would give point to certain properties of film" (31).

This provocative formulation leads to a paragraph that is a touchstone of Cavell's aesthetic philosophy. "This perhaps sounds like quibbling," the paragraph begins, but it means that the "aesthetic possibilities of a medium are not givens. You can no more tell what will give significance to the unique and specific aesthetic possibilities of projecting photographic images by thinking about them or seeing some, than you can tell what will give significance to the possibilities of paint by thinking about paint or by looking some over" (31).

Cavell's claim is not merely that you cannot know what would give significance to the aesthetic possibilities of film by thinking in the abstract about projected film images, or by simply looking some over; in those ways you cannot even know what film's aesthetic possibilities *are*. The claim is that only the significance films have *given* to these possibilities *makes* them aesthetic possibilities in the first place. To know the aesthetic possibilities of painting or motion pictures, "you have to think about painting, and paintings; you have to think about motion pictures. What does this 'thinking about them' consist in? Whatever the useful criticism of an art consists in" (31).

Panofsky errs by defining the aesthetic possibilities of motion pictures on theoretical grounds, in advance of criticism. A theory that validly determines the aesthetic possibilities of motion pictures cannot dictate terms to criticism; it must be motivated by discoveries that emerge through acts of criticism. Only the art itself can discover its aesthetic possibilities, in other words. And, Cavell adds, "the discovery of a new possibility is the discovery of a new medium" (32).

"Painters before Jackson Pollock had dripped paint, even deliberately," Cavell writes. "Pollock made dripping into a medium of painting" (31–32). This example leads Cavell to say—at least, to say he *feels* like saying—that "the first successful movies . . . were not applications of a medium that was defined by given possibilities, but the *creation of a medium* by their giving significance to specific possibilities" (32).

What motivates Cavell's impulse to speak this way is his understanding that a medium of art, like a form of speech, "provides particular ways . . . to make sense" (32). He holds it to be a fundamental condition of art that discovering ways of making sense "is always a matter of the relation of an artist to his art, each discovering the other" (32). (This is in the spirit of the Cavellian maxim, "Apart from the wish for selfhood [hence the always simultaneous granting of otherness as well], I do not understand the value of art.") And he understands "making sense" to mean expressing oneself in a medium. Apart from a medium, it is not possible to get through to others.

Film is itself a medium. It provides what Cavell will go on to call a "material basis" for the entire panoply of cycles and genres—each one a medium making possible particular ways of making sense—through which movies have given significance to a diversity of specific possibilities.

Cavell writes, "The familiar historical fact that there are movie cycles, which some film theorists have taken as a mark of unscrupulous commercialism, is a possibility internal to the medium; one could even say, it is the best emblem of the fact that a medium had been created. For a cycle is a genre (prison movies, Civil War movies, horror movies, etc.); and a genre is a medium" (36).

Cavell closes Chapter 5 by giving a surprising philosophical twist to his remarks about aesthetic possibilities and media. The remainder of the chapter leading up to this ending, though, dwells on the fact that "types are exactly what carry the forms movies have relied upon" (33). It is one of *The World Viewed*'s central *historical* claims that in the leading genres of film, the human somethings who take part in the drama have been types. This is why it is an important moment in the book when at the end of Chapter 4 the idea emerges that the creation of a screen performer is the creation of a type.

A type is a character of a certain kind ("Not the kind of character an author creates, but the kind that certain real people are"). A star is a type. And yet, in Cavell's view, what Panofsky calls "the well-remembered" figures of "the Vamp and the Straight Girl . . . the Family Man, and the Villain," characters with ancient roots in theatrical tradition, are types, too (*WV*, 33).

Panofsky believes that figures whose iconography operates according to a "fixed attitude and attribute principle" and whose conduct is predetermined accordingly became, as Panofsky puts it, "gradually less necessary as the public grew accustomed to interpret the action by itself and were virtually abolished by the invention of the talking film" (33). Cavell denies this. In movies, characters with fixed attitudes and attributes persist as long as there are Westerns, gangster films, comedies, musicals and romances. "*Which* specific iconography the Villain is given will alter with the times," he adds, but "that his iconography remains specific . . . seems undeniable: if Jack Palance in *Shane* is not a Villain, no honest home was ever in danger" (33).

Cavell expands on this in "More of *The World Viewed*": "On film the type is not primarily the character but primarily the actor. The sets of 'fixed attitudes and attributes' by which types are defined—as these are at work in the experience of film —are established by the individual and total physiognomy (of face, of figure, of gait, of temperament) of the human beings taking part in the drama" (174–75).

To say that in movies the characters in the drama are types is not to deny that they are individuals. "[T]his is the movies' way of creating individuals: they create *individualities*. For what makes someone a type is not his similarity with other members of that type but his striking separateness from other people" (33).

Again:

> Stars of every magnitude . . . have provided the movie camera with human subjects—individuals . . . whose individualities, in turn, whose inflections of demeanor and disposition were given full play in its projection. They provided, and still provide, staples for impersonators: one gesture or syllable of mood, two strides, or a passing mannerism was enough to single them out from all other creatures. (35)

On film, types are not defined by particular social roles. For screen performers to be types is for their individuality to project particular ways of *inhabiting* whatever social roles they happen to occupy in particular films. There is thus a general difference in film between types and stereotypes.

> Until recently, types of black human beings were not created in film: black people were stereotypes—mammies, shiftless servants, loyal retainers, entertainers. We were not given . . . individualities that projected particular *ways* of inhabiting a social role; we recognized only the role. Occasionally the humanity behind the role would manifest itself; and the result was a revelation not of a human individuality, but of an entire realm of humanity becoming visible. (33–34)

In films, the individuality naturally takes precedence over the social role in which that individuality is expressed. Because social roles appear arbitrary or incidental,

> movies have an inherent tendency toward the democratic, or anyway the idea of human equality. (But because of film's equally natural attraction to crowds, it has opposite tendencies toward the fascistic or populistic.) This depends upon recognizing film types as inhabited by figures we have met or may well meet in other circumstances. . . . As Hollywood developed, the original types ramified into individualities as various and subtle, as far-reaching in their capacities to inflect mood and release fantasy, as any set of characters who inhabited the great theaters of our world. We do not know them by such names as Pulcinella, Crispin, Harlequin, Pantaloon, the Doctor, the Captain, Columbine; we call them the Public Enemy, the Priest, James Cagney, Pat O'Brien, the Confederate Spy,

82

the Army Scout, Randolph Scott, Gary Cooper, Clark Gable, Paul Muni, the Reporter, the Sergeant, the Other Woman, the Fallen Woman, the Moll, the Dance Hall Hostess. Hollywood was the theater in which they appeared, because the films of Hollywood constituted a world, with recurrent faces more familiar to me than the faces of all the places I have lived. (36)

In "More of *The World Viewed*," Cavell expands on this splendid paragraph:

A type on the screen need not be established [as it is] in theatrical tradition, by the recurrence of a role in a corpus of plays; it can be established by the recurrence of an actor in a corpus of films. (This is why, in my sketching a list of Hollywood types, I mixed together the names of characters and stars.) This helped explain to me why I find that the distinction between actor and character is broken up on the screen; and I was led to speak of the individuals projected on the screen as individualities and, implicitly, to deny in the experiencing of them the distinction between types and well-rounded characters. (175)

Objecting to *The World Viewed*'s discussion of types, Sesonske had argued that the prevalence of types in Hollywood films had nothing to do with the ontology of film and everything to do with the limited creative imagination of American directors and audiences; while American films were populated with mere types, European directors like Renoir, Vigo, and Pagnol were creating well-rounded characters.[23] In reply, Cavell reiterates his conviction that film denies the distinction between type and well-rounded character (as it denies the distinction between character and performer). It obscures the differences between the films made by American directors and those by European directors to suggest that the American films keep to a concern with types and the Europeans do not.

I would find it hard to believe that anyone admires *Grand Illusion, Rules of the Game, Zero for Conduct* and *L'Atalante* more than I, but it seems . . . accurate to their intention and effect to say that they are explorations of types. . . . The figures in both Renoir films are insistently labeled for us: the Aristocrat, the Jew, the Officer, the Professor, the Good Guy, the Poacher, the Wronged Wife, the Impetuous Lover. (175–76)

Grand Illusion and *The Rules of the Game* depend on the fact that the human somethings taking part in their dramas are types, Cavell argues, because both films "are about the arbitrariness and the inevitability of labels, and thence about the human need for society and the equal human need to escape it, and hence about human privacy and unknownness. They are about the search for society, or community, outside, or within, society at large. So are the films of Vigo" (176).

The richness, beauty, and convincingness of Jean Vigo's *L'Atalante*, for example, "have nothing to do with anything I understand as a study of character," Cavell writes in "More of *The World Viewed*."

> Compared to Desdemona and Othello, Vigo's bride and groom are, well, mere types. We know and learn next to nothing about them. She is a village beauty who expects to find excitement in the world outside; he becomes frightened and jealous of her attention to attractions which are not within his power to provide; she leaves, more or less innocently; he retaliates by abandoning her; they long for one another; they are happy when they are reunited. (176)

The old man in *L'Atalante* is somewhat more developed, but Vigo's concern is not to explore his character very far.

> We learn that the old man is superstitious, appreciates women and is successful with them, that he is capable of natural courtesy but also of crudity and selfishness, and that he has been around. In short, an old sailor. We know he somehow holds the key to the plot or plight of the little community, but this is a function of his actions rather than of his character (if we are to have that distinction): If this marriage is to take effect—which the Church, and the community of the village, and apparently satisfactory sex, have all failed to insure—the old man will have to effect it . . . he will have to *give* the bride. He has authority in this because we have seen him win her for himself. (176–77)

The treasures in *L'Atalante* "are found here by the resonance that Vigo's camera, with wit, with tact, with accuracy, elicits from these temperaments in those actions in these settings at those times" (177). From the resonance Vigo's camera elicits from these human subjects, we learn more than we knew of

> wedding processions, how they can feel like funeral processions, presumably because they commemorate the dying of the bride to her past; we know more precisely and memorably than we had known of the daze and the remoteness of brides, of the innocence of grooms, of the daze and remoteness of a husband who recognizes that he has been no husband; we know more certainly that a man wins a beautiful young girl only when he wins her imagination, i.e., only when he can share his imagination with her, and that if he can do that he may even be ugly and not young. (177)

From the resonance Vigo's camera elicits from its human subjects, the viewer arrives at the culminating realization ("for the first time or the fiftieth, it makes no difference") that, as Cavell puts it, "one's responsibility toward one's desire is to acknowledge it, and acknowledge its object, i.e., acknowledge its object's separateness from you." The power of these last ideas, as they find "incarnation in the image of the husband searching under water for his love, is finally as inexplicable as the power of a phrase of music or of poetry. And the ideas are nothing without that power. Of course there is a sense of character explored. It is our own" (177).

By eliciting resonance from particular human individualities, from their particular ways of inhabiting social roles, films explore *our* character, the human character. With this idea, "More of *The World Viewed*" echoes the theme of one of the most eloquent passages in Chapter 5, which suggests that the significance of screen stars is that they realize "the myth of singularity"—

> that we can still be found, behind our disguises of bravado and cowardice, by someone, perhaps a god, capable of defeating our self-defeats. This was always more important than their distinction by beauty. Their singularity made them more like us—anyway, made their difference from us less a matter of metaphysics, to which we must accede, than a matter of responsibility, to which we must bend. But then that made them even more glamorous. That they should be able to stand upon their singularity! (35)

In reflecting, in "More of *The World Viewed*," on the way movies explore the human character, Cavell is reminded of Thomas Mann's

> description, in his essay on Freud, of the "point at which psychological interest passes over into the mythical," and of his assertion that "the typical is actually the mythical." Mann speaks of the step he took as a novelist when his subject-matter moved "from the bourgeois and individual to the mythical and typical" and he finds that "the mythical knowledge resides in the gazer and not in that at which he gazes." (177–78)

For a novel to take this step is a major achievement. For film, it is the natural mode of revelation. "That gaze of knowledge is the province of camera and screen; it is the power with which the director, in his pact with his audience, begins.—The mythical in the typical" (178). The fact that it is natural for film to reveal the mythical in the typical accounts for the "irrelevance of character and individual psychology in assessing the significance of screened figures" (178).

■ ■

Chapter 5 concludes with a paragraph about the great movie comedians Chaplin, Keaton, and W. C. Fields, a set of types who "could not have been adapted from any other medium" (36). (In saying this, Cavell knows full well that these performers enjoyed success on stage before making the transition to the screen.) They all depend, Cavell argues, on the condition of the film medium that screen performers do not project but are projected, and on the condition that photographs are of the world (in films, human beings are not ontologically favored over the rest of nature; objects are not props but natural allies—or enemies—of the human character) (37).

These conditions are necessities, not mere possibilities, of film, Cavell argues. "So I will say that two necessities of the medium were discovered or expanded in the creation of these types" (36–37). The emergence of the idea that film has not only possibilities but also necessities, natural limits, as it were, represents a significant new development in the philosophical investigation of the concept of medium with which the chapter began. This development moves increasingly into the foreground as *The World Viewed* proceeds.

III

■ ■ ■ ■

CHAPTERS 6–9:
FILM'S ORIGINS AND HISTORY

IN THE PREFACE, Cavell suggests that the completion of Chapter 5 marked
the end of the first stage of the writing of *The World Viewed*. Having got
this far with the work, he felt he had some words he could believe in to
account for his experience of film. He had enough faith in what he had
written to accept an invitation to give a public reading of this material,
in May 1968, at the University of Illinois. That is, he had faith that his
account of his private experience was capable of holding a public audience.

The opening chapter of *The World Viewed* begins with the question
of why movies are important, and ends with the question "What is film?"
As we have said, these questions are not separable for Cavell. It is a fact
about film, or our concept of film, as it is a fact about art in general, or
our concept of art, that what it is cannot be separated from what makes it
important.

In Chapter 2, as we have seen, Cavell addresses the question "What is
a photograph?" without, however, providing a definition or even a theory,
comparable to theories he examines and finds wanting, that explains the
ontology of the photographic image. Similarly, in the entirety of Chapters
1 through 5, he addresses the question "What is film?" without providing
either a definition or a theory that purports to make it less mysterious
what the medium really is. Rather, in this part of the book he calls upon
himself, and calls upon his audience, to stop forgetting how obscure the
ontology of film remains to us.

Cavell began the second stage of the writing of *The World Viewed* during a sabbatical he spent at the Humanities Center at Wesleyan University. The first topic he then took up, in Chapters 6–9, is the obscurity of film's history and origins, the medium's own "obscure promptings." If what makes film important and what film is are not separate questions, neither can be separated from the question of film's origins. In addressing this last question, and the further questions to which it gives rise, the writing of *The World Viewed* does not become more systematic, as Cavell had expected it would (and as he had assumed it *should*) after completing the first five chapters. As we have noted, the writing becomes more fervent, more subjective, more private, more absorbed with its own obscure promptings, as well as film's.

Chapter 6: "Ideas of Origin"

"It is inevitable that in theorizing about film one at some point speculate about its origins," Chapter 6 begins, "because despite its recentness, its origin remains obscure" (36).

Panofsky's study of film, for example, opens with a speculation about film's origins: "It was not an artistic urge that gave rise to the discovery and gradual perfection of a new technique, it was a technical invention that gave rise to the discovery and gradual perfection of a new art."[24] Panofsky assumes we know what has given rise to this new art. In response to this, Cavell writes:

> He mentions an "artistic urge," but that is . . . about as useful as explaining the rise of modern science by appealing to a "scientific urge." . . . Panofsky cites an artistic urge explicitly as the occasion for a new "technique." But the motion picture is not a new *technique*, any more than the airplane is. (What did we use to do that such a thing enables us to do better?) Yet some idea of flying, and an urge to do it, preceded the mechanical invention of the airplane. What is "given rise to" by such inventions as movable type or the microscope or the steam engine or the pianoforte? (36)

There is nothing particularly obscure regarding the facts about the invention of cinema, Cavell reminds us; but "a chronicle of the facts preceding the appearance of this technology does not explain why it happened when and as it did" (38). Noting that "it would be surprising if the history of the establishment of an artistic medium were less complex a problem . . . than (say) the rise of modern science," he adds, "I take Bazin to be suggesting this when he reverses the apparent relation between

88

the relevant technology and the idea of cinema, emphasizing that the idea preceded the technology, parts of it by centuries. So what has to be explained is not merely how the feat was technically accomplished but, for example, what stood in the way of its happening earlier" (38–39).

Surprisingly, Bazin does not include the contemporary arts "as a part of the ideological superstructure that elicited the new material basis of film." But "unless film captured possibilities opened up by the arts themselves, it is hard to imagine that its possibilities as an artistic medium would have shown up as, and as suddenly as, they did" (39). It is surely relevant that realism was the burning issue during the latter half of the nineteenth century in painting, the novel, and theater. And it is in this context that Cavell presents the oft-quoted formulation, "The idea of and wish for the world re-created in its own image was satisfied *at last* by cinema" (39).

It should be kept in mind that when Cavell formulates in this way the wish motivating the creation of film as an artistic medium, he is paraphrasing Bazin. It is Bazin, not Cavell, who calls the wish for the world re-created in its own image "[t]he myth of total cinema," who claims that this wish, or its fulfillment, is unique to film. Cavell's own view is that it has always been one of the myths of art. "Each of the arts had satisfied it in its own way. The mirror was in various hands held up to nature" (39). In some ways, theater more fully satisfied the wish; when we sit in the audience at a play the characters are in our presence and the dramatic events take place here and now. Cavell provocatively adds, in one of his signature parenthetical remarks, "Since theater is not on the whole . . . now a major art for us, it on the whole no longer makes contact with its historical and psychological sources; so we are rarely gripped by the trauma we must once have suffered when the leader of the chorus stopped contributing to a narrative or song and turned to face the others, suffering incarnation" (39).

Apart from a medium of art, the world as it exists cannot satisfy our wish for the world re-created in its own image. The world as it exists, apart from a medium of art, cannot satisfy our wish to re-create the world, to create a semblance of the world, the world's double, a world we can possess or at least feel connected to. For modern human beings like us whose consciousness has become unhinged from the world, whose subjectivity has become interposed between our selves and our presentness to the world, as Chapter 2 puts it, wishing for the world is like wishing for the moon. If the world re-created in its own image on film is to satisfy our wish for the world, it must differ, in this crucial respect, from the existing world. Film must transform the world as it exists into a world capable of satisfying our wish for the world.

Clearly, in Cavell's understanding, our wish for the world cannot be separated from what in Chapter 2 he calls our wish for presentness. This is why his formulation "The idea of and wish for the world re-created in its own image was satisfied at last by cinema" is designed not only to paraphrase Bazin, but also to echo the wording of one of Chapter 2's key sentences ("So far as photography satisfied a wish, it satisfied . . . the human wish, intensifying since the Reformation, to escape subjectivity and metaphysical isolation—a wish for the power to reach this world" [21]).

Cavell's claim in Chapter 6 is that the wish for the world re-created in its own image, a wish that prompted the creation of film as an artistic medium, is the same wish that since the Reformation has motivated the creation of artistic media in painting, theater, and other arts. It is the wish for presentness, the wish to reach this world and attain selfhood ("Apart from the wish for selfhood [hence the always simultaneous granting of otherness as well], I do not understand the value of art.")

Film did not satisfy this wish more fully than other arts. Film was never in competition with other arts. Each art satisfied in its own way our wish for the world re-created in its own image. Cavell argues in *Must We Mean What We Say?* ("The Avoidance of Love") that theater's traditional way of satisfying this wish is by enabling characters to be in our presence while we are in the presence of the actors who project those characters. Those characters participate in the events of the play that unfold in our presence. But if we do not remain hidden and silent and fixed, if for example we rush onto the stage to try to affect the course of events, we disrupt the play. Theater's traditional way of re-creating the world in its own image, in other words, requires that we perform the role theater traditionally allots to its audience. In theater, there is something we have to do to satisfy our wish for the world re-created in its own image. What we have to do is nothing. But that is something.

What is film's way of satisfying our wish for the world re-created in its own image?

Automatically, we said. But what does that mean—mean mythically, as it were? It means satisfying it without *my* having to do anything, satisfying it *by* wishing. In a word, *magically*. I have found myself asking: How could film be art, since all the major arts arise in some way out of religion? Now I can answer: Because movies arise out of magic; from *below*

90

the world. The better a film, the more it makes contact with this source of its inspiration; it never wholly loses touch with the magic lantern behind it. (39)

To say that movies arise out of magic is to say that they are not, for example, created miraculously—being photographic, movies re-create the world without the intervention of a human hand, and without God having to take a hand, either. Metaphorically or mythically, movies arise "from *below* the world," Cavell says; that is the way the art of film arises out of religion. (Another implication of this formulation is that, viewed from film's perspective, religion *is* "below"; in movies, religion and magic are one.)

As Chapter 2 argues, objects and persons in the world are displaced from their natural sequences and locales when they are photographed, projected, and screened. This displacement of objects and persons in the world, itself an acknowledgment of their physical reality, enables movies to depict the fantastic as readily as the natural. Film's way of satisfying our wish for the world re-created in its own image is to re-create the world *by* producing an image; the re-created world is literally *in* this image, and this image is, also literally, the world's own (it belongs to the world, it is *of* the world). Film's way of satisfying our wish for the world re-created in its own image is so fantastic, so *magical*, that "movies of the fantastic (*The Cabinet of Dr. Caligari, Blood of a Poet*) and filmed scenes of magic (say, materialization and dematerialization), while they have provided moods and devices, have never established themselves as cinematic media, however strongly this 'possibility' is suggested by the physical medium of film; they are technically and psychologically trivial compared with the medium of magic itself" (41).

Cavell adds, in a provocative footnote, "Dadaists and surrealists found in film a direct confirmation of their ideologies or sensibilities. . . . This confirmation is . . . sometimes taken to mean that dadaist and surrealist films constitute the *avant-garde* of filmmaking. It might equally be taken to show why film made these movements obsolete, as the world has" (41 n).

Film's way of magically satisfying our wish for the world re-created in its own image is by presenting us with the world's image, not by literally presenting us with the world. In film, the way objects and persons are present to us is also the way they are absent from us, the way we are absent from them. ("What makes the physical medium of film unlike anything else on earth lies in the absence of what it causes to appear to us; that is to say, in the nature of our absence from it" (166). Again:

"The depth of the automatism of photography is to be read not alone in its mechanical projection of an image of reality, but in its mechanical defeat of our presence to that reality" [23]). So far as film satisfies our wish for presentness, our wish to reach this world and attain selfhood, its way of doing so is not by acknowledging that endless presence of self—that is modernist painting's way—but by *overcoming* subjectivity in a way impossible for painting.

Cavell extends these thoughts, as earlier chapters have developed them, by entering the following claims: Film's way of overcoming our subjectivity is by magically satisfying our wish to view, unseen, the world re-created in its own image; and it is by magically satisfying our wish to view the world unseen, in a way that overcomes our subjectivity, that movies satisfy our wish for the world re-created in its own image (40).

Cavell further specifies the nature of the wish to view the world unseen that movies magically satisfy: "This is not a wish for power over creation (as Pygmalion's was), but a wish not to need power, not to have to bear its burdens. It is, in this sense, the reverse of the myth of Faust. And the wish for invisibility is old enough. Gods have profited from it, and Plato tells it in Book II of the *Republic* as the Myth of the Ring of Gyges" (40).

In viewing films, Cavell adds, our sense of invisibility is an expression of modern privacy or anonymity, "as though the world's projection explains our forms of unknownness and of our inability to know. The explanation is not so much that the world is passing us by, as that we are displaced from our natural habitation within it, placed at a distance from it. The screen . . . makes displacement appear as our natural condition" (40–41).

In a footnote to this passage, Cavell refers to "Knowing and Acknowledging," an essay in *Must We Mean What We Say?* that links the philosophical problem of other minds with ideas of displacement, of privacy, and of the inability to know. In the existing world, "Knowing and Acknowledging" argues, your suffering makes a claim upon us (as our suffering makes a claim upon you). "It is not enough that I *know* (am certain) that you suffer," Cavell writes, "I must do or reveal something (whatever can be done). In a word, I must *acknowledge* it" (*MWMWWS*, 263). If you know I am in pain, you must acknowledge my pain, or else be withholding the acknowledgment. One does not *acknowledge* another's pain the way one acknowledges one's own pain (that is, by expressing it). Since to know another is in pain is to acknowledge it or else to be withholding the acknowledgment, however, one does *know* another's pain the way one knows one's own pain.

The Tramp searching the eyes of the woman he loves (*City Lights*).

Viewing a film, we cannot but be invisible to the human somethings we are viewing. Our invisibility to them is mechanically assured. And it is mechanically assured that our feelings are unknown to those human somethings, since there is nothing they can possibly say or do which would count either as acknowledging our feelings or withholding acknowledgment of them. Our feelings make no claims upon those human somethings. And whatever claims their feelings may make upon us, we cannot possibly address an acknowledgment *to* them or withhold an acknowledgment *from* them.

Viewing the ending of *City Lights*, for example, we know that the Tramp suffers as he desperately searches the eyes of the woman he loves for a sign of her feeling.

We say and do nothing as we view the Tramp, but not for the same reason we say and do nothing as we watch Lear's suffering. Lear's suffering, like the Tramp's, makes no claim upon us to say or do something by way of acknowledgment. It makes no such claim upon us not because it is a convention of theater that its audience does nothing but sit and watch, but because it makes no such claim upon anyone. Again, to acknowledge Lear's tragedy as it unfolds before us is to acknowledge the awesome fact that there is nothing for anyone to say or do, the fact that it is not possible for any human being to do and suffer what it is another's to do and suffer.

The Tramp's suffering, by contrast, does make a claim upon someone to say or do something by way of acknowledgment. It makes a claim upon the woman (Virginia Cherrill) in his presence. But film mechanically assures that we are not in that woman's place, that we are at a distance, displaced, from the little man in her presence, that we are invisible to him.

When Cavell suggests that in viewing films the sense of invisibility is an expression of modern privacy or anonymity, he is reminding us that modern human beings like us, isolated by our subjectivity, already know how it feels to be trapped within our privacy, to be unknown, unacknowledged, invisible. Significantly, he sums up the sense of invisibility symptomatic of modernity by invoking not only our familiar forms of unknownness, but also our familiar forms of inability to know. Our feeling that others fail to acknowledge us is matched, after all, by our feeling that we fail to acknowledge others. More mysteriously, Cavell also speaks of the world's projection onto the movie screen as *explaining* these all too familiar forms of unknownness and inability to know.

If the existing world were only a projection, if other human beings were only human somethings projected on a screen, our forms of unknownness and inability to know would require no explanation. They would be mechanically assured, as it were, by the reality of our condition. But the existing world is not a mere projection. It exists. We feel that we are placed at such a distance from the world as to render us invisible, but this displacement is not our condition objectively; feeling displaced is an expression of our subjectivity. Our displacement is a condition we long to overcome, but it is also a condition we wish upon ourselves. The world's projection onto the movie screen makes "displacement appear as our natural condition," as Cavell puts it. What film is capable of bringing home to us is that displacement from our natural habitation within the world is anything but natural.

Chapter 6 concludes with the questions, "What do we wish to view in this way?" (that is, in the way we view movies, privately and anonymously, our displacement from the world appearing natural). "What specific forms discover this fundamental condition of the medium of film?" (41).

94

Chapter 7: "Baudelaire and the Myths of Film"

With a seamless transition, Chapter 7 begins, "This wish, and these forms, can be glimpsed in a famous but puzzling text of the nineteenth century: Baudelaire's *The Painter of Modern Life*" (42).

In turning to Baudelaire, Cavell singles out the historical moment immediately prior to film's emergence. Chapters 7 through 9 explore the significance of this historical moment by focusing on Baudelaire's way of thinking about the world of his time and the new types who inhabited it— the way these people looked, moved, and thought about the world and themselves. These chapters argue that the emergence of film is intimately linked to the emergence of modernity to which Baudelaire was responding in a modern way. If *these* types of people, *these* ways of moving, *these* clothes, *these* machines, *these* landscapes, had not emerged, what would have given rise to the wish to view the world the way we view movies?

Not coincidentally, in turning to Baudelaire Cavell is also returning to *The World Viewed*'s recurring theme of photography's relationship to painting. The central argument of Chapters 7 through 9 is that the burning issue of realism, which forced painting (in the works of Courbet and Manet) to change radically, is internal to film's origins.[25]

Cavell finds *The Painter of Modern Life* puzzling because in this most ambitious of Baudelaire's theoretical statements about art, the "prophet of the modern" can seem merely perverse or superficial. Baudelaire called for a realization of

> the other half of art whose first half is "the eternal and unchangeable." The half he wanted he named "modernity," that which is "ephemeral, fugitive, contingent upon the occasion," the "description of contemporary life," and in particular the "nature of beauty in the present time." And he says: "The pleasure we derive from the depiction of the present arises not only from the beauty in which it can be attired, but also from its essential quality of being the present." But the quality of presentness is exactly what Courbet and Manet themselves craved, and in establishing it as it could be established in painting, they were establishing modernist painting. (41–42)

Read as art criticism, *The Painter of Modern Life* is, indeed, perverse or superficial; Baudelaire praises Delacroix to the skies and fails to recognize what is modern in the paintings of Courbet and Manet. Read as an anticipation of film, however, Baudelaire's text takes on a visionary aspect. "Out of his despair of happiness, out of his disgust with its official made-up substitutes, and out of his knowledge and estrangement from the present and the foreignness of the past (and, I believe, in his experiments with hashish)"—movies arise from *below* the world, indeed!—"[Baudelaire] found the wish . . . for that specific simultaneity of presence and absence which only the cinema will satisfy" (42). In Baudelaire's prophetic text, Cavell glimpses answers to the questions posed in Chapter 6. What we wish to view in the way we view movies is that which is ephemeral, fugitive, contingent upon the occasion, the phenomena Baudelaire finds exemplary of what he calls "modernity."

"Nothing less than everything is new in a new period," Cavell observes, "not merely the attirements, but physiques and postures and gaits and nudity itself" (42). In Baudelaire's text, "the pleasure we derive from the depiction of the present arises not only from the beauty in which [the present] can be attired, but also from its essential quality of being the present" (41). *The Painter of Modern Life* presents a veritable catalogue of the phenomena of modernity—new types of objects, of settings, of human beings who inhabit those settings—which when viewed the way Baudelaire views them reveal the nature of beauty in the present. As Baudelaire views them, these phenomena are ephemeral, fugitive, contingent upon the occasion. They possess the quality *The World Viewed* calls "presentness," and in them, we might say, presentness is also beautifully attired.

Read as articulating and expressing the wish movies were created to satisfy, Baudelaire's little book seems to Cavell to take on the power it must have had for its author.

> Let me simply recall the titles of his chapters, pondering them against our knowledge of cinema: Fashion, The Man of the World, Crowds, The Child, War-Sketches, Pomps and Ceremonies, The Military Man, The Dandy, Cosmetics, Women and Courtesans, Carriages. Here are stores of cinematic obsession, and they are more convincingly so the more one appreciates the meaning they have for Baudelaire and the particular way they occur in movies. (43)

Cavell starts by considering Baudelaire's remarks about carriages: "Whatever the posture into which it may be thrown," Baudelaire writes, "whatever the gait at which it may be traveling, a carriage, like a ship, is lent by its movement a mysterious and complex grace which it is very difficult to note down in shorthand" (43). "Difficult?" Cavell interjects. "It is impossible to imagine its being seen on paper; but it is the very grain of moving pictures. Baudelaire's carriages carry the weight of all those conveyances and machines whose movements are so lovingly studied in film."

Carriages and trains appear again and again in movies not "because 'we like to see things move,'" Cavell argues, "but because their characteristic movements have that 'mysterious and complex grace' divined by Baudelaire." In lovingly studying those movements, "film returns to us

96

and extends our first fascination with objects, with their inner and fixed lives" (inner, in that objects have lives of their own; fixed, in that objects are not free to change themselves, to make themselves other than what they are).[26]

In lovingly studying the graceful movements of carriages and trains, movies view them as objects with inner and fixed lives. They also study "what is done in and with" these contrivances, "where they are placed and why—this is something with a drama of its own, its unique logic of beginning, middle and end; and they create the kind of creature who may use them" (43–44).

On film, carriages and trains are inhabited at particular times in particular ways by particular types of human beings. Thus they are part of the realm Baudelaire calls "Cosmetics," by which he means not merely makeup or even fashion in general but, as Cavell puts it, all the "artifices necessary to civilized life as a whole: its streets, parks, buildings, furnishings, commodities, the secretions and scaffoldings of our forms of life." For Baudelaire, these "secretions and scaffoldings" take on status of "specific *settings*." This is "their indispensable value in film," Cavell adds, "where sets must be in reality, whether genuine or counterfeit" (44).

As settings, carriages and trains are "vitalized and vivified" by the dramas—ephemeral, fugitive, contingent upon the occasion—for which they provide settings (44). They also participate in the creation of those dramas, hence the creation of the types of human creatures whose forms of life could not exist apart from them. Yet the human types who inhabit these settings are capable of inhabiting others; they have empirical existences that precede and follow their placement, at a particular moment, in a particular setting.

"Baudelaire's vision is confirmed," Cavell writes, "in his insistence that 'to appreciate fashions . . . one must not regard them as lifeless objects. . . . They must be seen as vitalized and vivified by the lively woman who wore them. Only thus can one understand their spirit and meaning'" (44). Baudelaire is not simply claiming that when a woman wears clothes they take on a life of their own, Cavell argues. "He is responding to the fact that [clothes] simultaneously conceal and reveal the body." In theater and painting, "clothes reveal a person's character and his station, also his body and its attitudes. The clothes *are* the body, as the expression is the face" (44).

Viewed in the modern way Baudelaire's text is heralding, a way that anticipates the way we view movies, "clothes conceal; hence they conceal something separate from them; the something is therefore empirically there to be unconcealed." In concealing, therefore, clothes also reveal. A woman in a movie "is *dressed* (as she is, when she is, in reality), hence potentially undressed" (44). In movies, as in the modern world when viewed in the modern way Baudelaire anticipates, it is the nature of human beings to be embodied.

Yet Baudelaire shies away from the full implications of his own intuition. Cavell criticizes as "uncharacteristically pious" a Baudelaire passage that describes "a woman and her garb" as "an indivisible whole." Cavell is not denying that, when viewed the modern way Baudelaire's text anticipates, a "lively woman" vitalizes and vivifies the garb she wears. Her attire takes on a life of its own, participates in creating the beautiful creature it is a delight to view. But a woman is her body, not her clothes. As Cavell puts it, "A woman and her garb are a divisible whole" (45).

This is the concluding line of a passage of Cavell's that might strike readers as uncharacteristically impious. "A nude is a fine enough thing in itself," the passage begins, and

> no reason is required to explain nakedness; we were born that way, and besides, "the human body is the best picture of the human soul." But to be undressed is something else, and it does require a reason; in seeing a film of a desirable woman, we are looking for a reason. When to this we join our ontological status—invisibility—it is inevitable that we should expect to find a reason . . . no matter how consistently our expectation is frustrated. . . . The million times in which a shot ended the instant the zipper completed the course down the back of a dress, or in which the lady stepped behind a shower door exactly as her robe fell, in which a piece of clothing fell into the view of a paralyzed camera—these were not sudden enticements or pornographic asides; they were satisfactions, however partial, of an inescapable demand. All the Hays Offices in the world could not prevent that; they could merely enforce the interruption. A woman and her garb are a divisible whole. (45)

Is Cavell egregiously sexist for offering the undressing of a woman as a paradigm, or for assuming that readers will share what may seem his distinctively male experience, when viewing a "desirable woman" on film, of looking for a reason for her to be undressed? Before rushing to condemn Cavell on feminist grounds, let us remember that his subject here is film's new way of regarding, and asserting, the *human*.

In referring to theater and painting, Cavell asserts that clothes reveal "a person's character and his station, also his body and its attitudes." This wording makes explicit that in theater and painting it is the case for all persons that "clothes are the body," although the use of the word "his" indicates that the example Cavell has in mind is that of a male. Perhaps

98

Cavell's wording is meant, in part, to register the historical fact that in painting women have so often been represented as nudes, as having no clothes—hence no social station—at all. In any case, when Cavell refers to film, he invokes the example of a woman. Again, his wording may be meant to register a historical fact (that at least until recently movies were more inclined to present women than men *as* creatures viewers might desire to be undressed). Perhaps it also registers that Cavell personally is more inclined to view women than men as "desirable" in the relevant sense. But, again, it must be kept in mind that he understands the condition he is characterizing—the fact that the body is the person, the fact that clothes are not the body—to apply to all human beings on film. Again, on film it is the *human* condition to be embodied. Insofar as film, historically, has emphasized the bodies of women, this fact suggests that the medium has singled women out as exemplars of the human. That movies have tended to envision women as exemplary of humanity is one of *The World Viewed*'s central themes.

Within contemporary film theory, it is widely assumed that in "classical" Hollywood movies women's bodies are subjected to the camera's gaze primarily to satisfy male desire. Cavell is not denying that here. What he is denying is that it was the Hays Office censorship, or the system of production that censorship helped support, that *caused* clothes to conceal and reveal the bodies of women on film, that *caused* (male) viewers to desire those bodies to be undressed. It is an ontological condition of the medium, not a contingent fact, that on film human beings are their bodies, not their clothes. As Cavell puts it, "The ontological conditions of the motion picture reveal it as inherently pornographic." When he adds "though not, of course, inveterately so," he is suggesting—his "of course" gives this suggestion a whiff of irony—that in most movies such satisfactions are a relatively marginal element of film's appeal (44).

Following Laura Mulvey, feminist film theorists have charged that film's attention to women's bodies is exemplary of Western society's systematic objectification of women. Cavell offers an alternative interpretation. Painting and theater, arts in which persons are their clothes, do objectify women (and human beings generally) by equating them with objects. Film is radically different: On film, the woman *is* her body, which means that her body is not an object; it is the woman herself, this particular embodied, lively, human existence. On film, the nature of a woman's beauty is "ephemeral, fugitive, contingent upon the occasion," in principle divisible from the garb in which she is attired and from the class or social position her garb may signify. What makes a desirable woman desirable

99

is the person, the human subject, she is. ("The human body is the best picture of the human soul"—Wittgenstein.)

This condition of the medium of film receives further articulation in *Pursuits of Happiness*, where Cavell notes that each of the principal films of the genre he calls the "comedy of remarriage" has "a way of acknowledging . . . the identity of the real woman cast in [the film]" (*PH*, 64). In *Pursuits of Happiness*, Cavell characterizes the genre's attention to its leading women as at once the narrative's emphasis on the heroine's identity and "an emphasis taken by the cinematic medium on the physical presence, that is, the photographic presence, of the real actress playing this part, an emphasis that demands, without exception, some occasion for displaying or suggesting the naked body of the woman to the extent the Production Code will allow" (*PH*, 64).

Cavell derives from this characterization the following provocative formulation: "Thus does film . . . declare its participation in the creation of the woman, a declaration that its appetite for presenting a certain kind of woman a certain way on the screen—its power, or its fate, to determine what becomes of these women on film—is what permits the realization of these narrative structures as among the highest achievements in the art of film" (*PH*, 140).

Films *can* exploit the anonymity of their human subjects and the invisibility of their viewers (and their wish to remain anonymous). The art of film *can* give way to pornography. And yet *The World Viewed* suggests that this has not generally been the case, that movies have ordinarily worked quite differently. They have participated in, and affirmed, the quest for a new form of human life that overcomes or transcends the alienation (from nature, from other people, from ourselves) that is a condition of human existence in the modern period. *The World Viewed* takes film's envisioning of human beings as embodied to be the medium's response to the modern wish for a radically transformed, more fully human, form of life. (Beginning with "What Becomes of Things On Film?," Cavell comes to use the word "photogenesis" to refer to film's capacity for transforming human beings, objects, and settings, for effecting their re-creation, or rebirth.)

The view that women in movies are systematically objectified, that patriarchal ideology fixes the camera's view of them in advance—itself a view an ideology has fixed in advance—fails to acknowledge Cavell's guiding intuition that what a human being, male or female, is capable of becoming on film is not determinable *a priori*. Film does not fix in advance the range of the human.

100

As we have noted, Cavell is by no means denying that in movies, as in the existing world, women are sometimes objectified. Nor is he denying the element of desire in film viewing (any more than he is denying the roles desire plays in our everyday lives). What he is denying is the claim that film itself, or some system of production to which film has been yoked, has *caused* women on film to be objectified. In Chapters 7 through 9, Cavell begins to address the way film's revelation that the woman is her body has led to explorations of possibilities specific to the medium, possibilities that acknowledge the humanity of the particular women who have been among the camera's leading subjects.

Chapter 7 concludes with an epilogue, written as Cavell was completing *The World Viewed*, occasioned by the introduction of the ratings system that marked the definitive end of the Production Code era. "An immediate result was to make nude scenes mandatory in adult films," he observes, reminding us that we cannot take for granted that the end of the old system of censorship automatically spelled increased freedom. In his experience, Cavell testifies, "the new half-freedom unhinges the camera; it either becomes fixated or skittish-lyrical. The interruption occurs at a more painful point" (46). He wryly concludes that "genitalia seem to be as difficult either to follow around or to ignore as the microphone was in early talkies. Will we learn really to take them for granted? And would that mean looking them over at every opportunity in no matter what company and alongside no matter what others?" (45).

Cavell does not speculate here as to the new artistic possibilities open sexuality may prove capable of creating (45). Such possibilities are for filmmakers to discover, not for theorists to legislate. Rather, he closes Chapter 7 with a paragraph about pornography that links up with Chapter 8's concluding reflections on explicitness and inexplicitness in sexual matters and with the conclusion of Chapter 9, which meditates in a different way on the crisis of privacy that in Cavell's view is intimately tied to the origin and history of film. This theme returns in Chapter 13, where the topic is film's ability to establish a world of private fantasy. And the theme motivates a central section of Chapter 19, which invokes the nightmarish possibility that the self has already been rendered fully recessed, completely private, absolutely inexpressive, utterly unknowable to the world.

"I find it said by more than one liberal," the paragraph begins, that the moral question about pornography is "its invasion of the last corner of privacy. From the point of view of the performers, this is ludicrous, like saying that the moral problem about child labor is that the kids worked

101

in poor light. From the point of view of the audience, it is bullying; pornography is more likely to be privacy's last proof" (46).

In a tone reminiscent of James Agee, Cavell notes that the members of an audience at a pornographic film are

> respectful of one another's needfulness, and though each is penetrated with the knowledge the others must be having, no one supposes this lessens his privacy. And even if you attend a pornographic film telling yourself you merely want to know what it's like, you ought to be impressed by the absolute attention, the common awe, when all holds are unbarred. An artist must envy that power. That such an experience . . . is for many people confined to the occasion of viewing a pornographic film, deprived of what it analogues in serious art or in actual sex, is an indictment of society's invasion and enforcement of privacy. (46)

In projecting views of anonymous sexual acts to anonymous audiences, in combining the "absolutely explicit with the completely unspecific," as Cavell puts it at the conclusion of Chapter 8, pornography, like serious art, confirms our longing to acknowledge and be acknowledged by others, to reach this world and achieve selfhood. Unlike serious art, pornography concedes our inability or unwillingness to satisfy our wish, condemns us to remain isolated by our private fantasies. Art is nourishing food; pornography is a drug, in Cavell's view. But pornography has not *caused* the crisis of privacy we are facing.

Chapter 8: "The Military Man and the Woman"

Chapter 8 singles out two of the types Baudelaire considers representative of modernity: the Military Man and the Woman. (The Dandy is the topic of Chapter 9.) Cavell writes that as Baudelaire describes them, the Military Man and the Woman "are not merely further items in cinema's daily sustenance," these figures "have been movies' presiding geniuses" (47). That they are presiding *geniuses* suggests that they are masterminds, wizards with mysteriously powerful and original ways of thinking (yet again: "[M]ovies arise out of magic, from *below* the world,"). That they are *presiding* geniuses suggests that they play active roles in movies, that they dictate the terms of their own appearances.

Cavell turns first to the Military Man, who represents "men in uniform, which is to say, men doing the work of the world, in consort. . . . This figure asserts the myth of community, the idea that society is man's natural state. There are many films—there are genres of film—with nothing but men in them, or with just one or two peripheral women" (47).

"Now listen to what Baudelaire says about Woman," Cavell goes on, eager to shift to this topic. This introduces a long quote from *The Painter of Modern Life* that begins, "The Being who for most men is the source of the most vivid and . . . most lasting delights; the Being towards whom, or for whose benefit, all the efforts of most men are directed," and ends with images especially evocative of film: "for whom, but especially *through whom*, artists and poets create their finest jewels; the source of the most enervating pleasures and . . . fruitful griefs; a ray of light, a look, an invitation to happiness, sometimes a watchword" (47).

"And so on," Cavell impatiently cuts Baudelaire off. For contemporary sensibilities, Baudelaire's passage is difficult to stomach, as when he describes the Woman as "that Being who is terrible and incommunicable as God (but with this difference, that the Infinite does not communicate because it would blind and overwhelm the Finite, whereas the Being of whom we speak is perhaps incomprehensible only because she has nothing to communicate)" (47). For all the Woman's apparent depth, Baudelaire's passage seems to suggest, intelligence is not one of her attributes. To be sure, the passage can also be read as suggesting that what is unfathomable about the Woman is something impossible to communicate, something beyond the reach of words, not something nonexistent. Even read that way, though, Baudelaire's words rankle, for we have learned the danger in equating women with the unknowable "Other."

It is important to keep in mind that Cavell is not equating his own thinking with Baudelaire's. In Chapters 7 through 9, he is arguing that it is a *historical* fact that in the modern period the figure Baudelaire calls "the Woman" emerged, as did Baudelaire's way of viewing this figure as at once the mysterious Other and as exemplary of modernity. In taking this fact to be a datum in investigating film's origins, Cavell is guided by his own intuition that for innumerable movies, the Woman—or the woman who incarnates the Woman on screen—far from being a bubble-brain, is a presiding genius.

It is also important to keep in mind that Cavell understands otherness to be a condition of *human* existence in the modern period. To exemplify the mysterious Other is to exemplify humanity. That the Woman, exemplifying otherness, is a presiding genius of so many movies manifests the depth of film's response to the crisis of subjectivity which, in Cavell's view, emerged with the modern. It reveals film's history to be, in part, a history of expressions of the isolation and the longing for a new intimacy that are conditions of human existence in the modern period.

Within the field of film study, it has long been an article of faith that

103

classical Hollywood cinema—in which (male) ideology, economics, and psychology allegedly cause women to be objectified by the (male) gaze of the camera—systematically subordinates women to men. To the contrary, Cavell finds that in most Hollywood films of the thirties and forties women are *not* subordinate. Rather, "the distribution of emphasis" between man woman "favors the woman, as in a *pas de deux*. Remarkable directors have existed solely to examine the same woman over and over through film. A woman has become the whole excuse and sole justification for the making and preserving of countless films; in many of Garbo's films, or Dietrich's, next to nothing may be memorable, or even tolerable, but these women themselves. The miracle is that they are enough" (48).

Baudelaire asserts that modern artists or poets—it does not occur to him that any might be women—create their "finest jewels" *through* a Woman. In a film whose creation is justified solely by the woman— Woman?—in it, however, she is no more subordinate to her (male) director than to her (male) costar. It might be apter to think of her *as* the artist or poet who creates her film through her director, rather than the other way around. (She is the movie's "presiding genius," after all.)[27]

The chapter's second paragraph claims that in movies the Military Man "asserts the myth of community, the idea that society is man's natural state." The third claims, if not in so many words, that the Woman is anti-community: When a man in a movie directs his efforts toward a Woman, he is not doing the work of the world in consort with other men, nor even breaking ranks with his comrades to do the world's work of procreation (nice work if you can get it); he is seeking private satisfactions. From these facts the fourth paragraph draws the moral that we had better stop drawing the "morals of movies" too hastily, had better reflect more thoughtfully on the stories movies are forever telling. What *are* the morals—the moral lessons—movies draw? What are *morals*—what is morality—in movies?

"Is it true in movies that virtue is always rewarded and vice vanquished?" Cavell asks, invoking a common example of drawing the morals of movies too hastily (48). This question initiates a long paragraph filled with ideas Cavell will continue to explore and develop in his subsequent writings.

One who draws the morals of movies too hastily might assume that movies depict the "woman outside," whose sexuality lures men to stray, as a creature of sin, and that she is punished (in "More of *The World Viewed*," Cavell cites Greta Garbo, Marlene Dietrich, and Mae West as the fullest embodiments of this figure in American movies [*WV*, 206]). Likewise, it might be assumed that movies depict the "woman inside," the faithful wife, as virtuous, and that she is rewarded (along with the straying man who atones for his sins and returns to the fold).

In movies, the woman outside suffers for her acceptance of sexuality, Cavell allows, while noting that civilization exacts its discontents on us all. Yet this woman is outside because she rejects a marriage that denies her sexual nature, not because she is unworthy of marriage or because she sacrifices her own desire. Her acceptance of her sexuality "permits her intelligence and depth and independence," rewards too valuable to trade for a lawful but sexless marriage (48).

By affirming her sexuality, the woman outside embraces self-realization as a greater good than social acceptance. That films do not condemn her for this is a crucial datum in pondering the morals of movies. Movies do not view the woman outside as morally inferior. Her commitment to being true to herself makes her superior—superior *morally*—to a society that lacks the moral standing to judge her.

And, in movies, when the man rejects the possibility of staying with the woman outside, the woman of intelligence, depth, and independence he really loves, and goes home to his wife, he reaps no reward; his life is over. The films Cavell cites (*Intermezzo, Now, Voyager, The Man in the Gray Flannel Suit*) offer different reasons for the man's inability, or unwillingness, to extricate himself from his loveless marriage, but in each he understands himself to have an obligation to return to his wife. However, these movies understand him also to have an obligation, perhaps an overriding one, to create a more authentic marriage with the woman outside, albeit one that requires that he acknowledge his own outsideness. In movies, it is a virtue—indeed, a moral imperative—to quest for human fulfillment. What Cavell has discovered, in discovering this fact about the morals of movies, is the depth of film's commitment to the moral outlook, or dimension of thought about morality, that in later writings he will call "moral perfectionism."

In *Pursuits of Happiness*, Cavell does not yet use the term "moral perfectionism," but this moral outlook is an implicit subject throughout. It becomes an explicit—if still unnamed—subject when that book invokes Matthew Arnold's idea of the "best self," Arnold understands as existing in each of us.

> [M]ore natures are curious about their best self than one might imagine, and this curiosity Arnold calls the pursuit of perfection. "Natures with this bent," Arnold says, "emerge in all classes . . . and this bent tends to take them out of their class, and to make their distinguishing characteristic not their Barbarianism or their Philistinism, but their *humanity*." . . . There is a visual

equivalent . . . of what Arnold means by distinguishing the best self from the ordinary self and by saying that in the best self class yields to humanity. He is witnessing a possibility . . . in the human self not normally open to view, or not open to the normal view. Call this one's invisible self; it is what the movie camera would make visible. (*PH*, 157–58)

Moral perfectionism, as Cavell goes on to develop it in his later writings, reformulates the terms of moral philosophy by locating the emergence of the best self at the heart of morality. For Cavell, moral perfectionism is not a theory of morality, but "something like a dimension or tradition of the moral life that spans the course of Western thought and concerns what used to be called the state of one's soul, a dimension that places tremendous burdens on personal relationships and on the possibility or necessity of the transforming of oneself and of one's society" (*CH&U*, 2). Cavell's goal is not to *define* moral perfectionism, because he has "no theory in which a definition of perfectionism would play a useful role." His goal is to develop what he calls "an open-ended thematics" of moral perfectionism. That is not to his mind "a mere or poor substitute for some imaginary, essential definition of the idea that transcends the project of reading and thematization I am undertaking. . . . That there is no closed list of features that constitute perfectionism follows from conceiving of perfectionism as an outlook or dimension of thought embodied in a set of texts spanning the range of Western culture" (*CH&U*, 4).

A Doll's House is one such text. Cavell's reading of Ibsen's play in *Conditions Handsome and Unhandsome*—like all of Cavell's writings, that book is itself a text that embodies moral perfectionism—focuses on Nora's outrage that hers is not a true marriage. Her "imagination of her future, in leaving," in rejecting her marriage in a way that makes her a prototype for the "woman outside" of so many movies, "turns on her sense of her need for education whose power of transformation presents itself to her as the chance to become human. In Emerson's terms, this is moving to claim one's humanness . . . , to follow the unattained" (*CH&U*, 115).

The theme of a woman rejecting a conventional marriage in order to follow the unattained is most fully explored in *Contesting Tears*, Cavell's recent book about the genre he calls "the melodrama of the unknown woman." In the essays that comprise *Contesting Tears*, he explicates different paths women take in these melodramas. At the end of *Now, Voyager*, for example, the woman follows the unattained by walking away from the man in her life, dismissing him while letting him believe she still loves him, whereas *Stella Dallas* ends with the woman walking not away but toward and then past the camera, declaring that she has embarked on a transcendental path of self-discovery.

Moral perfectionism is as internal to the remarriage comedies *Pursuits of Happiness* studies as it is to the unknown woman melodramas, to *A Doll's House*, to Shakespeare's plays, or to Cavell's own writings. As Chapter 8 makes clear, in *The World Viewed* it is already a central theme that there is a serious moral philosophy, or way of thinking about morality, which is not imposed on movies from the outside like the Production Code, but is internal to the stories movies keep telling.

The figure of the Military Man asserts "the myth of community," as Cavell puts it, the idea that society is the natural human state. Yet the imperative to perfect the self, typified by the figure of the woman outside, calls for an acceptance of sexuality that society, as it stands, denies. In innumerable films, the problem for both the woman and the man is that although it is natural for human beings to exist in society, society as it stands is unnatural.

In the paragraph of Chapter 8 we have been addressing, Cavell first cites films (*Intermezzo, Now, Voyager, The Man in the Gray Flannel Suit*) in which the woman, recognizing that in the world as it stands society and nature are incompatible, makes the (virtuous) choice of remaining outside, even as the man, not up to taking this difficult path, goes back to his sexless marriage.

Then the paragraph turns to films in which the problem is resolved, but in which the "solution," far from rewarding virtue, entails some terrible crime, a literal or symbolic theft, or murder, or devouring of one self by another. In *A Stolen Life*, "the good and bad mothers-lovers are literally twins, and nothing so perfectly declares the permanence of the stolen identity as the good sister's overt confession and outward sloughing of it." In *The Corsican Brothers, The Prisoner of Zenda, The Man in the Iron Mask, Shane,* and *The Man Who Shot Liberty Valance*, "the man's identity is doubled so that it is half of him who withdraws or is killed by the other half." In *Under Two Flags, Destry Rides Again,* and *High Noon*, "the woman outside suffers a death or withdrawal in time for the man's incorporation of her into his marriage" (49). In these last films, the man's life is not over when he goes home to his wife, but the woman outside dies, literally or symbolically, to make this possible. (The word "incorporation" suggests cannibalism, as if the woman outside must be consumed—not just her spirit but also her flesh incorporated into the wife—for the man's marriage to be redeemed.)

The sentence fragment "As though marriage itself is as illicit as sexuality outside" sums up the paragraph's crucial point that a valid marriage incorporates sexuality in a way that transgresses deep societal taboos (49). It also implies the idea, central to *Pursuits of Happiness*, that although a marriage requires validation, nothing outside the marriage itself—not church, or state, or society's need for children to perpetuate itself—is capable of validating it.

That in movies sex is illicit even if the partners are legally married is an idea *The Lady Eve* "manages comically," Cavell observes (surely thinking of that film's ending). *The Great Lie* handles it "with full hysteria." In *The Postman Always Rings Twice* and *Double Indemnity*, "the lovers die because they have killed, but also, since they transgress the deeper law against combining sex and marriage. In a thousand other instances the marriage must not be seen, and the walk into the sunset is into a dying star: they live happily ever after—as long as they keep walking" (49). (As long as they walk, the question of sex can be deferred.)

Tellingly, Cavell's wording invokes Thoreau's image, in the punning last sentence of *Walden*, of "the sun as but a morning"—and *mourning*—"star." The innumerable films that end with the couple walking into the sunset, into a dying star, are often said to have happy endings, but they do not end with a vision of virtue happily rewarded, do not make explicit the necessity of transforming ourselves that Thoreau insists upon.

> For *Walden's* writer . . . the morning of mourning, the dawning of grieving, [is] the proposed alternative, the only alternative, to what he calls "our present constitution," which he says must end. He means our political constitution, with its slaves, but he means more than this; he means what permits this constitution in our souls. He means that mourning is the only alternative to our nostalgias, in which we will otherwise despair and die. ("The Politics of Interpretation," *TOS*, 54)

The image of the movie couple walking into the sunset, their happy marriage asserted but not shown, provides the penultimate image of a paragraph that culminates—prophetically, in light of Cavell's subsequent writing—by invoking *The Philadelphia Story*, *Woman of the Year*, and *The Awful Truth*, three prominent instances of the comedy of remarriage, the genre *Pursuits of Happiness* studies, in which "the marriage is established from the beginning and is worth having at the end," the drama turning upon getting the couple back together (49). These films, *Pursuits of Happiness* argues, "take the experience of the end of a romantic comedy as a matter of a kind of forgetting, one that requires a passage, as it were, from one world (of imagination) to another, as from dreaming to waking. . . . Emerson and Thoreau call the passage to this experience, I take it, dawn" (*PH*, 261–62).

Acknowledging that they *are* creating the world, that heaven is under their feet as well as over their heads, the couples at the end of remarriage comedies arrive at an acceptance of their location on earth, as human. They are explicitly shown to be happily married, in contrast to the innumerable couples who "live happily ever after—as long as they keep walking." (And yet, as Thoreau also insists, walking is a gait natural only to humans.)

It is hardly an exaggeration to say that the entirety of *Pursuits of Happiness* can be glimpsed in Cavell's inspired gesture, in the paragraph of *The World Viewed* we have been considering, of linking *The Philadelphia Story*, *Woman of the Year*, and *The Awful Truth* to the culminating image of Thoreau's *Walden*. This is not to say, however, that when Cavell was writing *The World Viewed* he was fully conscious of the true dimension of these American movies or the genre they exemplify, as *Pursuits of Happiness* brings it to light. It is indicative of this that in *The World Viewed* the concept of acceptance surfaces not in this paragraph but in the next, devoted to Ingmar Bergman's *Smiles of a Summer Night*, which constitutes the most extended piece of criticism of a single film to this point in the book.

"Bergman's *Smiles of a Summer Night*," Cavell writes, "is close enough to the surface of this tradition"—the tradition of Hollywood romantic comedies—"for its brilliance to remember and confirm" the resourcefulness of the earlier films—the resourcefulness of women like the Irene Dunne character in *The Awful Truth*, who uses her powers of seduction to effect the reconciliation with her man, and the resourcefulness of the films themselves (49–50). *Smiles of a Summer Night* revolves around a woman who possesses the strength, intelligence, and independence of a Garbo, Dietrich, or West, American cinema's great exemplars of the woman outside. Yet unlike them she is rewarded with a marriage that is, like the marriages in remarriage comedies, worth having in the end.

Like Shakespeare's Cleopatra, the woman in Bergman's film finds a source of strength in theater. The "calculated set of arrangements" by which she effects the man's return allows marriage to be reinvented, just as the invention of marriage "*is* the (is Cleopatra's, whoever that is) response to Antony's abandonment," as Cavell puts it in *Disowning Knowledge*. "It is a return of the world through the gift of herself, by becoming, presenting herself as, whatever constitutes the world. She is herself her dowry, nothing less than a woman, one who will successively present herself as a queen, a goddess, an actress, a lover, a mother, a nurse, a bride" (*DK*, 28).

The woman in *Smiles of a Summer Night* is so strong, and the man so passive, that "one is not [at the end] suspicious of her drama but perplexed that she finds him worthy of it," Cavell observes. However, "the passiveness of her man is neither contemptible nor stimulating to the woman," but simply "a fact within her acceptance of him" (*DK*, 50). The woman's acceptance of the man declares her acceptance of her own sexuality, her acceptance of who she is. "The film's faithfulness to itself justifies the self-confident wittiness of its references to *A Midsummer Night's Dream*," Cavell writes, not yet prepared to recognize that films like *The Awful Truth* are themselves no less indebted to Shakespearean romance, allude no less wittily to that indebtedness, and are no less faithful to themselves. These facts about remarriage comedies become important themes in *Pursuits of Happiness*.

As we have noted, it is striking how much of Cavell's later writing is anticipated by the long paragraph that culminates by linking three American romantic comedies with *Walden*. It is no less striking, however, that this paragraph explicitly expresses so little of Cavell's full understanding of these films, as *Pursuits of Happiness* and *Contesting Tears* will go on to articulate it. The way the paragraph sweeps us from film to film to film is part of its strength. Yet by conspicuously *not* lingering on any particular film, much less any particular moment, the paragraph conveys the impression—an impression reinforced by the fact that *Smiles of a Summer Night* is accorded such a long paragraph of its own—that the American movies the paragraph cites do not call for being pondered. This impression comes through most strongly, perhaps, when Cavell refers to the "thousand other instances" in which "the marriage must not be seen, and the walk into the sunset is into a dying star" without deigning to name a single one of these films. This pointed omission intimates that these movies, by asserting a conventional happy marriage they do not explicitly show, render themselves interchangeable, forfeit their claim to being named—as if by oversimplifying or evading the morals of movies, they betray their own morality, fail to be faithful to themselves, fail fully *to be* themselves.

Perhaps remembering his own admonition not to draw the morals of movies too hastily, however, Cavell inserts a typographical break at this point. It marks the transition to the second part of Chapter 8, in which he probes his subject more deeply.

■ ■

"Critics of the movie's traditions of sexual or intellectual or political simplicities and evasions seem to have an idea that what is lacking is verbal or visual explicitness," the second part of the chapter begins. "No one will deny that inexplicitness can be abused, but so can explicitness. An avoided subject is not confronted by calling it names" (51).

Clearly with these words Cavell is distancing himself from the un-named critics of this ilk.[28] However, in criticizing "critics of the movie's traditions of sexual or intellectual or political simplicities and evasions," he is not exempting himself; he is also distancing himself from an impulse he recognizes in himself (the impulse that just surfaced in his own writing, perhaps, when he seemed to be condemning all but the most exceptional Hollywood movies for failing to keep faith with their own morality).

Cavell is not denying that film has its traditional ways of avoiding certain subjects. Simply to accuse movies of being simplistic and evasive— to call films names—is to continue avoiding those subjects, though. It is also to continue avoiding the subject of film itself. To be sure, in this passage Cavell is not explicitly naming the subjects film has traditions of avoiding. As always in Chapter 8, the overriding moral is that we must not draw the morals of movies too hastily. The corrective is to turn to the films, as Cavell does when he sketches an extended comparison between the two versions of Lillian Hellman's *The Children's Hour.* This gives rise to the first passage of *The World Viewed* that reveals Cavell's full powers of "reading" movie moments, of homing in on their concrete particularity, on what is explicitly seen and heard in them, and on what the-explicitly-seen-and-heard implies.

The sixties version, titled *The Children's Hour,* refers explicitly to the homosexual attachment that had to be cast into heterosexual terms in *These Three,* the thirties version. Nonetheless "the homosexuality in the relation between the two women, at least their genuineness and exclusiveness of feeling, is much plainer in the first movie version, in which we see the women as roommates in a girl's college, about to graduate into the unwelcoming and depressed world of male competition. . . . Their strategy is to avoid entering it, to reproduce their world of women by

111

starting their own school for girls" (51). Because it "depends upon a pact to expel desire and fruitfulness," it is desire itself—heterosexuality no less than homosexuality—this world of women finds threatening.

> It was a valid insight that produced the male's entrance (Joel McCrea) through the rafters of the decaying house (now the niece's) enveloped in beekeeper's clothing. He frightens the young arrivals, both because of the eeriness of his appearance and the unexpectedness of his place of invasion, but surely also because he presents maleness as the source of stings, and as impervious to their repulsions. To introduce homosexuality in such an environment merely shows it as a deeper strategy to avoid the intrusive company of males. That may be part of some theory of homosexuality; but these events cannot confirm it, they can merely purvey it, and with no idea . . . about why such a choice should ever be made. (52)

By comparison, the sixties version shows "an external, peeping treatment of the subject," Cavell observes in another passage in which he homes in both on what is explicitly seen and heard, and on what is implicit, in a moment on film.

> The dominant friend has a close-up premonition, upon which she runs back to the house to prevent her vision of her friend's self-destruction. But where did she get this vision? From her wish? And where did her friend get it? Must she kill herself because she cannot live with the knowledge that she is homosexual? That destroys our sense of the moving confession of love she has just given. Is it because she has brought destruction upon her friends? But she has not, unless they will it. (52)

"The two versions meet," Cavell asserts, "at a piece of business the later preserves almost intact—the point at which, in the interview between man and woman that sends the man away, a hand of one covers the mouth of the other to stop a question" (52). In the thirties version, the man, courteously and tenderly, "touches the woman's mouth to stop her from the explicit question that would mean her distrust of him. It was to be a simple question of fact: Did you succumb to the vulgarest of temptations and betray me with my best friend? It is more humiliating to ask than to answer; but he answers." The hand over her mouth leaves the woman "asking herself what has brought her to this question. When she answers that, she can accommodate her love" (52–53).

In the sixties version, it is the woman who stops the man's question. "But it is no longer a question of external fact; it is not, did you or did you not?, but, do you return her love or do you not? That may be painful, but it is not humiliating to ask or answer, and he has a right to know, and a reason to want to know." The woman's stopping this question is "an evasion, and her explicit denial of it is a further falseness." Whereas in the earlier film the surviving woman is willing to pay the price of social ostracism to be faithful to her desire, hence to herself, in the sixties version the woman's "isolation [is not] ostracism but . . . the sealing of secret victory; she was loved, someone died of love of her, and she returns the love, but now it will never need to show; vulnerability is bypassed" (53). The quest for selfhood, which calls for acknowledging one's separateness from others, is abdicated. The moral point is lost.

The Children's Hour has an unhappy ending that "stops at what the surviving woman wishes to be accepted as the truth: the society of women and the world of men and the views of children have wronged her and are miserable things compared with her purity" (53). *These Three* has an ending that is deeper, more faithful to the "morals of movies," in that it "shows that happy endings require trust and a faithfulness to one's desire which overcomes what faithfulness must always overcome—the meanness and maliciousness of opinion" (53–54).

If trust and faithfulness, in a democracy such as ours, must always overcome the meanness and maliciousness of opinion, how can the Good State ever be achieved? What *causes* opinion to be so mean and malicious, to deny or repress desires that are a natural part of being human? *Mr. Smith Goes to Washington* is not explicit about the causes of political corruption, Cavell notes in Chapter 8's penultimate paragraph, which makes clear that he understands the morals of movies to have a public or political as well as a private or personal dimension. It does not seriously detract from the paragraph's significance that it ends with a vivid description of a scene that does not take place quite the way Cavell remembers it.

> Still, the image of its abrupt close marks out the region which will have to be explored for details of a further significance. On the floor of the Senate, Jean Arthur kneels beside Mr. Smith's prostrate, rejected form, supporting his head in the ambiguous birth-death posture of a Pieta. The corrupted senator (Claude Rains) flies to their side, his life of respectable conspiracy broken into by the scene, to confirm to the gathered world the truth of the swooned man. One of the senator's hands points down to the couple, the other is raised up in an oratorical dedication, like Liberty's ambiguous upraised, threatening arm. Whom does the truth kill? Who is in a position to speak it, or hear it, or to act upon it if he knows he has heard? (54)[29]

The writing of *The World Viewed* is predicated on its author's faith that he is in a position to speak truths he wishes readers to hear and act upon. The rhetorical questions Cavell poses here—Whom does the truth kill? Who is in a position to speak it, or hear it, or to act upon it if he knows he has heard?—cut to the heart of his own understanding and practice of philosophy. In closing Chapter 8 by returning to the topic of desire, Cavell

113

extends these questions to the realm of sexuality. "If inexplicitness in sexual matters invites the itch of suggestiveness, explicitness cuts feeling from an attachment to anything beyond itself" (54). Then how are the truths of desire to be spoken, by whom and to whom, and whom do they kill? (Is *The World Viewed* undertaking to speak such truths?)

"[S]ickened, rightly, at the world's furtiveness about certain words and deeds," Cavell observes, D. H. Lawrence wrote *Lady Chatterley's Lover* to "try to exorcize the bad magic of certain words and deeds with a magic of repetition and literalness." However admirable, that leaves the "importance of the subject incomprehensible, the metaphysical facts of sexuality, as in his *Women in Love*, in which moon and water and meadows and beasts and snow peaks are not symbolic evasions but tracings of that universe of feeling in which each of us finds or loses the space of our desire" (54–55).

That we each have our own desires is a metaphysical fact of human sexuality, one that above all reveals our condition as separate, finite beings. Justice will be done, the Good State will emerge, we will reach a happy ending, not when we become merely more explicit about sexual, intellectual, and political matters, but when we become faithful to our own desires, and find the trust that others will be faithful to their desires, too.

Only we can speak for, or from, our own desires, and, in doing so, there is no telling, beforehand, how explicit our words must be. As Cavell puts it in the chapter's wonderful closing lines, "From the fact that the birds and the bees become insufficient it doesn't follow that all we ever need are the ABC's. What you need is the tact in each case to be specific enough. (Pornography, so far at least, combines the absolutely explicit with the completely unspecific.)" (55).

Part of what Cavell's tactful words are just specific enough to say is that in the writing of *The World Viewed* it is a continuous issue, a matter requiring tact, how explicit, and how specific, the words must be.

Chapter 9: "The Dandy"

The Military Man wears a uniform; the Dandy, whose "personal appearance and material elegance" are "symbols of the aristocratic superiority of his personality," looks like no one else in the world (55). The Military Man does the work of the world in consort with other men; the Dandy is alone, and he does not do the work of the world at all. The Dandy is ruled by his passion, and his ruling passion is a burning need

to acquire originality, within the apparent bounds of convention. . . . It is the delight in causing astonishment, and the proud satisfaction of never oneself being astonished. . . . The characteristic beauty of the Dandy consists . . . in his air of reserve, which in turn arises from his unshakable resolve not to feel any emotion. It might be likened to a hidden fire whose presence can be guessed at; a fire that could blaze up, but does not wish to do so. (55)

Observing that we still feel the power of this figure who stakes himself upon a passive potency, Cavell calls Bogart and the Western hero our most brilliant representatives of the type. He cites Peter Fonda in *Easy Rider* as its latest avatar, "self-proclaimed and claiming to be the last" (56).

For Cavell, the feature of the hidden fire is essential, not only to the Dandy's beauty but also to his strength, apart from which he could not be a hero. "Our conviction in the strength of the hero depends upon our conviction in the strength and purity of character he has formed to keep his fires banked. Otherwise he is merely physically indomitable, and no man is; in that case, his success over evil would be arbitrary, an aesthetic and moral cheat. He does not *know* he will succeed; what he knows is himself, his readiness" (56).

The Dandy's strength is a function of the purity of the character forged in the crucible of his inner fire. As Cavell's imagery suggests, there is about the Dandy an aura of religion or magic. (Then again, religion and magic, in film, are not separate realms.) Baudelaire emphasizes the Dandy's characteristic beauty, while Cavell insists on his *moral* dimension, or, rather, in keeping with the outlook of moral perfectionism, in Cavell's view the Dandy's private heroism, his heroism of privacy, transcends the distinction between aesthetics and morality. The Dandy's morality no less than his beauty resides in his keeping faith with his burning need to acquire originality, to re-create or originate himself as his own man, ruled by his passion. What makes the Dandy beautiful also makes him strong, makes him an enemy of evil, and a powerful one.

Where we find a Hero, we expect a Villain. In each of the cases Cavell cites, Dandy and Villain have a connection so intimate as to suggest that they are less separate individuals than aspects of a single self.

The Villain of the piece may either be a lout or a swell—generally, some combination of the two. . . . The hero faces one of his doubles and comes to his kind of terms with it. In the first case he kills brutishness, false masculinity (*Stagecoach, My Darling Clementine, Hombre*); in the second he kills vanity, false dandyism (*Destry Rides Again, Shane, The Appaloosa*). The Villain of *The Maltese Falcon* is the woman, another range of the Dandy's double, and she is both brutish (hence a false man) and so wholly caught up in appearances that she can't tell a Dandy from a brute. But one's love must not wait for justification by its object, and Bogart-Spade loves her. He tells her when it has all come

115

out, in some of the best dialogue ever set to film, that she is "going over" for what she has done, that he is sending her over for the way she is. But in finishing her he does not finish his love for her, and this makes him true to type (his feeling is not dead, but banked); and because that shows the depth of his strength, he is the greatest instance of the type. (57)

Although it is within the bounds of convention that Dandies strive to acquire originality, they remain outside society. They "are not outside society because they have been pushed out," Cavell observes, "or because society holds them, by its own force, above its head." They have stayed out. "There is therefore about them," he intriguingly adds, "the suspicion that their freedom is never more than fantasy, like Huckleberry Finn's, that while their profession is risks, their selves are never chanced" (56). What makes Cavell nominate Bogart-Spade as the greatest instance of the Dandy is the unfathomable depth of feeling—hence the unfathomable strength it takes to keep such feeling banked—he so convincingly projects. We do not doubt that *this* man really takes risks, chances his self, that for him staying out comes at a high price, and that he knows, and accepts, that cost.

In invoking the principle "One's love must not wait for justification by its object," Cavell's wording implies that this is a principle the Dandy affirms (57). And it implies that Cavell, too, affirms this principle, that this maxim gives expression to a knowledge the Dandy and the author of *The World Viewed* share (and, presumably, share with us). In any case, by invoking this principle within the context of his remarks about Bogart-Spade, Cavell links this "greatest instance" of the Dandy to the equally exemplary Woman in *Smiles of a Summer Night*, who possesses a comparable knowledge. In *The Maltese Falcon*, Bogart-Spade loves the woman (Mary Astor) he is sending over. We might say, mimicking Chapter 8's wording, that her brutishness is neither contemptible nor stimulating to him, but a fact within his rejection of her; his rejection of her declares his acceptance of his own sexuality, his acceptance of who he is.

The Bogart-Spade example brings out what seems to be a difference between Cavell's and Baudelaire's understanding of the Dandy. Cavell agrees with Baudelaire that the Dandy "does not make love his special aim" (unlike the Military Man, whose prototype is Shakespeare's Antony). However, Cavell does not concur that the Dandy's burning need is to avoid or deny feeling. Bogart-Spade does not aim to fall in love, but neither does he aim to avoid it. Fall in love he does. When he does, he does not deny his feeling, either to the woman or to himself, or attempt to extinguish it. Rather, he manifests that exemplary capacity for self-knowledge ("what

116

he knows is himself") crucial to the strength and purity—and beauty—of the Dandy's character.

In Cavell's understanding, the Dandy's burning need, his unshakable resolve (to use another of Baudelaire's terms), is not to avoid or deny feeling but to recognize his feeling as a condition he accepts about himself. Cavell's word "resolve" makes it seem as if by sending over the woman he loves Bogart-Spade is following society's rules, not obeying his own ruling passion. In truth, when he rejects this woman he loves, he is not denying but keeping faith with his desire, his burning need to be his own master, to master his feelings, not be slave to them.

In Cavell's understanding, feeling—passion, desire—*is* the inner fire separating the true Dandy from the false Dandies he calls "swells" and also from the false masculinity of "louts" or "brutes." The Dandy's heroism is inseparable from his commitment to achieving a true masculinity, to becoming a true man (a truly human male, a truly male human being). What qualifies the Dandy to be a hero is thus akin to what qualifies the woman outside to be a heroine. Her quest for selfhood, which likewise has a moral dimension, requires that she accept her sexuality, which society would have her deny. The Dandy accepts his sexuality, too. There will be moments "in which the hero's emotion blazes up, showing that what is happening takes place over fire," Cavell reminds us, adding that this "is the meaning of Bogart's familiar mannerisms (the lips caught back, the distracted tug at the ear lobe)" and that "the Bogart character also has a fixed attribute that indicates its depth—the occasion usually found for him, when he is alone, to laugh at himself, as if at all types and their confinement, putting him and them in perspective" (57).

The next paragraph deepens the terms of the discussion by linking up with the questions prompted in Chapter 8 by the ending of *Mr. Smith Goes to Washington* ("Whom does the truth kill?" "Who is in a position to speak it, or to hear it, or to act upon it if he knows he has heard?").

In *The Man Who Shot Liberty Valance*, the John Wayne character knows that when he kills the brute (and Lee Marvin's brute is also a false Dandy, with his silver-handled whip) he is killing half of himself. He has to do it because he knows that the James Stewart character is incapable of preserving himself either from the brute or from true or false dandies; and he must survive because he is the only real man around who has left room for the woman in himself . . . ; hence only he is capable of preserving civilization, marrying privacy with society. So Wayne breaks not only society's law but his own, murdering in secret in order to establish justice. This is the best that can be done so long as men go on believing that the force of force is greater than the power of justice, and that justice comes from nowhere. *Liberty Valance* is

Bogart laughing at himself (*To Have and Have Not*).

the fullest expression of the knowledge of the cost of civilization to be found
in this genre of film, and therefore it is the greatest instance of it. . . . In so
fully opening the legend of the West, it ends it. Shane's beauty is of a different
valence. What Shane knows, as he rides back out of the valley, is only that *he*
is not made for civilization, which he finally learned, as we did, when after
his climactic duel he twirled his brilliant pistol (the whole screen looming it)
back into its holster. His satisfaction pins him to his fate; he recognizes that
he cannot forgo his mark of mastery, his taste for distinction, the privilege in
his autonomy. (57–58)

The ending of *Shane*, as Cavell reads it, invites comparison with the ending
of the sixties version of *The Children's Hour*, in which the surviving woman's
"isolation [is not] ostracism but . . . the sealing of secret victory." She
denies the truth of her feeling—it is a truth about the world and about
herself, and she denies it to the world and to herself—in favor of what she
wishes to be accepted as the truth (by the world, by herself): that society

118

and the world "are miserable things compared with her purity." In denying her feeling, she proves herself to be as miserable, and as impure, as the society she would condemn. By contrast, Shane recognizes and accepts the truth (that he is not made for civilization, that it is not to his taste). In staying out of the society he lends his power to protect, he accepts this truth about the world and about himself, preserves the integrity of the character forged in his inner fire. (Barbara Stanwyck's Stella Dallas, as she emerges in *Contesting Tears*, is a comparable figure.)

Shane knows that he is not made for civilization, that he cannot forgo his mark of mastery, his taste for distinction, the privilege in his autonomy that society would have him deny. What Shane does not know, does not even question, is why, given that civilization is not to his taste, he fights to preserve or establish it. Because *The Man Who Shot Liberty Valance* seriously addresses this question, Cavell singles it out as the "fullest expression of the knowledge of the cost of civilization to be found in this genre," hence as the genre's "greatest instance" (58).

In these formulations, Cavell's precise wording is crucial. What *Liberty Valance* expresses more fully than other instances of its genre is "the knowledge" of civilization's cost. This use of the word "knowledge" implies that what *Liberty Valance* gives full expression to *is* knowledge, is something *The World Viewed accepts* as knowledge. Cavell is claiming that there *is* something about the cost of civilization, about the establishment of legitimacy, about the traumatic birth of law in the new world, that *Liberty Valance* knows and expresses even more fully than other films of "this genre." In entering this claim, *The World Viewed* is claiming to possess—and expressing—this knowledge, too, and is calling upon us to acknowledge that we possess it as well, that we accept as an instance of *knowledge* this "something" that *Liberty Valance* expresses.

When Cavell refers here to "this genre," he has in mind films like *Shane* and *Liberty Valance*, whose stories revolve around knowledge of the cost of civilization. Whether by this criterion all Westerns are to be counted as instances of "this genre," or only certain Westerns (and perhaps also certain movies we would not classify as Westerns), is a question Cavell pointedly leaves unanswered. Identifying the members of a genre is a task for criticism, in Cavell's view. In leaving this question open, in particular, Cavell is leaving the door open for the critical procedures he will go on to follow in *Pursuits of Happiness* and *Contesting Tears*. In those books, he singles out a number of films, from the large body of Hollywood romantic comedies and melodramas of the thirties and forties, as exemplary instances of genres whose members revolve around particular stories or myths. These stories or myths, which give expression to particular regions of knowledge, account for the fact that the members of each genre have innumerable features in common.

The Wayne character in *Liberty Valance*, when he murders in secret to establish justice, "breaks not only society's law but his own," as Cavell puts it. This hero knows he is "killing half of himself," but also knows he has to do this. He knows that the James Stewart character, the tenderfoot incapable of protecting himself, "must survive because he is the only real man around who has left room for the woman in himself," the only masculine figure capable of "marrying privacy with society," as civilization requires (58).

Powerless to fight the Villain single-handedly, the tenderfoot believes so strongly in justice that his faith attracts to his side a hero who commands a force of arms even greater than the Villain's. And yet this hero not only kills half of himself in killing Liberty Valance, he also "kills the identity of the tenderfoot, because the secret transforms the tenderfoot into 'the man who shot Liberty Valance'" (58). By killing the Villain in secret, Wayne frees the tenderfoot to marry the woman Wayne himself loves, and who secretly loves him. This woman's marriage to "the man who shot Liberty Valance," a marriage society recognizes as legitimate, as confirming society's own legitimacy, is a marriage that denies her desire.

Hero kills Villain in *Liberty Valance*; justice is done. And justice— the rule of law—is established. But it requires this problematic "transfer of identity," as Cavell calls it, which establishes the limits of each man's identity, to effect that outcome. "This is the best that can be done," Cavell laments, "so long as men go on believing that the force of force is greater than the power of justice, and that justice comes from nowhere." The order of civilization established in America, as *Liberty Valance* envisions it, is one in which false beliefs are given a veneer of legitimacy, not overthrown. "And a stern moral is drawn," Cavell observes, in a passage that speaks eloquently to the question of what is *American* about American movies:

> Justice, to be done, must be seen to be done; but justice, to be established, must not be seen to be established. No single man can establish it, only men together, each granting the other a certain right over his own autonomy. Were there still a place beyond our lives from which Athena might appear, the just city could be seen to be established, all could recognize the justice of justice. Such are the traumatic births of law in the new world. In the old world, at once less new and less primitive, the homologous trauma lay in the deaths of kings, not in the establishment but in the replacement of legitimacy. (58–59)

120

The above passage distinguishes "this genre" from, but also links it to, a European tradition that can be traced back through Shakespeare to Greek tragedy. At this point in the text, Cavell reflects on this distinction in a footnote—the longest in *The World Viewed*—in which he returns to the figure of the Woman, largely in the background in Chapter 9.

> In "Greek Tragedy: Problems of Interpretation," Jean-Pierre Vernant speaks of . . . Greek tragedy as a moment in which two ideals of conduct clash: the hero necessary for the establishment of justice must disappear after its establishment, and because of it. He also speaks of the women of Greek tragedy as possessing individual "character" despite their lack of social character, i.e., citizenship. In Westerns, this is true of the bad woman [i.e., the "woman outside"], not of the good woman. (If the woman is not bad but nevertheless mildly interesting, she is a "visitor from the East," usually Boston, and usually serving as a schoolteacher.) (59 n)

In terms strikingly prophetic of *Pursuits of Happiness* and *Contesting Tears*, this passage characterizes "the inner relation" in Westerns between the hero and the "bad woman" by spinning out a scenario meant to highlight certain features of the story, or myth, Cavell takes to underlie *Liberty Valance* and other films of its genre.

> The inner relation between the hero and the bad woman lies in their relation to their own feelings. . . . Their feelings are strong and clear enough to judge the world that thinks to size them up. They know their inner lives are unknown to the world at large, and because they are unmoved by the opinion of others (which . . . is too compromised to value seriously), their respect for themselves demands scrupulous respect in the way others treat them. . . . They are not contemptuous, i.e., afraid, of weakness; they come to its protection. They do not force or buy feeling, in particular not love from one another. This is more important as an impediment to their marriage than anything called the Hollywood code. The sanction they lend one another outside society cannot function within it. Inside, there is no room for absolute autonomy; the opinion of others must be ceded some control over one's conduct. This is the end of the woman, whose sense of worth depends upon an absolute freedom from the control of reputation; but it merely limits the man, in favor of society's future, with his children in it, to whom, to perpetuate his name, he must limit his autonomy. Naturally there is an indictment of society in this. . . . But the indictment is lodged earlier than in the man's desire to enter society, and hence to forgo the woman. It is implied in the value of that relationship itself, in society's incapacity to provide, or to live according to, the terms in which honor can be honored. . . . That [the hero] must leave the woman outside permanently questions whether the light of civilization is worth the candle. The impediment to this marriage is a psychic incestuousness; they are halves of one another. Their relation, in its combination of mutual independence, lust, knowledge, and narcissism, is a serious modern equivalent of the Platonic. (59 n)

121

Not all Westerns, not even all John Ford Westerns, correspond as fully as *Liberty Valance* to the above scenario. In *Liberty Valance*, the leading woman is a homespun product, as the scenario dictates, but in *My Darling Clementine*, for example, she is very much of the visitor from the East persuasion, as is the leading woman in *Rio Bravo* (a Howard Hawks Western). *Stagecoach* (an earlier Ford Western featuring a much younger Wayne) follows the scenario to a point, but then departs from it. Ringo, the Wayne character, has no desire to forgo the "bad woman," Dallas, in order to enter society. Because he gives precedence to avenging his murdered family, he risks forgoing Dallas. But after he kills the Villains, his lawmen friends allow him to ride off with her to his ranch in Mexico, where it is possible for the couple to marry and yet remain "outside."

In the scenario he presents in this footnote, Cavell does not seem to be tracing the story line of existing films. Rather, he seems to be discovering a story or myth—or it seems to be revealing itself, unfolding on its own—by working through its internal logic. Perhaps that is why the resulting scenario turns out to be so revelatory of Cavell's own ways of thinking about Hollywood movies, ways of thinking he will flesh out in *Pursuits of Happiness* and *Contesting Tears* by marrying them with particular films and film moments.

Even *Liberty Valance* departs from the scenario, we might note, insofar as the hero does not forgo the woman in order to enter a society she cannot enter without its being the end of her. Rather, by murdering in secret, he establishes an order of society within which she has a place (she is the wife of "the man who shot Liberty Valance") but he remains outside. Nonetheless, we may discover an intimate relation between *Liberty Valance* and Cavell's scenario. Just as the hero kills part of himself when he kills the Villain, and just as part of the tenderfoot's identity dies when he incorporates the hero's identity and becomes "the man who shot Liberty Valance," so part of the woman's identity (the part not made for civilization, the part that desires and is desired by Wayne) is killed when Wayne murders in secret and thereby gives her no choice but to marry Stewart rather than Wayne himself, the hero she loves.

At the heart of *Liberty Valance*, in other words, is a story that hinges, as Cavell's scenario does, on the "inner relation" between the hero and the woman outside (a relation, abhorred by society, that combines "mutual independence, lust, knowledge, and narcissism") and on the "psychic incestuousness" that is the impediment to their marriage, an impediment they are unable to overcome, or transcend. And *Liberty Valance*, like Cavell's scenario, registers a devastating indictment of society, not only in the hero's desire to forgo his relationship with the woman, but "in the value of that relationship itself, in society's incapacity to provide, or to live according to, the terms in which honor can be honored" (59 n).

At the heart of the remarriage comedy, too, *Pursuits of Happiness* argues, is a story or myth that hinges on the inner relation between a hero and a "woman outside," figures who are halves of one another, who are like brother and sister. However, what makes the remarriage comedy unique, what leads Cavell in his later writing to accord it a privileged status within the constellation of Hollywood genres, is the fact that it envisions the couple as overcoming or transcending this impediment, as achieving a marriage worth having in the end.

The Western hero and the "bad woman" are as close as brother and sister, and yet, Cavell's scenario suggests, there is an asymmetry in their relation to each other and to society. The man can accept the limitations on his autonomy that society imposes, can even forgo the woman he loves, because he wishes to raise his sons within society and thereby perpetuate his name. The man is implicated in society, has a stake in it that the woman does not have. For the woman, entering society would completely destroy her autonomy, not merely limit it. It would be the end of her, Cavell argues, because "her sense of worth depends upon an absolute freedom from the control of reputation" (59 n). That the man's sense of worth does not depend on this reflects the fact that society, as it stands, holds men and women to unequal standards. In *Stagecoach*, Ringo knows that once he serves out his jail time, society will accept him back. Society will never accept Dallas, no matter what price she pays.

The remarriage comedy minimizes this asymmetry. For one thing, the woman's father is on the side of her happiness. Because she is his daughter, not his son, perpetuating his own name can be no part of what motivates this father to wish to "give her" to the hero who loves her. For another, in remarriage comedies the criteria for what makes a marriage worth having in the end—mutual trust and mutual desire, as reflected in the quality of their conversation—have nothing to do with having children, nothing to do with perpetuating the patriarchal line of a society they remain outside. Yet even in these comedies, in which the woman has the good fortune to love a hero capable of acknowledging his inner relation to her, an asymmetry remains: It is the woman, not the man, who undergoes a metamorphosis tantamount to death and rebirth. As Cavell's reading of *Adam's Rib* in *Pursuits of Happiness* makes explicit, even in the remarriage comedy there seems an element of villainy inherent in the male role, perhaps inherent in masculinity itself.

One might think that the Hays Office simply dictated by fiat that the world of classical Hollywood movies be a good world, a world in which it is a foregone conclusion that good always defeats evil. That is to draw the morals of movies too hastily, however. The world of *Liberty Valance* is no more a good world than is the world of *Mr. Smith Goes to Washington*, or, indeed, the world of *Adam's Rib*.

> If we accept the inner relation of the bad and the good man—that both are outside the law, the one because he's strong enough to get away with it, the other because he's strong enough to impose his own code upon himself and have it respected . . . —then it cannot be true that the satisfaction of powerful Westerns consists merely in viewing again and again the triumph of good over evil. If that were all, the arbitrariness of victory would have only the anxious pleasure in watching a game of chance. The anxiety in the Western is a deeper one. . . . The victory is *almost* arbitrary, and the hair's-breadth lets in the question: What is the fate that chooses the stronger to defend the good? Evil is always victorious in the short run, why not forever? Why is it the fate of good in an evil world *ever* to attract strength in its behalf, and strengthen it? (59)

As the chapter's penultimate paragraph nears its conclusion, Cavell increasingly summons up his powers of eloquence ("And in the all but complete absence of public virtue, and the all but invincible power of the empty demagogue and the empty mass filling one another's spirits . . .") to describe the world of Westerns and Frank Capra movies, a world in which "evil is always victorious in the short run," in which good loses every battle before it wins its perhaps only pyrrhic victory (59).

As we find ourselves swept up in the passion of Cavell's prose, we may well begin to sense that the world he is invoking in this paragraph, in which "men go on believing that the force of force is greater than the power of justice, and that justice comes from nowhere," is not only the world of Westerns and Capra movies, in which fate still chooses the stronger to defend the good, it is also the world of the present, as Cavell was writing these pages—a world in which America was tearing itself apart over a war in which it was far from clear that we were using our strength to defend the good.

It is characteristic of the modern, as Baudelaire envisions it, that it transcends or overcomes the distinction between aesthetics and morality. It is keeping faith with his ruling passion that gives the Dandy, that exemplar of modernity, his strength, purity, and beauty. The Dandy would not be moral at all, would not champion the good, unless he found goodness *attractive*, unless there was for him "a point at which the desire for good appears fairer than the taste of rancor and the smell of power,"

124

Vacant landscape and sky (*My Darling Clementine*).

as Cavell puts it (59). The morals of movies depend upon there being—or our believing there to be—such a point.

The question that the anxiety underlying the Western motivates, the chapter's penultimate paragraph concludes, is not "Why should I be moral?" To that question "the answer may be that you are too cowardly for much of anything else." The pertinent question is whether goodness will "lose its power to attract, whether all men and women will despair of happiness" (59).

Since the Western's heyday, the deep anxiety underlying the genre has surfaced. The possibility that goodness is losing—or has lost—its power to attract is suggested by the closing paragraph of Chapter 9:

> Every American city has someone in it who remembers when part of it was still land. In the world of the Western there is only land, dotted here and there with shelters and now and then with a dash of fronts that men there call a city. The gorgeous, suspended skies achieved in the works of, say, John Ford, are

as vacant as the land. When the Indians are gone, they will take with them whatever gods inhabited those places, leaving the beautiful names we do not understand (Iroquois, Shenandoah, Mississippi, Cheyenne) in place of those places we will not understand. So our slaughtered beauty mocks us, and gods become legends. (59–60)

In a John Ford western, the skies are as vacant as the land, as vacant as the expression of a Dandy who delights in causing but not showing astonishment. When the events of *Liberty Valance* begin, Native Americans still inhabit these places, as do their gods, whose presence, like a Dandy's ruling passion, may be likened to a hidden fire that could blaze up but does not choose to do so. When these events end, the rule of law is established, but the Native Americans and their gods are gone. They are slaughtered, like the identities of the tenderfoot and the hero and the woman. All the places Americans call cities were once beautiful places inhabited by gods we have slaughtered, the chapter closes by reminding us. Can we ever be at home in this landscape, when we do not, cannot, understand the places we inhabit, when our slaughtered beauty mocks us?

IV

■ ■ ■ ■

CHAPTERS 10–11:
THE END OF THE MYTHS

THE ENDING OF Chapter 9 marks the first passage in *The World Viewed* whose tone is poised between elegy and harsh judgment. This tone will be repeatedly sounded in the two chapters that follow, which inaugurate the book's reflections on the fact that the traditional media of movies are losing their power to compel conviction, and that film has begun moving into the modernist environment inhabited for generations by the other major arts.

Chapter 10 dwells on the ways recent traditional movies are "dressed up" to cover the loss or baffling of conviction in their myths. Chapter 11 reminds us that the traditional myths are still capable of carrying conviction when *certain* flesh and blood human beings incarnate the genres' presiding geniuses, and when they are placed against and within *certain* settings.

Chapter 10: "End of the Myths"

"I assume it is sufficiently obvious," Chapter 10 begins, "that the media of movies exemplified by familiar Hollywood cycles and plots that justify the projection of types are drawing to an end" (60). Why this has happened calls for no less complex an explanation than comparable events in other arts. "To say that the 'conventions have become exhausted' is no explanation. . . . It merely restates this historical fact" (60). Another

127

way of restating the fact is to say that "within the last decade film has been moving into the modernist environment inhabited for generations by the other major arts" (60). Each of those arts, its traditional media no longer carrying conviction, has had to justify its existence in its own way, to discover altogether new ways of making sense, previously unexplored possibilities within the medium of the art itself.

Although film has recently begun moving into this modernist environment, movies are still being made in traditional genres. But, as Cavell observes, there no longer is the same continuity between them "and the films we take seriously, or between the audiences awaiting each." The fact that traditional movies continue to be produced, he argues, "provides evidence at once for their completion as media of seriousness and for an examination of what we mean by 'cinematic' and by 'exploration of the possibilities of the medium itself'" (60–61).

The traditional movies now being made tend to be "dressed up" with "fancier cutting and dreamier color and extremer angles and more explicit dialogue," as Cavell puts it.

> This is sometimes taken as an investigation of new possibilities of the cinematic medium. But what is new in these products? It is hardly news that the camera can move, even rapidly; that it can subtend varying directions and distances from its subject; that a story can be told by abrupt editing from scene to scene. One takes mechanical extensions of these known quantities as explorations of the cinematic to the extent that one accepts these quantities as constituting the significance of "cinematic." (61)

The possibilities traditional movies have explored are *certain* possibilities, not *the* possibilities, of film; they do not constitute "the significance of 'cinematic.'" Mechanical extensions of these "known quantities of film" thus bear "roughly the relation to the history of cinema that late-nineteenth century chromaticism bears to the history of music," Cavell argues (61). When composers after Wagner pushed chromatic alteration and modulation to the limits of the human organism's capacity to hear tones as alterations of other tones, certain possibilities of music came to an end. But such mechanical extensions of traditional possibilities of music became new possibilities for music only when Mahler, Schoenberg, and Debussy discovered new musical forms that gave them significance *as* music.

Just as there are physical limits to the human capacity to hear tones as alterations of other tones, "there are physical limits upon how fast a camera can move or a scene change, how far a lens can blur and still depict human actions and events to the unaided eye" (62). To push such known

128

quantities to their physical limits is to bring to an end certain possibilities of film, not to discover new possibilities. Then why are filmmakers "led to push possibilities (or why are they pushed by them) to their limits?" One answer is that mere extensions of known quantities are an effort on their part "to retain interest in movies—their interest in making them and their public's interest in viewing them. But interest is not enough to keep an art alive. . . . It requires belief, relation to one's past, conviction that one's words and conduct express oneself, that they say what one means, and that what one means is enough to say" (62).

Cavell's implication is that filmmakers "dress up" their films to cover the fact that conviction in the originating myths of traditional movies—the public world of men, the private company of women, the secret isolation of the dandy—has become "lost, or baffled" (62).

In the remainder of Chapter 10, Cavell considers, one by one, the fate of these myths in recent movies.

The Public World of Men

"We no longer grant, or take it for granted," Cavell writes, "that men doing the work of the world together are working for the world's good, or that if they are working for the world's harm they can be stopped. These beliefs flowered last in our films about the imminence and the experience of the Second World War, then began withering in its aftermath" (62). He goes on to characterize that aftermath as America's "knowledge, and refusal of knowledge" of the war's real outcome. In a passage of searing intensity, he asserts that our belief in the public world of men began withering, specifically, in the "knowledge, and refusal of knowledge" that, although we had rescued our European allies,

> we could not preserve them; that our enemies have prospered; that we are obsessed with the ally who prospered and prepared to enter any pact so long as it is against him; that the stain of atomic blood will not wash. . . . It is the knowledge, and refusal to know, that we are ceding to Stalin and Hitler the permanent victories of the war . . . , letting them dictate what shall be meant by communism and socialism and totalitarianism, in particular, that they are to be equated. We lash ourselves to these ideas with burning coils of containment, massive retaliation, . . . yellow perils, red conspiracies, in order that in the spasms of our fixed fury we do ourselves no injury, in order not to see the injury we have done, and do. So the mind tears itself apart trying to pull free. (62–63)

The World Viewed was written during the Vietnam War. Cavell might well never have written a book about movies, and would surely not have written the book he did write, were it not for his sense that Americans were reaping the tragic consequences of the "knowledge, and refusal to know" that was the outcome of the Second World War. What Americans knew, and refused to know, was our *separateness*, the fact that we exist in the world among others who make claims upon us (as we make claims upon them). By our desperate efforts to avoid recognizing our responsibility for the suffering we were causing and the limits of our power in the face of that suffering, we were inflicting harm on others and tearing ourselves apart. This is the knowledge, and refusal of knowledge, that was "fixing"— immobilizing, emasculating—America, as Cavell puts it. America was "lashing itself" with "burning coils" from which it was also violently struggling to free itself. And the passage culminates with a haunting image: "So the mind tears itself apart trying to pull free."

The sentences leading to this climactic line explicitly address a specific case of "knowledge, and refusal to know"—the case of America in the aftermath of the Second World War. By extension, they are about the Vietnam War, one tragic consequence of that case of "knowledge, and refusal to know." The line "So the mind tears itself apart trying to pull free" marks a shift to a more universal formulation, however. It invokes a general principle, the principle this specific case exemplifies.

The human mind has limits and is divided, as Kant discovered; we are creatures of soul and sense. The splitting of the human mind is not an objective fact; the mind splits itself to avoid recognizing the limits to its freedom. Like the capacity for skeptical doubt, the capacity to "tear itself apart trying to pull free" is internal to the human mind, as Cavell understands it. The specific case of America's "knowledge, and refusal to know" that is the Vietnam War exemplifies a tragic possibility inherent in the condition of being human.

During the Vietnam War, the killing and the stifling of dissent at home were authorized and performed by "men in uniform." Half of America believed that these men were "doing the work of the world together," that they were working for the world's good, but doubted they would succeed in stopping the evil forces joined against them. The other half believed those men in uniform were working for the world's harm, but doubted that they would be stopped. Yet it is not enough to say that the myth of the public world of men had become capable only of splitting and not uniting America. For neither half of America was capable any longer of simply *believing* in this myth.

To believe during the Vietnam War that America's actions at home and abroad exemplified the myth of the public world of men, one would have had to deny that America was in the throes of tearing itself apart. Both halves of America knew, even as they refused to know, the tragedy that America was inflicting on itself and others. Both halves knew, and refused to know, the awful truth that they were not capable of existing separately. Only together were they capable of becoming the more perfect union that was America's promise. Only together were they capable of existing among others in the world; only together were they capable of being separate. But separateness, Cavell argues in "The Avoidance of Love," is what America, which had uniquely "exerted its existence in a war of secession and asserted its identity in a war against secession," has never been able to bear. "*Union* is what it wanted. And it has never felt that union has been achieved. Hence its terror of dissent, which does not threaten its power but its integrity. So it is killing itself and killing another country . . . in order not to acknowledge its separateness" (*MWMWWS*, 345).

It is a striking feature of the way Cavell characterizes the tragedy of the Vietnam War in both "The Avoidance of Love" and *The World Viewed*— and this is exemplary of Cavell's way of thinking philosophically—that he does not take sides in the argument tearing America apart. Rather, his writing achieves a philosophical perspective capable of acknowledging the motivations of both sides, and capable of acknowledging, as well, the inner relation between their positions. In this spirit, Cavell does not characterize one half of America as knowing and the other half as refusing knowledge; both halves know, and both halves refuse to know. And it is the *same* knowledge both halves fail to acknowledge. How could it be otherwise, since in Cavell's vision both halves are harbored within every American family, within every American, are two halves of the American mind?

Cavell's dissatisfaction with Marxism derives in part from Marxism's inability to read the American mind. Marxists hold that America's actions in Vietnam can simply be accounted for in terms of the wish for material gain. Cavell observes in "The Avoidance of Love" that America is *the* anti-Marxist country, "in which production and possession are unreal and consciousness of appreciation and of its promise is the only value" (*MWMWWS*, 345). But America is not *the* capitalist country. To suppose that Americans are capitalists like any other is to deny what Cavell calls the metaphysical dimension of our actions. It is to deny how Americans think, who Americans are, what the American character is. America has a problem, in Cavell's view, but it is not one a Marxist revolution could solve. Our problem is that we do not see our, or the world's, "true need." For us to see this would only take a change of consciousness. Thus the barrier to our seeing it is internal to our consciousness. We do not simply fail to see, we refuse to see, fail to acknowledge what we

131

cannot help seeing. Our problem is a matter of "knowledge, and refusal of knowledge."

Every sentence of this section of "The Avoidance of Love" expresses Cavell's passionately-held convictions about these matters. Its culminating line—"So phenomenology becomes politics"—declares his writing to be committed to the promise of America, to enabling America to keep its promise. Cavell's writing is committed to achieving that change of consciousness which might enable Americans to see our, and the world's, true need, and thus enable metaphysics—here called "phenomenology"—to become practical after all. And in this aspiration to make philosophy practical, Cavell is embracing the tradition of philosophy founded in America by Emerson and Thoreau, those two most metaphysical, and practical, Yankees.

The Private Company of Women

This section of Chapter 10 of *The World Viewed* begins with the startling words "We no longer grant, or take it for granted, that stylish dumb women are as interesting as stylish intelligent ones; we don't even think they look alike" (63). Sympathetic readers may be taken aback by this line, which seems to imply that traditional movies required us to grant, or take for granted, that our interest in women on film had nothing to do with their intelligence. But Cavell is not claiming that it made no difference to viewers that the likes of "Carole Lombard and the young Rosalind Russell and Katharine Hepburn and Audrey Hepburn," or the "leading women of the Bogart character—Mary Astor, Ingrid Bergman, Lauren Bacall," or the great courtesans Garbo and Dietrich, were "possessed of an intelligence that animates their presence" (63). Cavell is not wavering in his conviction that it is their intelligence that gives such women "an independence from men, hence makes them worth winning, worth yielding independence for" (63). And yet, as he here reminds us, many Hollywood "leading ladies"—he singles out Madeleine Carroll, Anita Louise, and Hedy Lamarr—lacked, on screen, a comparable intelligence. Evidently, it seemed natural to take an interest even in "dumb" women in movies, women with whom no marriage of true minds could be imagined. Is Cavell suggesting that we are no longer interested in unintelligent women? Rather, he is suggesting that our interest in them has become perverse.

Just as "we no longer grant, or take for granted, that a man who expresses no feeling has fires banked within him," Cavell argues, "we no longer take it for granted that a demonstrative woman is capable of

132

intimacy," or "that a superficially cold one probably is" (64). He illustrates this point in a series of remarks that trace a line of development in Hitchcock films from *Notorious* to *The Birds*.

It has often been said that the heroine of Hitchcock's later films— Grace Kelly, Kim Novak, or Tippi Hedren—excites a promise of passionate intimacy "by the very coldness of her surface." But Cavell denies that these women invite a promise of intimacy at all. What they invite is a lust whose perverseness is heightened by their having in common a certain *crudity* of intelligence (64).

> A nice registering of this occurs in . . . *To Catch a Thief*, in which the girl (Grace Kelly) catches the thief (Cary Grant) by lifting her necklace at him . . . upon which the camera lifts up to a display of fireworks outside the window. One's first response is to laugh at the . . . movie cliche, but then one realizes that Hitchcock . . . has converted this conventional movie dodge into a specific display of this girl's imagination. . . . Here the conventional symbol exposes a conventional imagination of the deed. (64–65)

That this woman's imagination is so conventional means "she can be won by satisfying her crudity, which is child's play compared with commanding the attention of a free woman" (65). Her love can easily be stolen. Then again, she is a thief.

Marnie continues Hitchcock's examination of what Cavell calls "our world of stolen love, a world whose central figures are thieves of love." In *Marnie*, Hitchcock

> reactivates his long obsession with the phony psychological explanations we give ourselves to ward off knowledge. *Psycho* is some ultimate version of this obsession; the brutal rationality of the "psychiatrist" at the end, tying up the loose ends of our lives, exhibits one form in which our capacity for feeling, our modulation of instinct, is no longer elicited by human centers of love and hate, but immediately by the theories we give ourselves of love and hate. (65)

The Birds takes a different dialectical step. "Explanation is stifled, the universe now sees to it that the consequences of our actions hunt us to a conclusion. Now when love is teased nature is not amused, but aroused" (65). At the end of *The Birds*, Tippi Hedren has "flown into her own imagination," as Cavell puts it. "[S]he and her man will never be equal to one another. . . . No man is a bird of her feather. We believe this without explanation, shown what has happened to nature in our culture" (66).

Two decades earlier, in *Notorious*, another Hitchcock hero rescued another

> sickened lady from a dangerous house, supporting her dazed body on the long walk to his car. But that lady will stand again on her own feet, facing her lover. From a woman enacted by Ingrid Bergman we can hardly withhold

the power of love: she may be disloyal to her feelings (out of loyalty to her country, and to spite her lover), but she is not forgetful of them or detached from them. (66)

Notorious was made when the traditional myths of movies still divined our nature. It was natural for Cary Grant and Ingrid Bergman to love each other and for us to accept their love as natural. Hitchcock's later films, as Cavell views them, examine what has since happened to nature in our culture. What has happened to *our* nature, these films tell us, is that "instinct has gone a bit funny" (65–66).

The Secret Isolation of the Dandy

"We no longer grant, or take it for granted, that a man who expresses no feeling has fires banked within him; or, if we do grant him depth, we are likely not to endow him with a commitment to his own originality, but to suppose him banking destructive feeling. Antonioni's leading men come to mind, and most of Bergman's and Godard's" (67). We no longer grant, or take for granted, that men like Bogart inhabit our world. Is it the world that has changed, or have we changed? As times change, *everything* changes. (This is a major theme of *The World Viewed*.) "[U]nexpressed masculine depth" has made something of a comeback in recent movies, Cavell suggests, but what makes this possible is not a revival of the Dandy, but a "rebound of culture that created the new possibility of the cool; the young Montgomery Clift and Marlon Brando are early instances of it; James Dean and Paul Newman and Steve McQueen count on it; its latest original was Belmondo" (67).

> Conviction in their depth depends upon their being young, upon the natural accuracy of their physical movements . . . , suggesting unknown regions of physical articulateness and endurance. . . . In this figure, the body . . . is the expression of selfhood, of the ability to originate one's actions. . . . The vanity in the young man's careless slouch has perhaps not been sufficiently appreciated; but it should also be recognized that this is not the vanity of personal appearance or fashion, but the vanity of personal freedom; of distinctness, not distinction. (67–68)

The figure of the cool young man is, in a sense, "the democratic equivalent of the Dandy," Cavell observes. "When society requires greater uniformity, consensus crowding out the claims of consent, then the strategy of individuality and distinctness is to become identifiable within uniform"— Brando's black leather jacket in *The Wild One*, for example—"not by it, adopting its identity, but despite it, accepting no privilege or privation

The cool young Jean-Paul Belmondo (*Breathless*).

accruing from it" (68). The guiding myth of this type "is the myth of youth itself, that life has not yet begun irretrievably, that the time is still for preparation" (68). The Dandy has already staked out his individuality. The cool young man has not yet declared himself, but he is sure that, when the time comes, he will be recognized.

■ ■

The World Viewed was written more than a quarter of a century ago. Reading Chapter 10, especially, that fact may well leap out at one. What was the present when Cavell was writing *The World Viewed* is now the past. Indeed, it is so far in the past that, when we teach the book these days, we can reasonably expect that none of our students were even born when that past was the present. Not only for them but for all readers of *The World Viewed* today, the question inevitably arises as to that past's relation to our present.

Keeping in mind Cavell's view as articulated in *Must We Mean What We Say?* that the sense that "history will not go away except through our perfect acknowledgment of it (in particular, our acknowledgment that it is not past)" is internal to the modern, one Cavellian response to that question is to say that the past that was the present when *The World Viewed* was written will not go away, we will not be able to put it behind us, except through our perfect acknowledgment of it, our acknowledgment that it is not yet past. *The World Viewed* characterizes the historical moment in which it was written as a moment in which film was beginning to move into a modernist environment, a moment in which traditional movies were still being made, but in which conviction in the original myths of movies was becoming, or had become, lost or baffled. Can it be possible that this description still applies to the present world over a quarter of a century later? Can it be possible that it does *not* still apply? Some would say, of course, that ours is a postmodern age, that film, like the world, has left modernism behind. But what could it mean to move beyond modernism, if we understand modernism the way Cavell does?

Reading Chapter 10, one may well feel prompted to ask oneself whether traditional movies are still being made in the present, and, if so, whether they (some? all?) are still being "dressed up" to cover a loss or baffling of conviction in their myths. Are we to think of the high-tech special effects in so many recent movies as new, even fancier ways of "dressing up"? What are we to think of so-called postmodernist films, which flaunt, rather than cover, their loss or baffling of conviction? Have the traditional figures of the Military Man, the Woman, and the Dandy rebounded in the decades since *The World Viewed* was written? What has become of the figure of the cool young man? Who, mythically, are the men, and the women, in the movies of the seventies, eighties, and nineties, or in today's movies? Who, on screen, is Robert Redford or Robert DeNiro or John Travolta or Brad Pitt or Arnold Schwartzenegger (the body as the expression of selfhood, indeed!)? Who is Jane Fonda or Sally Field or Sissy Spacek or Meryl Streep or Sigourney Weaver or Sharon Stone? Have new types—hence new genres, new myths—emerged? What types? What genres? What myths?

The most fruitful way to read *The World Viewed* is not to set out to "refute" Cavell, but to check his words against one's own experience—to allow Cavell's words to prompt one's own thoughts, and to attend to those thoughts with the kind and degree of attention necessary to follow Cavell's thinking.

Chapter 11: "The Medium and Media of Film"

Chapter 10 focuses on the loss or baffling of our conviction in the film's originating myths. Chapter 11 reflects on the fact that traditional movies are not only expressions of particular myths, they are also "fixed" (here the word reminds us that photographic images, too, are fixed) in a particular set of human beings and in the "particular streets and carriages and chambers against which and within which those specific beings had their being" (69). This fact follows from the ontological condition of film that "the physical basis of movies, being irreducibly photographic, necessitates or makes possible the meaningful use of human reality and of nature as such" (68).

The apparent completion of traditional movies as media of seriousness, which reflects the loss or baffling of our conviction in the movies' originating myths, also reflects the fact that the particular human beings who helped "fix" the media of movies are now old, or dead. "When they and their particular locales are gone, Hollywood is ended. Its ending is the end of its media, of those arrangements whose significance was unquestioned, conviction in which was immediate" (69).

One strategy for discovering performers capable of sustaining conviction in traditional movies is to exploit the historical fact that, as Chapter 5 puts it, "until recently, types of black human beings were not created in film." Satisfying traditional movies have recently been made that revolve around, for example, "a black man and woman working a straight forties romance, as in *For Love of Ivy* . . . ; a black city-slicker detective impounding the admiration of a southern sheriff in a fifties murder mystery, as in *In the Heat of the Night*; a personally impeccable and cosmically successful black doctor confronting a liberal family with its values in a thirties problem picture, as in *Guess Who's Coming to Dinner*" (69).

Dressing movies up with mechanical extensions of known quantities of the film medium has a counterpart, however, in recent films which make no attempt to discover performers so individual they convincingly incarnate a traditional genre's leading types, but by casting people who have a contemporary "look" although they lack the individuality of traditional stars (70). When its stars are chosen for their look, not their individuality, Cavell argues, the resulting film is likely to "run up against a problem quite unforeseen in what we had experienced of film's possibilities." The problem is that the human somethings on screen emerge indistinctly ("not merely . . . their faces and trappings, but . . . their demeanor and posture and cadences, the way they inhabit their trappings").

> I hope I am not alone in simply being unable to recall the names or faces or presences of so many of the men and women who have come to people American movies over the past five or ten years. . . . The fact is that many of them look alike to me, or each resembles one of those upsetting composite drawings of, say, the Presidents of the United States or one of those face-shapes that run through various hair styles on a barber shop chart. . . . Baudelaire's perception of union between a woman and her cosmetics is here realized with perfect literality. (70)

Unlike a film "dressed up" with fancier cutting, dreamier color, extremer angles, or more explicit dialogue, a movie that suffers indistinctness by virtue of its indistinct performers is not cloaked in a garb meant to cover absence of conviction. Absence of conviction is plain on its face, or, rather, on the indistinct faces of its interchangeable performers. Rather than cover up a lack of conviction in the traditional media of movies, such movies openly *negate* those media.

> The interchangeability of the new performers—and of course, not merely of their faces and trappings, but of their demeanor and posture and cadences, and the way they inhabit their trappings—is a perfect negation of that condition of movies I described as one in which an individuality is the subject of film. These figures no more lend themselves to such study than they do to imitation. To impersonate one is to impersonate all; their personalities are already impersonations. This, further, negates or literalizes the condition I characterized as the ontological equality of objects and human subjects in photographs; for these figures are no longer the human part of nature. (71–72)

■ ■

"What needs accounting for," Cavell writes, returning us to his overarching theme, is that the tradition is still

> available to current successful films, and also that serious works are in the process of questioning their relation to the tradition, that they are moving into the modernist predicament in which an art has lost its natural relation to its history, in which an artist, exactly because he is devoted to making an object that will bear the same weight of experience that such objects have always borne which constitute the history of his art, is compelled to find unheard-of structures that define themselves and their history against one another. When in such a state an art explores its medium, it is exploring the conditions of its existence; it is asking exactly whether, and under what conditions, it can survive. (72)

138

What *are* the conditions apart from which the art of film cannot survive? What are the possibilities, and what are the necessities, of the *medium* of film? What *is* film's medium, that is, its material basis, which, in a modernist environment, the art of film has no choice but to explore?

With these questions on the table, it is incumbent on Cavell to formulate a definition of the medium of film, a definition of "the material basis of the media of movies (as paint on a flat, delimited support is the material basis of the media of painting)" (72). One might expect the formulation of such a definition to be a climactic moment in *The World Viewed*, but it is not, for this definition charts no new territory; it is composed entirely of terms that have already made their appearance:

> The material basis of the media of movies . . . is . . . *a succession of automatic world projections*. "Succession" includes the various degrees of motion in moving pictures: the motion depicted; the current of successive frames in depicting it; the juxtaposition of cutting. "Automatic" emphasizes the mechanical fact of photography, in particular the absence of the human hand in forming these objects and the absence of its creatures in their screening. "World" covers the ontological facts of photography and its subjects. "Projection" points to the phenomenological facts of viewing, and to the continuity of the camera's motion as it ingests the world. (72–73)

Cavell concludes Chapter 11 by observing that categories of succession and projection are "most emphasized in what I have . . . read about the aesthetics of film."

> [T]hey include what many take to be the basic question of the subject, namely, whether it is the possibility of cutting from one view to another (one sense of succession) or the possibility of continuous projection of an altering view . . . which is the essence of the cinematic. I have not made myself trace the experience and the philosophy which led, say, Eisenstein to opt for montage and Bazin for continuity. . . . My excuse for speaking in ignorance of this question is that I have a hypothesis about it, namely, that it is not *a* question. (73)

It is not a question for Cavell whether it is montage or continuity that constitutes "the essence of the cinematic," for in his view the cinematic *has* no essence. The concept "cinematic" cannot provide a criterion for judging movies.

> It is not to be expected that a given discovery shows the significance of an isolated possibility of the art, or that a given possibility yields up some single significance. For whatever is meant by a medium's "possibilities," each is what it is only in view of the others. This is why the general answer to the common question, "In what ways do movies differ from novels or from theater?" ought to be: "In every way." It is why the idea that a movie should be "cinematic" is either as bad or as special or as empty as the idea that a poem should be poetic. (72)

139

V

■ ■ ■ ■

CHAPTERS 12–13:
THE WORLD AS A WHOLE

THE IDEA THAT emerges at the end of Chapter 11, that each possibility of a medium is what it is only in view of the others, is yet another quintessentially Cavellian principle. It is akin to the idea, crucial to *Pursuits of Happiness*, that instances of a genre—for Cavell, a genre *is* a medium—do not share a set of features that can in principle be enumerated; they share *every* feature. Like a language (in which, as Emerson and Thoreau claimed, each word is what it is only in view of all the other words of the language), and like a world (in which "nothing less than everything is new in a new period," as Chapter 7 puts it), a medium is a *whole*, a *totality*. (The epigraph of *The World Viewed* is from *Walden:* "Why do precisely these objects which we behold make a world?" For Cavell as for Thoreau, this is tantamount to the question, "Why do precisely these words which I speak make a language?")

Cavell begins Chapter 12 by asserting that two recent developments in moviemaking acknowledge the *a priori* condition that film is photographic and that its subject is reality, that is, the world as a whole. The second of these developments, the use of color to declare that the projected world is a total world, is the topic of Chapter 13.

Chapter 12: "The World as Mortal: Absolute Age and Youth"

The development Cavell considers in Chapter 12, which declares the projected world to be the real past world of photography, has to do with the fact that the particular human beings "whose characteristics helped to fix the media of movies are now old or gone. . . . However unclear the issue of the artistic age of the movie, its absolute age is acknowledged in the use of these familiar faces explicitly as familiar ancients" (74).

Cavell cites Buster Keaton in *Sunset Boulevard*, Andy Devine in *Liberty Valance*, and Bette Davis in *The Star* (all films, we might note, *about* returning, making a comeback, or going back to beginnings). And when in *Sunset Boulevard* we watch Gloria Swanson "watching her young films, the juxtaposition of the phases of her appearance cuts the knowledge into us, of the movies' aging and ours, with every frame," as Cavell poignantly puts it (74).

"The nostalgia of old photographs is the perception that mortality is at some point to be stopped in its tracks," Cavell writes. "The figures in them seem so vulnerable, so unknowing of what we know about them, of the knowledge in store for them. We could know this about ourselves, if we could turn the force of nostalgia toward an anticipation of the fact that every moment is always stopped from every other" (75).

At first glance, the opening sentence of this paragraph seems to be saying something like, "The nostalgia of old photographs is the perception that mortality is stopped in its tracks." Yet what Cavell's words literally say is that the nostalgia of old photographs is the perception that mortality is at some point *to be stopped* in its tracks. The figures in old photographs seem so vulnerable because they seem not to know what we know about them. We know that they are fated to age and die. We also know that they are fated to know this about themselves. At some point, mortality is to be stopped in its tracks by the knowledge that they *have* aged, that they *are* dying.

"We could know this about ourselves, if we could turn the force of nostalgia toward an anticipation of the fact that every moment is always stopped from every other." Cavell's striking formulation implies, first, that such self-knowledge is a worthy aspiration. Second, that what we could know is not something we simply fail to know, but something so obvious we cannot simply fail to know it, something we keep ourselves from knowing. What figures in old photographs seem not to know, the knowledge that is in store for them, is something we are fated at some point to know, something about ourselves we are capable of acknowledging *now*. To acknowledge this "something," we must "turn the force of nostalgia toward an anticipation of the fact that every moment is always stopped from every other" (75). We can achieve such self-knowledge if we do not look back nostalgically to a past that never really existed, but look forward

141

Gloria Swanson watching her young films (*Sunset Boulevard*).

to the future in a spirit of adventure, accepting each new moment, as it comes, as the unique moment it is.

When we watch the aging Gloria Swanson watching her youthful self on film in *Sunset Boulevard*, the knowledge of mortality is painful (every frame "cuts the knowledge into us, of the movies' aging and ours"). In movies, the knowledge of mortality also has room to live happily, as Cavell puts it, as it does in the moments he goes on jauntily to evoke, each "stopped from every other." (Cavell does not explicitly state this, but they are from Astaire's early dance number in *The Band Wagon*, another movie about returning, or making a comeback, or going back to beginnings.) "In the very vulnerability of that embarrassed laugh, in the tilt of the hat, in the way the foot is turned, in the dust that lies on the shoe or in its hopeful shine, in the crook of the arm where the baby nods, the knowledge of mortality has room to live, even jauntily" (75).

There is no better place than film for the knowledge of mortality, Cavell argues. For one thing, the projection of a movie is itself a natural metaphor for human mortality.

> The roundness of clocks is convenient, but it naturally misleads us about something clocks tell, because its hands repossess their old positions every day and every night. The reels on a projector, like the bulbs of an hourglass, repeat something else: that as the past fills up, the future thins; and that the end, already there against the axle, when the time comes for its running, seems to pick up speed. (75)

The recent use of aging stars *as* aging stars explicitly declares the condition that "movies depend upon the appearance in them of living men and women, mortals," a condition naturally registered in the fact that the individuality of stars was always defined by their self-identity through repeated incarnations (75).

> Hollywood was an enormous stock company. . . . Though at first it seemed the reverse, those recurring figures in the films of Bergman, Godard, Resnais, Antonioni, Fellini, were part of what made them acceptable as movies, not merely as foreign films. And they were able to count on the power of recurrence after Hollywood, to achieve it, had to declare it by the assertion of age—that is, by nostalgia. (76)

In the Hollywood stock company, recurrence assured the distinctness of bit players as well as stars. Whether or not we remembered their names, we remembered the faces and temperaments of countless bit players. This is not the case, Cavell finds, in what he calls "neo-Hollywood" films.

> I cannot call back the faces of critical minor leads in several of the best recent neo-Hollywood films—in *In the Heat of the Night, The Detective, Petulia, Pretty Poison, Bullitt*. In itself this may not be surprising. These figures just

haven't been in enough films to have become memorable. But . . . my feeling is that they *could* not become memorable. I have no sense of the range of temperament they may occupy, and these isolated films have been insufficient to establish that sort of resonance for them. But without that, there is no world before us. Neo-Hollywood is not a world. (76)

In Cavell's experience, *Bonnie and Clyde* stands out among neo-Hollywood movies in achieving "at least three supporting players, enough to survey a whole and specific world" (76). By contrast, the supporting players in *The Graduate*, for example, fail to "accept and fill and specify the types they project. So their characters are thin and imposed—stereotypes" (77). This observation segues into a set of remarks about *The Graduate*, the longest concrete discussion of a film to this point in *The World Viewed*, which in turn segues into the reflections on "the myth of modern romance" that conclude Chapter 12.

There is no reason for the minor characters in *The Graduate* to be as mean as they appear to be, Cavell argues. Anne Bancroft is "caught up in the most elaborated arbitrariness," since she is the most powerful and accomplished of the performers. "For example, if her seduction of the graduate is the pure bad faith she enacts, why in her meetings with him is she so explicit in her wishes and humiliating in her unseducibility? And if she is really alcoholic or in painful sexual need, why is she so deliberate and indifferent in the event?" (77).

One could make up explanations for this woman's behavior, but they would all be arbitrary, "not because we don't know enough about her character, but because we aren't convinced that we have been given a character to respond to" (77). Is that because what we are given is meant to be taken as a series of projections from the graduate's point of view? That is clearly going on, Cavell observes, "in the well-realized passage radiating his new experience of his body shown in . . . cuts between the hotel room and his parents' house and the swimming pool." As surely as the graduate's parents do, the film denies the graduate's life of private fantasy.

> The hotel sequence . . . is a set piece of lobby-to-bedroom farce, depending for its effect upon the known quantities and rhythms of suspicious hotel clerks, lugubrious hotel receptions, the unfamiliar geography and properties of expense-account rooms, and upon a known source of audience response, its morbid appreciation of its own prejudice and tawdriness. Here the film's talented director takes revenge on all sides responsible for his success—on his audience, with whom he identifies and whom he despises; and on his hero, with whom he identifies and whom he patronizes. (77–78)

"But miracles are likely to be costly," Cavell writes, adding a miraculous twist of his own through which he unifies the chapter by effecting a

144

transition from reflections on aging stars and mortality to the "miraculous appearance," in the figure of Dustin Hoffman's graduate, of "the myth of youth itself, soliciting an investment of feeling in every inflection of the young man's behavior out of all proportion to any feeling of his own" (78). This investment fully justifies itself in the film's final act, Cavell maintains. From the graduate's announcement to his parents that he is going to marry to the end of the film, *The Graduate* acknowledges its debt to, and invokes the power of, "several huge moments in the history of films about young love."

For one, the graduate in flight "takes upon himself the Belmondo figure in *Breathless* . . . : a real modern hero, equal to his demand for happiness." Cavell specifies the heroism of this figure, who knows "that a woman may be more trouble than any public knowledge of her could rationally justify"; who is "able to take the trouble"; and who undertakes to win a woman worth winning. The woman the graduate undertakes to win is one of film's "daughters without fathers, or with defeated fathers," who "need to be won without anyone to award them" (78).

It is a notable feature of the remarriage comedy, as *Pursuits of Happiness* characterizes the genre, that its leading woman is fortunate to have a father who, unlike the woman's father in classical comedy, is on the side of his daughter's happiness. If she chooses to marry against her father's wishes, as occurs in *It Happened One Night*, and almost occurs in *The Philadelphia Story*, he ultimately has no choice but to accept it. But his wish is to award her to a man who really loves her, a modern hero to whom she might freely award herself. So it is appropriate that the interrupted wedding scenes that climax both these films are clearly among the "huge moments in the history of films about young love" that *The Graduate*, in its final act, acknowledges.

The graduate wins this woman, she awards herself to him, but not because he passes her tests of love. Her tests cannot be passed (any more than Othello's, or Lear's, tests of love can be passed) by human mortals. "We are not swans, not showers of gold, neither real beasts nor real princes," Cavell writes (78). By slipping into the first person plural here, Cavell's prose rhetorically identifies the graduate with himself—and with us. (As human mortals, we are in the same boat when it comes to winning people who must award themselves.) This rhetorical device is a response to the fact that, as Cavell has suggested, the director of *The Graduate* (Mike Nichols) identifies—calls upon us to identify—with his protagonist. Cavell means his own words here to be readable as projected from within the graduate's point of view.

145

Cavell has charged that, at least until the film's final act, the film's director patronizes the graduate even as he identifies with him, at once exploits and denies the primacy of his life of private fantasy, which "wants to be the subject of the film" (77). In the final act, the graduate is no longer patronized, or patronizable. And Cavell's passionate words, readable as projected from within the graduate's point of view, are anything but patronizing. They affirm the graduate's fidelity to the life of private fantasy, apart from which it is not possible to be a modern hero.

The long sentence that concludes this paragraph sustains the first person plural until its final clause, when it shifts, dramatically, from "we" to "I": "We win only by overcoming the woman's power of testing altogether, by showing her that her destructiveness has not destroyed us, that her worth is no longer in need of proof; that her treasure, which she more and more fears may have been lost, is merely hidden, as befits grown women, and that I know this because I seek it and will not be lost" (78).

In the first person plural, Cavell cites a general principle ("We win only by . . .") he takes to apply to himself and to us no less than to the graduate. The woman's tests of love cannot be passed because they are meant to prove something—her worth—which cannot be proved in such a way. To show the woman that "her treasure"—not a treasure she owns but the treasure she *is*—is not lost—that she is not lost—but only unknown to the world, we must show her—overcoming her power of testing, her capacity for skeptical doubt—that her worth, her existence, is no longer in need of proof. If we do not succeed in showing this to her, if she does not recognize it, we lose her. Then she is not merely hidden, she is lost.

It is around this point that the shift from "we" to "I" occurs. Anyone who claims to know this woman's worth claims knowledge that cannot be doubted, that is no longer in need of proof. In entering such a claim, one cannot speak for anyone but oneself; one cannot base such a claim on a general principle, which can always be doubted. On such a claim one must stake one's life. So Cavell's prose, if it is to continue to be readable as projected from within the graduate's point of view, must shift from first person plural to first person singular.

If it is also to be readable as an expression of his own conviction, Cavell's prose must shift as well from citing a general principle he believes in, a principle he calls upon us to acknowledge that we also believe in, to a declaration of knowledge it is not possible for one to claim without staking one's life on that claim. The paragraph concludes: "I know this"—I know this woman's treasure is not lost, only hidden; I know this woman is not lost, only unknown to the world—"because I seek it"—I know this

146

woman's worth because she is the one I have been seeking, this is the knowledge I have been seeking—"and will not be lost"—if I do not win her, I will be lost, and I will not be lost. The author of *The World Viewed* is declaring that *he* will not be lost. Unknown to the world, *he* is seeking to win the knowledge that he is not lost. And *he* will not be denied, will not deny himself this victory.

Beginning a new paragraph, Cavell pulls back from this personal declaration, which is a huge moment in *The World Viewed*, to cite another "moment in the history of films about young love" that the final act of *The Graduate* acknowledges.

> The closing image of the young pair, at the back of the municipal bus, calls upon the great movie image of leave-taking in wedding: Vigo's bride in *L'Atalante*, standing alone on the distant night-deck of her husband's craft— the boat, the shore, the water, the sky infiltrating one another, mixing their stars, suspending the lone figure still in her wedding gown, drifting into the unknown territory of marriage. . . . We know they do not know what they are headed for . . . ; we do not know that they will not survive together. (78–79)

Readers of *Pursuits of Happiness* may recognize that the language Cavell marshals in invoking this transcendental image from Vigo's masterpiece ("the boat, the shore, the water, the sky infiltrating one another, mixing their stars") echoes yet another huge moment in the history of films about young love: Clark Gable's speech near the end of *It Happened One Night*, in which he expresses his longing to find a woman who hungers for the things he hungers for (" . . . those nights when you and the moon and the water all become one . . . Where the stars are so close you feel you could reach right up and stir them around . . ."), prompting the woman he loves (Claudette Colbert) to step around the blanket and declare her love for him.

This echo of *It Happened One Night* leads directly to the two concluding paragraphs of Chapter 12. They are about what Cavell calls "the myth of modern marriage, which is the modern myth of romance" (79), a myth that can be said to be the central theme of *Pursuits of Happiness*.

"So far as we can grant" that this couple might survive together, that they might have achieved a marriage worth having, the penultimate paragraph begins, *The Graduate* "reinstates the myth of modern marriage, which is the modern myth of romance." The paragraph goes on, "In classical comedy, the stage at the end is littered with marriages, tangled pairs that have at last been sorted out, age accepts its place, youth takes its own, and families are present to celebrate the continuance of their order. At some point, perhaps when the world went to war"—World

147

Drifting into the unknown territory of marriage (*The Graduate*; *L'Atalante*).

War I, that is, the Great War which left Europe shattered and provided the opportunity for America to claim the starring role in film's history— "society stopped believing in its ability to provide that continuity. It needed to know what modern romance asserted, that one couple can make it alone, unsponsored" (79).

Thirties comedies and musicals, which Cavell calls "the great movie genres of this idea," do not restore society's lost belief that it can assure the continuity classical comedy affirmed, that society can legitimize a marriage worth having. "What the community needed to know, in reduced circumstances," Cavell writes, was "that [society] is worth acknowledging . . . , that it still allows those meant for one another to find one another, and that they can accomplish happiness within the law," where this now means, in practice, that "it has allowed people who have found one another to be meant for one another" (79).

Subsequent to the thirties, this "myth of modern romance" has died a thousand deaths in movies. But each is equivocal.

> In *Holiday Inn* Astaire loses the girl to Bing Crosby; but that is perhaps because this girl requires comfort before all and is willing to go into exile to pay for it (e.g., into the Connecticut countryside with a crooner, subjected to "White Christmas" for the rest of her days). In *Damsel in Distress* Astaire wins, ludicrously, Joan Fontaine, but that just shows that not all girls can dance to this piper. In *Sabrina* Audrey Hepburn is won by the older, reliable brother, and *that* is felt as magic; but he is Humphrey Bogart, the cards were stacked. (80)

"So it was not unthinkable," Cavell concludes, "that the myth should flare up again" as it does in *The Graduate* (80). (The fire was not dead, only banked.) His tone abruptly shifting, he closes the chapter by remarking, "I am reminded that the graduate is introduced to us as . . . a track man." He adds, "If Lévi-Strauss is right"—invoking Lévi-Strauss in connection with *It Happened One Night* is another way this passage anticipates *Pursuits of Happiness*—"to relate a mythic question about walking to the fact of being human, a reminder that we are earthlings (an insight recaptured by Thoreau, who recognized walking as a gait natural only to man), then perhaps a man for whom running (or dancing) is natural"—or doing back flips, we might add, placing Cary Grant beside Fred Astaire and Dustin Hoffman's graduate in this discussion—"has a claim to our spirituality" (80).

This passage extends Chapter 10's suggestion that, in the unexpressed male sexuality of a youth like Marlon Brando, "conviction in his depth depends upon his being young, upon the natural accuracy of his physical movements (like athletes between plays), suggesting unknown regions of physical articulateness and endurance." When the passage ends with the epigrammatic line, "Whether or not there is a man in the moon, and whether or not there is life, or we put life, on the moon, it is analytically true that men do not inhabit the moon," it is sustaining the thought, central to the entirety of *The World Viewed*, that a world—like a language, like a medium, like a form of life—is a *whole.* Neo-Hollywood is not a world, Cavell asserts, and neither, for us, is the moon (80). Creatures that may inhabit the moon do not differ from us in certain ways but not others. Their form of life is different. They differ from us in every way.

Chapter 13: "The World as a Whole: Color"

The second recent development in moviemaking that acknowledges the condition that film's subject is reality, Chapter 13 suggests, is the use of color to declare a total world. In considering this complex chapter, the longest in *The World Viewed,* the typographical breaks on pages 89 and 94 of the Enlarged Edition will serve to divide our reading into three parts.

I.

The theatrical and financial success of *Gone with the Wind* "depended upon its appearance as a luxury item," Cavell writes; "this is merely the best cinematic instance of those romancings of history that have always tapped the popular purse: Technicolor was the natural visual equivalent of the Scott-descended prose such matters require when they take the form of books" (80–81).

Cavell cites *The Wizard of Oz* and *Robin Hood* as two films of the thirties that went beyond using color as a luxurious form of packaging to explore color as an *aesthetic* possibility of film. "These films discovered that color can serve to unify the projected world in another way than by direct reliance upon, or implication toward, the spatial-temporal consistency of the real world. The world so unified is obviously not the real past world of photography but a consistent region of make-believe" (81).

Cavell contrasts these classic films, which use color to create a projected world of make-believe (it is no accident that they are children's tales), with *The Cabinet of Dr. Caligari.* The famous German silent film creates an artificially unified environment not by filtering reality "through a normal stage of fantasy" but by *opposing* reality with "images that compose a conventional expression of madness." *Caligari's* sense of constriction "is a function of its existence in black and white" (82). (The chapter will return to this idea.)

At this point, Cavell presents the central assertion of the first part of Chapter 13, which is that recent films, when the fact that they are in color "becomes a declared condition of a medium," use color not to create a past world, or a world of make-believe, but a world of an immediate future (82).

Cavell cites Antonioni's *Red Desert* and Truffaut's *Fahrenheit 451*, two "modern" films, and *Petulia* and *Bullitt*, two neo-Hollywood movies, whose declaration of color envisions the world we inhabit as *already* the future. *Bullitt's* world does not look different from ours. The lives it presents are what ours may fully become when the "subtlety and sensibility that human relations require are no longer negotiable. The action does not take place against an independent world, as gangster and police movies take place against the normal life of a city, or Westerns beyond outposts of civilization; it forms a complete and abstract world" (82–83).

Beginning an extended aside, Cavell observes that *Bullitt's* sense of futurity is enhanced by the "extraterrestrial quality" the telephoto lens accords to the car chase, whose particular effect depends "on the accuracy of perception which realizes the hills of San Francisco as the ultimate site for the ancient motif of a car chase through a city. The narrative mode is not 'Once upon a time . . .' but 'What if one day . . .' " (83).

Continuing the aside, Cavell notes that Hitchcock is the master at perceiving a familiar locale "as a natural setting for a hitherto unrelated individual task or predicament: the tennis match in *Strangers on a Train*, the cymbal crash in *The Man Who Knew Too Much*, the crop-dusting plane in *North by Northwest*" (83). In each, an environment we associate with conventional goings-on becomes a setting for a dramatic event that unexpectedly, but quite naturally, takes place there. (*Of course* the Great Plains is a region in which people are unprotected from the sky!) "The effect is as of a revelation of the familiar," Cavell writes. What is revealed is "the radical contingency of convention." It is as though "society's web of expectancies may at any moment be torn, as though to span the abyss of the unexpected (that is to say, the future) were society's only point, and its work about to come undone unless . . . one or two ordinary souls are successful" (83–84).

In *Must We Mean What We Say?*, Cavell suggests that ordinary language philosophy is "about" whatever ordinary language is about, and that ordinary language is about "the necessities common to us all, those necessities we cannot, being human, fail to know. Except that nothing is more human than to deny them" (*MWMWWS*, 96). What Cavell is now calling "the radical contingency of convention" is such a necessity.

151

Black and white functioning like colors (*Alphaville*).

Returning to the chapter's main argument, Cavell considers two "satisfying modern works" that appear to counter his assertion that in recent films the declaration of color establishes a world of futurity. The first is Godard's *Alphaville*, which depicts the cities we inhabit as already the future, yet pictures them in black and white. But in *Alphaville*, Cavell argues, the black and white function like colors. Godard accomplishes this "by confining the interiors largely to bright metallic and glass and plaster expanses or passageways, and the exteriors to scenes at night"; he makes the black and white function, the way colors do in other of his films, to "de-psychologize," or "un-theatricalize," the characters (84). (In invoking *Caligari*, Cavell had alluded to color's de-psychologizing or un-theatricalizing effect. Again, he postpones development of this idea.)

152

Rosemary's Baby is the other modern work Cavell cites which appears to counter his assertion that the declaration of color establishes futurity. Firmly rooted in the immediate past, it uses color to establish a world of private fantasy, the point being to "juxtapose opposing moods and to symbolize mutually exclusive environments" (84). Like Hitchcock's *Vertigo*, *Rosemary's Baby* establishes the moment

> of moving from one color space into another as one of moving from one world into another. In *Rosemary's Baby* this is accomplished by showing the modernizing of one apartment in the Dakota building, then moving between its open chic and a darker elegance. An instance in *Vertigo* is James Stewart's opening of a storage-room door—the whole car-stalking passage leading up to this moment shot in soft washed-out light—into a florist shop alive with bright flowers, predominantly red. (84)

This moment in *Vertigo* "is almost comic in its display of assured virtuosity," Cavell remarks (84–85). Hitchcock's virtuosity here reflects his longstanding interest in using color to juxtapose opposing moods and symbolize mutually exclusive environments. (In his silent films, Hitchcock already tinted certain passages blue-green—the color associated with Judy's final transformation in *Vertigo*—to establish a world of private fantasy.)[30]

Beginning another extended aside, Cavell remarks that *Vertigo* and *Rosemary's Baby* not only use color to establish a world of private fantasy, but are also *about* fantasy, "in particular about its power to survive every inroad of science and civility intact, and to direct the destiny of its subject with, finally, his active cooperation" (85).

Vertigo is about the power of the man's fantasy not merely to forgo reality "but to gear every instant of his energy toward a private alteration of reality. . . . It is a poor idea of fantasy which takes it to be a world apart from reality, a world clearly showing its unreality. Fantasy is precisely what reality can be confused with. It is through fantasy that our conviction of the worth of reality is established; to forgo our fantasies would be to forgo our touch with the world" (85).

That fantasy is precisely what reality can be confused with, and that to forgo our fantasies would be to forgo reaching the world (hence to forgo selfhood), are ideas, crucial to *The World Viewed*, which Chapter 14 will develop.

"And does someone claim to know," Cavell asks, abruptly shifting tone, "the specific balance sanity must sustain between the elaborating demands of self and world, some neat way of keeping soul and body together?" (85). When he invokes Freud's advice ("To retrieve stifled fantasy so that its annihilating power can command the self's self-esteem, the admiration of men, and the love of women, to insist upon a world with room in it for fruitful work and love"), Cavell's point is that the founder of psychoanalysis, who devoted his life to developing methods for "retrieving stifled fantasy," recognized that no theory can enable us to know *a priori* the powers and limits of fantasy.

Articulating one of the philosophical principles that underwrites his own work, Cavell writes, "Analyses of ideology are bound to be external when they fail to honor—I do not say share—the ineradicable weave of fantasy within ideology. Marx thought it was separable and called it Utopianism, not seeing his own" (85–86). Cavell follows this dismissal of Marx's claim to have overcome fantasy with an equally devastating statement about what, after a century of ideological wars, has "happened to us." After politics "retrieved the fantasy of brotherhood orphaned in God's abandonment," Cavell writes, "the realities of politics so brutalized and specialized their charge that the orphan withdrew on its own; and now fantasy and politics each try to devour the other" (86). After we abandoned our faith in God, after God abandoned us, the fantasy of brotherhood, now orphaned, was claimed by politics. In the political realm there has been so much brutality, however, that the fantasy of brotherhood, like the fantasy of a transcendent God, has become stifled.

In an obscure but striking transition, Cavell turns his attention back to *Vertigo*. "*Vertigo* is just a movie, but no other movie I know so purely conveys the sealing of a mind within a scorching fantasy," Cavell writes.

> The totality of [the Stewart character's] longing—and the terrorizing deface-ment of his object's identity which his longing comes to require—mimics that convulsion of consciousness which transcends idolatry in favor of the fantastic reality of God, that point past imagination at which happiness and truth coalesce. (Not happiness and *virtue*, as Kant childishly thought. *That* conjunction takes place on earth or nowhere.) The modern Pygmalion re-verses his exemplar's handling of his desire, and turns his woman to stone. (86)

When Cavell says that the totality of the Stewart character's longing (and the defacement of the woman's identity it comes to require) "mimics that convulsion of consciousness which transcends idolatry in favor of the fantastic reality of God," what does he mean? Part of what he means, we take it, is that Madeleine is not one among other gods and goddesses to this man; she is the one deity around whom his whole existence revolves. Judy, as she is, does not satisfy this man's desire, so he transforms her into a more perfect semblance of Madeleine. But no semblance will satisfy him. He will not be satisfied until he can believe that the woman before him is not a stand-in or representation, a graven image, as it were, but the

154

real Madeleine—the Madeleine of his fantasy, the dead Madeleine, the transcendent Madeleine, the Madeleine whose reality is unimaginable. Rather than bowing to an idol, he undertakes to create or re-create the woman he loves, taking upon himself the powers of a transcendent God. (This is another part of what Cavell means by saying that the Stewart character "transcends idolatry in favor of the fantastic reality of God.")

The reality of a transcendent God is beyond imagining because the imagination, alone, cannot make a fantasy real, and because a God it is not possible to represent cannot even be imagined. The fantasy of a transcendent God can become real only if there exists an unimaginable reality, "a point past imagination at which happiness and truth coalesce," a point it takes a "convulsion of consciousness" to reach. The Stewart character's fantasy cannot become real (Judy cannot become Madeleine, the transcendent Madeleine cannot exist) unless through such a convulsion of consciousness he reaches this "point past imagining at which happiness and truth coalesce."

Reality that is past imagination is not beyond the reach of film, however. Because it is reality itself, not a stand-in for reality, that appears to us on film, reality does not have to be imagined, or even imaginable, to be filmed. For us to accept at the climax of *Vertigo* that the human something on the screen is at once the eminently immanent Judy and the transcendent Madeleine, we must acknowledge at once film's capacity to transform the world into a reality beyond imagining, and film's capacity to transform a reality beyond imagining into a world that seems naturally to present itself to us. We must acknowledge, as well, our own participation in transforming Judy into Madeleine and Madeleine into Judy. ("The casting of Kim Novak in this role seems to me inspired," Cavell writes. "The featurelessness of her presence and nonexistence of her acting allow full play to one's perversity" [86]—to *our* perversity as well as the Stewart character's.)

The Stewart character defaces Judy's identity not because he believes this will bring Madeleine back, but because he believes Madeleine is irretrievably lost, and is perversely denying what he has no doubt he really knows. This is part of what Cavell has in mind, we take it, when he ends this paragraph with the obscure line, "At the least, Hitchcock trades on an idea that even Freud could not stomach—that the fantasy of a transcendent God is not, is perhaps the central experience which is not, original in childhood, but is the product of adults, of creatures whose knowledge is of childhood past" (86).

155

Freud was prepared to accept an idea of childhood sexuality his contemporaries could not stomach. What made this idea palatable to him was his belief that the sexual experiences of early childhood confirm the ideal of a monogamous relationship between a man and a woman, confirm that it emerges naturally in the course of human development. Freud believed that the fantasy of a transcendent God, too, is so deeply rooted in human nature that it emerges naturally in the experience of childhood. What Freud could not stomach is the possibility that it is adults, "creatures whose knowledge is of childhood past," who produce the idea of a transcendent God, and that they produce it not to express what they know about themselves and their world, not to keep faith with their experience of childhood, but to deny their knowledge (their knowledge of childhood past; their knowledge that childhood is past; their knowledge that it is they who have produced this fantasy). The idea Freud could not stomach, in other words, is that the fantasy of a transcendent God did not arise naturally, but is an expression of the perversity of human nature, of the human tendency to turn away from nature, from our own nature, to deny "the necessities common to us all, those necessities we cannot, being human, fail to know."

As Cavell has suggested, one of these necessities, the radical contingency of convention, is revealed in those Hitchcock passages which perceive a familiar locale as a natural setting for a hitherto unrelated individual task. Movies arise "from below the world," Cavell argues in Chapter 5, and, on film, religion *is* "below." Hence the rightness of the church tower setting for the dramatic events which in *Vertigo* unexpectedly but quite naturally take place there ("Kim Novak's final fall from the tower being tripped off by the sudden fluttering of a nun, Stewart's world snapping at the high point of a church . . ." [87]).

Hitchcock loves to explore a zone "in which superstition, expectancy, explanation and obsession cross one another," and is preoccupied with nuns and churches, Cavell notes.

> The Hitchcock heroine is, as it were, a defrocked nun; . . . one already sees more of her than is normal. When to a nun's habit Hitchcock adds high heels (as in *The Lady Vanishes*), we have an overt acknowledgment of voyeurism, which is not merely one of his special subjects (explicit in *Rear Window* and *Psycho*) but a dominant mood of his narration as a whole (most blatant in the films with Tippi Hedren, in which we spy full length on her inner life). Voyeurism is a retracted edge of fantasy; its requirement of privacy shows its perversity. Narrative voyeurism is Hitchcock's way of declaring the medium of film, a condition of which is that its subjects are viewed from an invisible state. (87)

Hitchcock films are about the perversity of voyeurism, but voyeurism is also an irreducible element of the mode of viewing movies call for. Because it is a condition of film that "its subjects are viewed from an invisible state," there is an element of perversity in all movies. "Narrative voyeurism is Hitchcock's way of declaring the medium of film," Cavell asserts (87). On this basis, Hitchcock's serious art can be distinguished from pornography. Indeed, Hitchcock's narratives, in which everything in the world assumes an aspect of sexual suggestiveness, are at the furthest possible remove from pornographic movies, which project views of anonymous sexual acts to anonymous audiences, and thereby combine the "absolutely explicit with the completely unspecific," as Chapter 8 puts it. Like art, pornography confirms our wish to reach this world and achieve selfhood. Unlike art, pornography concedes—and exploits—our inability, or unwillingness, to satisfy this wish. In *Vertigo*, the Stewart character is isolated by and within his private fantasy. In Hitchcock's eyes, this is a tragedy.

From the observation that there is an irreducible aspect of perversity in all movies, Cavell turns to a set of remarks—packed into a single dense paragraph fully two pages long—about *Rosemary's Baby*, a "modern" film which uses color to establish a world of private fantasy, as *Vertigo* does, and which is likewise about the power of fantasy to direct the destiny of its subject with, finally, the subject's active cooperation.

In *Rosemary's Baby*, Roman Polanski's narration is such, Cavell observes, that we "try to see the story" both from its protagonist's point of view "and from just outside, as though there were a radical ambiguity between the events as they may be and her consistent interpretation of them" (87–88). The hellish goings-on that Rosemary imagines are happening really *are* happening. In her interpretation, however, the cause of hell's power is her husband's pact with it, whereas what really "produces her world," in Cavell's view, is the power of Rosemary's own fantasy. Rosemary is another of those "daughters without fathers, or with defeated fathers," as Chapter 12 puts it, who "need to be won without anyone to award them." Succeeding where her husband had failed, the Devil wins her when she succumbs to her fantasy of motherhood, a fantasy like that which reached its height with the birth of Christianity (as Cavell observes, its great modern version is Kleist's *The Marquise of O . . .*): "natural fatherhood essentially external to the fact of birth, pregnancy the condition of mystery, any woman may be singled out among women to carry God within her—as if to justify, or deny, her sense of violation" (88).

When Rosemary finds a *Time* magazine with "Is God Dead?" on the cover, the headline does not merely suggest to her what her husband may be doing; it is "an annunciation of what she has until then obscurely felt called upon to do. In the absence of God, it is up to her to create God. And what is thus created, in isolation, is not God" (88).

In *The Joyful Wisdom*, Cavell reminds us, Nietzsche had predicted "that the news of God's death will take a century to reach our ears. The century is now about finished, and the news has reached our ears. Only it has come as news, i.e., as gossip, and in that form the knowledge Nietzsche speaks of cannot come to us at all, is further from us than ever" (88). Nietzsche's intuition is that God no longer calls us, no longer comes upon us, not because God has abandoned us, but because we have killed God. If that is true, it is not a truth we could learn by reading *Time* magazine; it is a truth about our world, and ourselves, that we cannot simply fail to know. Not to know it is not mere ignorance; it is "the absence of conscience, of so much as the possibility of self-knowledge."

Rosemary's "is the original sin of mothers, to regard what they give birth to as their *own*—it is *Rosemary's* baby" (88). She comes to know that this baby is a separate creature when she is "drawn at the end by the need of the child, too late, after she had already sacrificed it" (89). Only Rosemary is in a position to sacrifice this child, for it is only "from within a fantasy of possession that the child could (logically) have been given." Her husband knows the child is not his to give, and that he is in no position to give Rosemary—whom he has never won—to the Devil, either. All he can do is "help arrange for Rosemary to confuse herself about whether she had in fact given herself to the Devil or only dreamed she had—as if that was the difference that mattered."

"Some say the Devil may have already taken power over the world without our knowledge," Cavell writes, in his best epigrammatic style. "He may have, but it is not beyond our knowledge." God's medium "is the covenant, or promise," and He "calls us, and comes upon us, unbidden." But the "Devil deals in pacts and bargains, and we must call him up" (89). It is by dreaming she has given herself to the Devil that Rosemary calls up the Devil, and their pact is sealed when she allows her destiny to be directed (with, finally, her active cooperation) by her fantasy of giving birth to a child, the God of her world, who will be hers alone. Rosemary is not prepared to satisfy her husband (who is not prepared to satisfy her, either). She "does not allow her husband to penetrate her dreams, allow him to be her devil, and give him his due. So children can go straight to the devil," as Cavell puts it. Nor is she prepared, until too late, to satisfy her child. She is prepared to satisfy no one. Thus, she satisfies the Devil.

With the assertion that the issue at the heart of the film is to know whom one is prepared to satisfy, Cavell closes out his remarks about *Rosemary's Baby*, which are as immersed in individual psychology and as theatrical as the movie itself. Abruptly pulling back from these almost hyperbolic remarks, he ends the first part of the chapter with a quite dispassionate summary—"I have recorded my experience of the work of color in serious films as a de-psychologizing or un-theatricalizing of their subjects. My hypothesis in that . . . this would account for the feel of futurity in them (when, that is, the point is not the coloration of make-believe or the color symbolism of private fantasy)" (89). In turn, he formulates a question the second part of the chapter undertakes to answer: What is the connection between the feel of futurity in these films and the de-psychologizing, or un-theatricalizing, effect of color?

II.

Cavell gets directly to the point: "Black and white was the natural medium of visual drama. This is painting's underlying legacy to photography: value contrast in painterly modeling is a means by which depicted gestures and posture takes on individual (as opposed to hieratic or symbolic) significance and in so doing became humanly dramatic" (89–90). When value contrast makes subjects humanly dramatic, theatricalism is not opposed to realism; the experience of theatricalism becomes "a condition of our accepting a work as the depiction of human reality."

From the beginning, it has been an impulse of photography to theatricalize its subjects. "The photographer's command, 'Watch the birdie' is essentially a stage direction," as Cavell points out (90). The direction is given "precisely to give the impression of the natural, that is to say, the *candid*," by distracting the subject from focusing on the camera lens. But why should this theatrical technique give the impression of naturalness? And why, because a subject "turns his eye into the eye of the camera," should a sense of the candid be denied? (90).

Black and white film is inherently dramatic, and this elucidates why film invited the "outline clarity" of types around which revolved those decades of melodramas, comedies, and so on, which have been the traditional media of movies. "In accepting these works as movies," Cavell argues, "we accepted what they depicted as reality." The world that presented itself on film in those works *was* reality, but it was reality *dramatized*. We accepted what movies depicted as reality because we had already come to take reality dramatically. "The movie merely confirmed what the nineteenth century completed" (90).

In one of the rare occasions in which *The World Viewed* indulges in an autobiographical anecdote, Cavell tells a story about the time in his early adolescence—it was around 1940—when he was told by a man whose responses he cared about that he "did not like movies to be in color because that made them unrealistic."

> Already a philosopher, I denied what I felt to be the validity of his remark and refuted it by pointing out that the real world is not in black and white, explaining further that his idea was only the result of having grown accustomed to the look of black and white films; I went on to prophesy that all films would eventually be made in color. I now have an explanation of the truth of his idea, of my sense then of its truth. . . . It was that film color masked the black and white axis of brilliance, and the drama of characters and contexts supported by it, along which our comprehensibility of personality and event were secured. Movies in color seemed unrealistic because they were undramatic. (90–91)

This anecdote brings home Cavell's point that in black and white movies the axis of brilliance helped gestures and expressions to take on individual significance, to depict a human reality, and in so doing to become humanly dramatic; movies in black and white seemed more realistic because they were more dramatic, and we had already come to take reality dramatically.

The story also bears on three concerns—philosophy, childhood, and education—that repeatedly surface in this chapter (and, indeed, in the whole of *The World Viewed*). Unlike the fantasy of a transcendent God, philosophy is original to childhood, or, at least, to early adolescence, a period of his life when Cavell, by his own testimony, was "already a philosopher," if a childish one. (Even Kant, perhaps the greatest philosopher of all, sometimes thinks childishly, Cavell suggests, as when Kant argues that it is happiness and virtue, not happiness and truth, that coalesce at the point past imagination that constitutes the fantastic reality of God.)

When Cavell was told that color made movies unrealistic, the young philosopher sensed the validity of this point, but lacked an explanation of its truth. So he offered, perversely, a "refutation" meant specifically to deny what seemed inexplicable, not only in the man's experience, but in his own, too. And so the explanation that he has since come to recognize as the truth, an explanation that accounts for the mystery in his experience rather than denies it, failed at that time to dawn on him.

When Cavell characterizes his adolescent self as "already a philosopher," we might think he is simply being ironic. For when the young Cavell "refuted" the truth of his own experience, surely this was sophistry, not philosophy. (And yet, as he goes on to observe, the sophist and the philosopher have always had the most intimate of relationships.) The adolescent Cavell took the task of philosophy to be the marshaling of

160

arguments to refute irrational assertions. In 1940, it was natural for Cavell to envision philosophy in such dramatic terms; this confirms, in a surprising way, that then, when most movies were still in black and white, dramatic explanations were still our natural mode of understanding human behavior. It also confirms what the chapter goes on to suggest, that it is no coincidence that now that movies are no longer in black and white, dramatic explanations no longer satisfy us, and Cavell no longer envisions philosophy's task in dramatic terms.

In confessing their pasts, St. Augustine and Rousseau declared the changed conditions of their present forms of life. In writing *The World Viewed*, Cavell, too, declares that the conditions of his life are changed. Declaring itself to be the work of a creature whose knowledge is of childhood past, *The World Viewed* achieves an adult perspective, as we might put it. The conditions that must be satisfied for such a perspective to be achieved are part of what the book is about.

From Cavell's little story about his adolescence, which no one but he could have written, there is a sudden cut, as it were, to a sweeping overview of the history of the nineteenth century, breathtaking in its scope yet almost comic in its sustained display of assured virtuosity. No one but Cavell could have written this passage, either. It begins, "When princes and kings were thrown from the stage, what happened was not that the theater emptied but that it came to encompass social intercourse as a whole; you could not tell the stage from the house" (90); (that is, you could not tell the characters or players from the audience; you could not tell the events on stage from what goes on, in private, in people's homes). Events on stage did not stop being dramatic; drama came to pervade all corners of human life. "If religion, as it left heaven, became drama, then drama, as it left art"—as it pervaded social intercourse as a whole—"became politics." And politics, pervading society and the self, "became religion."

When politics came to pervade society and the self, Reason, having conquered heaven, turned its attention "to each social detail and personal relationship, not just globally . . . but intimately (exemplified by . . . William Morris's projected design for every article of use and of decoration)," leaving no realm of mystery "to men's necessities, or any arbitrariness in their decisions." Under this nineteenth-century reign of Reason, mysteries, in practice, did not vanish; they were shoved "deeper into wastes of the mind and into more decorously veiled environments of cities," where they were left to spread.

> If knowledge and practice were more and more united to produce the décors and *mise en scène* of cultures, they were as far as ever from meeting at the

161

conditions of social life. But since these conditions were now theoretically subject to question, one's failure to change society presented itself as impotence. The need for theoretical explanation of social behavior accordingly became unlimited. Everything was changing, but nothing can be changed; so everything, including those facts, stands in need of interpretation. And because society, though revealed to Reason, remained cold and unyielding, and because the abyss between heaven and earth deepened as it narrowed (since there *is* no reason and no place for which the good city is to be postponed), and because God was reabsorbed and became an eye and a roar in the wings of the mind—our total explanation of our condition, to be convincing, had to be dramatic. (90–91)

As this account unfolds, Cavell's metaphors become more and more charged, culminating in his final images of the abyss between heaven and earth deepening as it narrows, and of God, mysteriously "reabsorbed," becoming "an eye and a roar in the wings of the mind." It is as if Cavell's prose is animated by the spirit of the age it characterizes, hence as if his own "total explanation," to be convincing, has had to become more dramatic.

When Cavell suggests that God became an eye, we might note, he pointedly does not specify whose eye God became. He leaves open the possibility that God became our eye, that our eye became God's eye (as when we came to view the world from within our private fantasies, perhaps). He also leaves open the possibility that God became the eye that we feel is forever upon us (as when we feel we are always playing to an audience). And when Cavell suggests that God became "a roar in the wings of the mind," his idea, clearly, is that we hear this roar, we sense the reality of God, when our minds are flying high (as Cavell's mind surely was when he was wrote this inspired passage). His idea is also, perhaps, that we cannot tell whether it is our own voice we are hearing, roaring at the world from our Godlike height, or whether we hear God roaring at us for flying so high.

Marx's theory of revolution, which relies on ideas such as "class conflict" and "classlessness," is an example of a "total explanation" of the condition of the age that is couched in terms which, as Cavell puts it, "while not necessarily theatrical, are inherently liable . . . to theatrical employment" (92). Shrewdly and wittily Cavell remarks, "When, to Hegel's comment that historical events occur twice, Marx added the tag, 'the first time as tragedy, the second time as farce,' he was expressing both the genius that set him apart from his age and the genius that placed him inside it." At the precise moment Marx was calling for the end of philosophy's interpretation of reality in favor of a start toward changing reality, theory and practice were already joined (in service of isolated opportunities for expansion or social experiment), and philosophy was already becoming the possession of men at large (as a more impenetrable set of justifications for one's deadly sins [92]).

In the course of the nineteenth century, in other words, philosophy, like drama, came to pervade social intercourse as a whole. Everyman become a theatrical character, an actor, and a philosopher as well. But "when everyman becomes his own philosopher, he simultaneously becomes his own sophist," Cavell observes. "The sophist remains philosophy's most intimate enemy, only now he does not take his form within a separate profession, but pervades every profession of reason" (92). And so the condition of philosophy, and of serious writing generally, changes in the course of the nineteenth century. "Philosophy, and serious writing generally, no longer knows to whom to direct its voice, no longer quite believes that a message in a bottle will find its way to another shore. Then it stands on darkening straits, casting unsystematic lines, in hopes of attracting to the surface some darting wish for sense" (92).

Cavell's metaphor—the philosopher as angler—would be at home in Thoreau's *Walden*. And Cavell incorporates a Thoreau-like pun. Writers, like anglers, literally as well as metaphorically "cast lines." The serious writer, no longer quite believing "that a message in a bottle will find its way to another shore," knows that his lines must lure the reader, must "attract to the surface some darting wish for sense." That is, the writer knows he must lure the reader to the writing's "surface," the particular words he has written. He also knows that, if they are to be able to do so, those words must attract to the surface the reader's wish for sense (a wish, evidently, that has become submerged).

When this paragraph concludes with the line "I am without authority to excuse myself either for, or from, that position," it declares what we had surely already intuited, which is that Cavell views philosophy as still standing "on darkening straits, casting unsystematic lines, in hopes of attracting to the surface some darting wish for sense." This is precisely Cavell's position when he writes these sentences, casts these lines.

This brings out another level of Cavell's punning language. "Lines" and "casting" are words at home in a theatrical context, too. To "attract to the surface some darting wish for sense," the serious writer has to *cast* his lines—has to discover a character who can convincingly speak them, a voice in which they can convincingly be spoken. Cavell is summing up this new condition of philosophy, and of serious writing generally, with a theatrical tableau. In the role of angler/philosopher in this tableau, he casts himself.

By casting the line "I am without authority to excuse myself for, or from, that position," Cavell might seem to be saying that his position as a serious writer is simply inexcusable (the point of luring readers, after all, is to hook them), or simply inescapable (what other position is open to him?), or both. However, what his words literally say is not that he cannot be excused, but only that he cannot excuse *himself* from this position. *We* cannot excuse Cavell from it, to be sure. But we can excuse him *for* it by acknowledging that he *is* a serious writer, that this *is* his position, and that it is necessary for him to keep faith with it.

"Movies begin as Victorian theater," Cavell writes, adding that "part of the meaning of 'Victorian' is the insane and independent energy of reason." Another part is "the moralization of morality—as if to justify, after faith in faith, faith in the appalling consequences of the reign of reason, e.g., in the calculated ruin of generations and continents." In the Victorian era, "society and the perception of society move past drama into melodrama. . . . Nietzsche's calling for an attainment beyond good and evil is a prophecy against this melodrama of progress" (92–93). Cavell goes on:

> If Machiavelli first described the theatricalization of politics—the Prince and the paupers, the General and the general, the man and the woman, the black and the white, the young and the old, depending for their position, their very social existence, upon their externalized . . . views of one another—then Marx first planned the recovery from this mortal slapstick; whatever the fate of "class consciousness" in a theory of revolution, its significance stands as a permanent goal of social epistemology. . . . For its claims are that history alone has excavated what we recognize as social position, that our place in society has become unknown to us, that knowledge of the self is acquired only together with knowledge of the self's society, of its stand in society—as though what is "unconscious" in an adult is not merely his psychic past but his social present, equally painful and difficult to recognize—and that just as having a self requires taking a stand upon the self, so having a social place means assuming that place. (93)

"In this condition," Cavell continues, beginning a new paragraph, "for the foreseeable future, self-consciousness will start, and mostly continue, as embarrassment" (93). Whether in Machiavelli, Rousseau, or Marx, the discovery of modern society "is the discovery of modern individuality, whether as isolated, as homeless, or as dispossessed." When Cavell adds, "But we are as capable of knowing our individuality, or accepting the individuality of another, as we are of becoming Christ for one another," we might think his point is that we are *not* really capable of these things. Yet Cavell is not *assuming* either that we are, or that we

164

are not, capable of "becoming Christ for one another" or of "knowing our individuality, or accepting the individuality of another." On what grounds could we really rest assured that we know, *a priori*, the truth about these matters?

Having a self requires taking a stand upon the self, but taking a stand upon the self requires the simultaneous acknowledgment of others. Having a social place means assuming that place. And yet, if history has excavated a place for us without allowing us our say, if modern society has already displaced us, we cannot at the same time assume such a place, which grants us no standing, and also take the stand upon the self necessary to achieve selfhood. To achieve selfhood, we must discover (inside, outside, or on the fringe of society) a community of others prepared to acknowledge our individuality, as we are prepared to acknowledge theirs.

"If it makes sense to speak of the Greeks as having discovered the self, or of the eighteenth and nineteenth centuries as having discovered childhood," Cavell writes, "we can say that our recent accomplishment"— as recent, perhaps, as the emergence in movies of Brando, Dean, and Belmondo—"has been the discovery of adolescence, the point at which one's life is to be chosen and one gives oneself a name, and that our task is to discover the existence of community" (93–94).

In his anecdote about his encounter with the man who found movies in color unrealistic, Cavell characterizes himself as in his "early adolescence." He would not have characterized himself that way then. Already a philosopher, already a sophist, he thought he was already an adult. In 1940, the world had not yet accomplished "the discovery of adolescence"—the discovery that there are such creatures as adolescents; the discovery of what it is that adolescents have discovered, what they cannot simply fail to know, the knowledge that makes them no longer children, which is that they are to choose their life, give themselves a name, discover the existence of community.

"Revolution, which begins the nineteenth century, is society's self-dramatization," Cavell goes on, "as romanticism, which continues it, is the self's self-dramatization. But then drama was still a form of acknowledgment" (94). To adolescents, drama remains a form of acknowledgment, or, as we might also put it, acknowledgment remains a form of drama. Insofar as we take adolescence to be a stage of development that is naturally transcended or overcome when the individual completes the transition to adulthood, the "discovery of adolescence" enables drama to remain alive, but on borrowed time.

Returning the discussion to its main theme, the concluding paragraph of this part of the chapter begins:

> When dramatic explanations cease to be our natural mode of understanding one another's behavior, whether because we tell ourselves that human behavior is inexplicable, or that only salvation (now political) will save us, or that the human personality must be sought more deeply than dramatic religions or sociologies or psychologies or histories or ideologies are prepared for— black and white ceases to be the mode in which our lives are convincingly portrayed. But since until yesterday dramatic modeling was the mode in which the human appeared, and its tensions and resolutions were those in terms of which our human understanding of humanity was completely satisfied, its surcease must seem to us the vanishing of the human as such. (94)

Painting and sculpture can "cede human portrayal in favor of the unappeasable human wish for presentness and beauty." They can do so, for example, by "finding ways to make paintings without value contrast among their hues" (94). Movies cannot simply cede "human figuration or reference (though they can fragment it, or can animate something else)." But movies in color do "cede our recently natural (dramatic) grasp of these figures." They do so "not by denying so much as neutralizing our connection with the world so filmed."

Thus, Cavell completes his answer to the question, posed at the end of the chapter's first part, of the nature of the connection between the sense of futurity in certain recent films and their use of color to de-psychologize, or un-theatricalize, their subjects. Since it is our world, after all, "that is presented to us, and since those figures . . . do after all resemble us, but since nevertheless they are no longer psychically present to us, we read them as de-psychologized, which, for us, means un-theatricalized. And from there it is only logical to project them as inhabiting the future, a mutation away from the past we know (as we know it)" (94).

III.

"Because I evidently require such clouds of history in order to adumbrate my conviction about these topics, let me at least avoid the appearance of thinking I have established more than is here," Cavell writes (94–95), beginning the third part of Chapter 13 on an embarrassed note (as if acknowledging his point that self-consciousness now starts, and mostly continues, as embarrassment). "I have described certain uses of color in film—as packaging, as unifying the worlds of make-believe and of fantasy, and as projecting a future."

Pointing out that he has not claimed these are all the uses of color, Cavell cites the passage in *Contempt* in which Brigitte Bardot is lying in bed and her body is bathed in "centerfold or calendar hues" (95). Godard uses color here not merely to register "our taste for mild pornography, but that our tastes and convictions in love have been pornographized, which above all means publicized, externalized—letting society tell us what to love, and needing it to tell us whether we do."

Neither has he claimed, Cavell reminds us, that futurity can be projected only through color ("In Bergman's harsh black and white mysteries, the future began a long time ago; it is already old"). Nor that all directors must be involved in projecting futurity ("The greatest will probably resist it, for the future has replaced the past as the object of timely elegy").

An innovator like Antonioni will have his own ways of projecting the future, Cavell continues, "beginning with *L'avventura*, with his spacing of film time, in particular by his fermata over single shots, which enclose an air of *presentiment*" (95). He goes on to chart some of the iconographic and thematic features of Antonioni's films that "show him to be an inheritor of surrealism from painting"—his obsession with the facades of uninhabited new buildings, say, or juxtapositions of old and new. For Antonioni as for surrealism, absence is obviously a root topic; absence

> is registered by the sheen or finish of the frames, which, along with the clean, deep lines of perspective, perfects the avoidance of human clutter or arbitrariness; nothing is behind this space. In the Monica Vitti trilogy, there is the absence of not merely feeling, but of so much as the effort to explain that absence. . . . When love is altogether over, unable even to stir a fantasy of future redemption, then we have forgone the futurity of our future. (95–96)

Cavell cites the ending of *L'avventura* as an instance of Antonioni's envisioning of a future in which all sense of a future is forgone. (As he describes it, this ending is strangely reminiscent, except for its mood, of the ending of Bergman's *Smiles of a Summer Night* and the endings of remarriage comedies.)

> [T]he woman puts her hand on the man's shoulder not because she forgives his betrayal, or even his inability to offer tears and beg forgiveness, but because she accepts that there is nothing to forgive, to forgo, no new place to be won on the other side of this moment. There is no man different from any other, or she will seek none. Her faithfulness is to accept their juxtaposition in a world of uneventful adventure . . . and to move into that world with him. (96)

In Godard's films after *Breathless*, by contrast, there is for his characters no longer any problem of ending, or of change, Cavell remarks, beginning a critique of Godard's post-*Breathless* work that provides Chapter 13 with its conclusion.

Godard's characters "are somewhere else, already in a future" (96). He establishes this by depersonalizing them from the outset, rather than by

167

Absence (*L'avventura*).

altering their psychology, or through their responses, or lack of responses, to their own inability to respond. Thus it would be antithetical to Godard's effort to use color to neutralize drama, or to create worlds of make-believe or fantasy. Godard does not envision the people in his films as inhabiting another world. They are "without fantasy (hence pastless and futureless, hence presentless), and the sort of depersonalization he requires depends both upon our responding to these characters as persons and upon our continuously failing to read their motions within the stresses of ordinary human emotion and motivation" (96–97).

Some admirers have taken Godard "to have established in some such way a cinematic equivalent to Brecht's call for a new theater in which the actor forces and maintains a distance between himself and his role, and between stage and audience" (97). Without denying that there could be a major discovery for film in this idea, Cavell does not find that Godard achieves it. "For a film director does not begin with a medium in which actor and character have conventionally or momentarily coalesced, nor with a conventional or passing denial of the distance between the stage and a coherent audience," Cavell reminds us. "Actor" and "audience" lack clear application to film. Thus one reads the distance from and between Godard's characters "as one does in reality, as the inability to feel, and we attribute our distance from the filmed events . . . to Godard's position

168

toward them. And because the events of the films do not themselves justify or clarify his position, it remains arbitrary. That alone would deprive him of a Brechtian justification" (97).

Cavell anticipates the objection "that the demand for a 'position' from an artist is an archaic . . . holdover from a romantic or moralistic view of art. Why can't the artist *simply* provide us with pleasure or merely show us the ways things are?" (97). Cavell does not counter this objection by arguing that we *are* justified in demanding of artists that they have a position. Rather, he testifies that Godard's post-*Breathless* films do not on the whole provide him with pleasure, and that they give him a sense of the way things are "only from the position of one who cannot see his responsibility in those ways—first of all his responsibility in approaching an audience on his topics." He also testifies that works that do provide him with pleasure or knowledge of the way things are also provide him "with a sense of the artist's position toward this revelation—a position, say, of complete conviction, of compassion, of delight or ironic amusement, of longing or scorn or rage or loss" (97–98).

Cavell is not faulting Godard for failing to have a position, but for failing to justify, or even clarify, the position he does have. This leads to one of *The World Viewed*'s benchmark statements of its author's own position on such matters: "The fact is, an artist, because a human being, does have a position and does have his reasons for calling his events to our attention. What entitles him to our attention is precisely his responsibility to this condition" (98).

In traditional arts, "apprenticeship and mastery in a discipline could take care of individual responsibility." When, in modernism, "an art demands that its disciple call its existence into question and then affirm it," the artist's responsibility, too, is in question (98). Echoing *Must We Mean What We Say?*, Cavell writes, "In art—as now in politics, as formerly in religion, as in personal relations—finding the right to speak the truth is as difficult as finding the truth. One could say that the *right* to speak, in these arenas, is gone."

In art, the condition that entitles one to speak is, again, one's responsibility to one's position, to one's reasons for saying what one has it at heart to say, for calling upon others to listen. "Where the silence of attention is not maintained by force, it is gathered through personal standing," Cavell asserts (98). (That art calls for a *silent* attention is an idea taken up in the remaining chapters.) Significantly, he adds, "When three stand on the same ground, there is a community"—a remark that makes explicit

169

a feature of the concept of community, a concept *The World Viewed* as a whole investigates.

Those who take Godard's works to constitute an authentically radical critique of our culture "read his withdrawal of feeling as a combination of knowingness and objectivity toward the corruption of the world," Cavell writes.

> The Belmondo figure in *Breathless* has achieved objectivity by winning his subjectivity; when he refuses the girl's rejection of his love, saying "There is no unhappy love," his position has the power to turn that apparently empirical claim into a definition of his world. His last words to her ("You are a coward") are accordingly not an accusation but, backed by his achievement, an observation. (98)

After *Breathless*, Godard seems to have regarded such an achievement "as impossible or unnecessary for his characters or for his art." Yet without it Godard has no standing as a radical critic of our culture.

> If you believe that people speak slogans to one another, or that women are turned by bourgeois society into marketable objects, or that human pleasures are now figments and products of advertising accounts and that these are directions of dehumanization—then what is the value of pouring further slogans into that world (e.g., "People speak in slogans" or "Women have become objects" or "Bourgeois society is dehumanizing" or "Love is impossible")? And how do you distinguish the world's dehumanizing of its inhabitants from your depersonalizing of them? How do you know whether your asserted impossibility of love is anything more than an expression of your distaste for its tasks? Without such knowledge, your disapproval of the world's pleasures . . . is not criticism (the negation of advertisement) but censoriousness (negative advertisement). (99)

When he follows this blistering passage with the remark "I do not wish to deny Godard's inventiveness, and no one can ignore his facility," Cavell might seem to be giving Godard his due (99). But when he adds, "the forms of culture he wishes to hold in contempt are no less inventive and facile," it becomes clear that, in Cavell's view, Godard's very inventiveness confirms his implication in those cultural forms, not his superiority to them; Godard's inventiveness is no less compromised. Cavell ends the chapter by considering two examples of Godard's compromised inventiveness.

The first is Godard's way of staging of an "eyes on interview" with, for example, Anna Karina (99). He does not do this "by justifying a subject's acceptance of the camera—that is, by establishing a character capable in a given context of accepting her own self-awareness, knowing the effect she has on others (as, say, in Manet's *Olympia*)." Rather, he establishes "a subject with no character, from whose person he has removed personhood, a subject incapable of accepting or rejecting anything. That is the

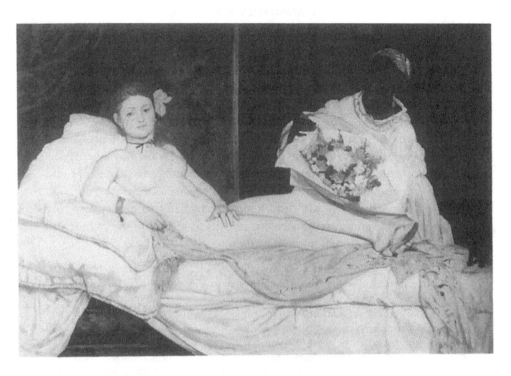

Manet's *Olympia*; Anna Karina in *Vivre sa vie*

condition of prostitution, and of advertisement. And Godard has created it, not captured it" (100).

The second is "Godard's use of the sound of philosophy, in those long dialogues his women elicit from actual philosophers" (100). Cavell praises Godard's perception in finding "this sound for the cinema," in recognizing that "in an environment of nonsense and insinuation and evasion the sound of sense still falls sweetly upon the human ear." The problem is that Godard listens to it the way his women do, "or the way a bourgeois audience does, somewhere within embarrassment, envy, contempt and titillation," not caring whether the philosopher speaks the truth. Although Godard's "talent and wit" lead him to recognize that attractive young women now stimulate philosophy, he fails to recognize the humor and sadness of this, or sees nothing further.

> From Plato on, sexual attractiveness has been an open motive to philosophy, as if to acknowledge the intimacy and mutuality of one soul's investigation of another. And if sexuality is the dialogue's conclusion, this need not mean that its point was seduction; it can acknowledge that the only successful conclusion of such investigation is mutual satisfaction, and that what remains between the participants is not a thing left unsaid. Where philosophy is foreplay, that at least refuses intellectuality as a *substitute* for sexuality. . . . The love that philosophy can teach is the power to accept intimacy without taking it personally. Its opposite is vanity, which takes every attention personally and none intimately. (Naturally, these states are commonly mistaken for one another.) Godard's girls walk away intact from these confrontations. Is this supposed to show that they are unseducible? So are prostitutes. Anyway, they are seduced—by slogans, advertisements, and illicitness. (100)

"Philosophy ought to be a nobler seduction," Cavell writes seductively, beginning Chapter 13's final paragraph, "or else its acceptance of separateness ought to be acknowledged as its power, its capacity to forgo further proof of love" (100). Cavell faults Godard for avoiding the choice, "most distinctly in *La Chinoise*, where the color suggests make-believe and so provides the out that the whole thing is child's play." At the end of the film, the philosopher speaks to the woman with real intelligence. But since we have been shown that she is

> an unloving and dangerous nitwit, we have to conclude either (1) that the man cannot tell this, or (2) that he doesn't care because he wants her and is willing to pay out intimacy and intelligence to get what he wants, tickling her fancy that she has a mind and is capable of serious action, or (3) that this is the fate of intelligence in the capitalist world, or the fate of old intelligence upon the young, or (4) that men and women have lost all ear for the difference between words (and deeds) of love, lust, instruction, valor, meanness, hope, or play.

172

> That all this is common in our world (and if you like commonly deserved) is not news, and to spread its commonness is not art. (101)

These uncompromising words speak difficult truths. What entitles Cavell to speak these truths can only be his responsibility to his position, to his reasons for saying what he has it at heart to say, for calling upon us to attend to his words. What gives him standing to write *The World Viewed* cannot be separated from what *The World Viewed* is about.

Godard claims the right to criticize our culture for treating people as if they had no souls. Yet that is precisely how films like *La Chinoise* treat their subjects and viewers, Cavell charges.[31] As we have seen, Cavell closes his remarks about *Rosemary's Baby* with the assertion that the issue, for that film's characters as for human beings in the world, "is to know who it is one is prepared to satisfy" (101). And he closes this longest chapter of *The World Viewed*, with these eloquent words: "Some people once thought that women do not have souls. Some thought that a group of people has its own soul. We no longer say such things. But just whom, or what group, does each of us treat as though it had a soul?" (101).

VI

■■■■

Chapters 14–15:
Automatism

"I HAVE SPOKEN of film as satisfying the wish for the magical reproduction of the world by enabling us to view it unseen," the first paragraph of Chapter 14 begins (101). What we wish to view in this way "is the world itself—that is to say, everything," Cavell goes on (102), invoking and answering the culminating question of Chapter 6 ("What do we wish to view this way?"). This answer resonates with a number of earlier formulations: "Photographs are of the world, of reality as a whole"; the medium of movies "is photographic and its subject reality"; film records "a total world"; and so on. But with this answer, the writing of *The World Viewed* takes a metaphysical turn that is also a turning inward.

With this development, readers who have been following all the twists and turns in Cavell's thinking may well be feeling a bit dizzy. Yet halfway through Chapter 14 the book takes an even more dizzying turn.

Throughout, Cavell has been using the word "medium" to refer both to the physical basis of an art and to the artistic discoveries of form and genre and type and technique that give significance to that physical basis. Because it is by virtue of the automatism of photography that moving pictures satisfy our wish for the world re-created in its own image, the power of the film medium can be said to be the power of its automatism. To say that until recently film has been traditional is thus to say that film's traditional forms and genres and types and techniques have until recently been able to tap into the power of film's automatism.

In the course of Chapter 14, however, Cavell announces his intention also to call those forms, genres, types, and techniques "automatisms." He devotes the remaining half of Chapter 14 to explaining why it is right to use the word "automatism" this new way, however confusing it might seem. And he devotes the entirety of Chapter 15 to going "further into a region of modernist painting" in order to develop further the concept of automatism.

Only after this extended detour will *The World Viewed* return its focus to film and bring to a conclusion its reflections on such questions as how movies were able to remain traditional for so long and how they might now acknowledge the loss of conviction in their traditions while continuing to tap the power of the medium.

Chapter 14: "Automatism"

When we wish for film, what we wish to view is everything, the world itself. That is why it takes magic for our wish to be satisfied, Cavell argues. For it is the starting point of modern philosophy, its accommodation with Cartesian doubt, that we cannot know (cannot grasp, cannot see) everything—the totality of the world, the world as it is in itself. "Nothing less than that is what modern philosophy has told us (whether for Kant's reasons, or for Locke's, or Hume's) is metaphysically beyond our reach or (as Hegel or Marx or Kierkegaard or Nietzsche might rather put it) beyond our reach metaphysically" (102). Kant's reasons, we might note, pertain to the inaccessibility of "things-in-themselves"; Locke's and Hume's, to our limitation to ideas derived from our experience. For all three philosophers, our metaphysical condition—our finiteness, our separateness, our limitation to the forms of our own experience—precludes our grasping what is "metaphysically beyond our reach." For Hegel, Marx, Kierkegaard, and Nietzsche, the totality of the world is "beyond our reach metaphysically." That is, it is beyond the reach of metaphysics—to reach it would take a fundamental change not only in our consciousness but in our form of life.

"To say that we wish to view the world itself is to say that we are wishing for the condition of viewing as such," Cavell continues (102). We wish to view the world unseen because that mode of perception feels natural to us. It feels natural because we have become displaced from our natural habitation within the world. Our way of feeling connection with the world is not so much to look *at* it as to "look *out at* it, from behind the self."

175

Cavell's compelling picture of the modern human being looking out at the world from behind the self, as from behind a camera, is a picture of the self as something interposed, something one interposes between one's true being (one's invisible soul, as it were) and the world. One's so-called self, in this picture, is only a mask, not who one really is. To view the world from behind the self, we have to hide our private fantasies, render them invisible. That this is our way of feeling connection with the world means that keeping our private fantasies hidden, giving no outward sign of our private desires, has come to feel natural to us. Indeed, we feel we *must* keep our private fantasies hidden, for they have become "all but completely thwarted and out of hand" (102). We keep our private fantasies hidden because we feel they have become so widely shared, so public, that they are no longer ours, and because we feel they have become so utterly private that they cannot be shared at all. We keep our private fantasies hidden "as if we could no longer hope that anyone might share them— at just the moment that they are pouring into the streets, less private than ever."

The last line may be read as alluding to the moment in the nineteenth century when the new human types that were to become the "presiding geniuses" of traditional movies were "pouring into the streets" of Paris, the historical moment of Baudelaire's original premonitions of cinema. Read this way, the line reminds us that the origins of movies were intimately bound up with the crisis of privacy Cavell is characterizing. Hence the passage's echoes of his account, in Chapter 1, of the conditions of moviegoing that fostered the "natural relation" to movies he had enjoyed for a quarter of a century.

The line may also be read another way. In "The Avoidance of Love," Cavell speaks of America's past as being "in its streets" (*MWMWWS*, 345), clearly thinking of the political protests taking place at the time he was writing the last essays of *Must We Mean What We Say?* This suggests that, when Cavell refers to our fantasies as "pouring into the streets, less private than ever," he is again alluding to the fateful historical moment in which he is writing: America is tearing itself apart, our thwarted fantasies are pouring into the streets. It is a fateful moment in the history of film. A century after Baudelaire's premonitions of cinema, our conviction in the myths of traditional movies has become lost, or baffled, and the author of *The World Viewed* finds that his own "natural relation" to movies has been broken.

The line's openness to being read as invoking either or both of these historical moments, separated by a century, brings home the fact that the entire history of movies has been bound up with our modern displacement from our natural habitation within the world. Movies originate as a response to this condition. In the course of the history of movies, this condition has not been cured; it has become more intense, or extreme, than ever.

Because our private fantasies have become all but completely thwarted, hiding them feels natural to us. And yet, how can our fantasies not be thwarted if we hide them? If we render our private fantasies completely unseen, unseeable, in an effort to establish connection with the world, we seal our withdrawal from the world. Thus, the culminating sentence of the chapter's second paragraph is also its strictly logical conclusion: "So we are less than ever in a position to marry [our private fantasies] to the world" (102).

As often in Cavell's writing, this culminating sentence not only draws a strictly logical conclusion from what precedes it, it contains a "kicker" that deepens the terms of the discussion in a surprising way. The "kicker" here is the idea that "marrying our fantasies to the world" is what we really long to do.

It is of the nature of fantasies that they are thwarted if we keep them hidden. The Clark Gable character in *It Happened One Night*, for example, longs to find a woman with whom he can share the life of adventure he dreams of. Even when he finds such a woman, his private fantasy is doomed to be thwarted if he fails to acknowledge that she is a match for the figure he dreams of finding. Marrying his private fantasy to the world, in this sense, is an act he must perform for himself; no one is in a position to perform it for him.

In "More of *The World Viewed*" Cavell writes, "One's responsibility toward one's desire is to acknowledge it, and acknowledge its object's separateness from you" (*WV*, 177). To acknowledge an object of one's desire as separate from oneself, one needs to acknowledge one's private fantasies about that object. One needs to acknowledge that they are fantasies (that they are thwarted unless one "marries them to the world"). One also needs to acknowledge that they are *one's own* fantasies (that one's own desires are manifest in them). To fulfil our responsibility toward our desire *is* to "marry our fantasies to the world," in other words. (What it takes to achieve such a marriage is one way of characterizing the central subject of *Pursuits of Happiness*.) If our private fantasies have become all but completely thwarted, we have all but completely failed to "marry them to the world." "To fulfil our responsibility toward our own desire," "to marry our private fantasies to the world"—these are new formulations

177

in *The World Viewed* of what is required to reach this world, to achieve selfhood, to attain presentness.

Viewing the world from behind the self feels natural to us because we have become displaced from our natural habitation within the world. Yet by viewing the world from behind the self, we consign our private fantasies to being thwarted, displace ourselves from our natural habitation within the world. We are responsible for what is unnatural about our condition, and that *is* what is unnatural about our condition. Because they *automatically* displace us from the world, movies relieve us of our unnatural condition. They seem more natural than reality to us because they take responsibility for our displacement out of our hands. They are not "escapes into fantasy," they are "reliefs from private fantasy and its responsibilities, from the fact that the world is *already* drawn by fantasy," as Cavell puts it (102).

Movies cannot be escapes into fantasy, in any case. That our fantasies have become all but completely thwarted is the condition we wish to escape *from*, and it is not possible for us to escape from that condition *into* fantasy. Fantasies promise us escape only if we fulfill our responsibility toward them, only if we "marry them to the world." When, in *It Happened One Night*, Claudette Colbert steps around the hanging blanket, the "Wall of Jericho" separating her side of the motel room from Clark Gable's side, his responsibility toward his desire, and toward this woman who has by this act declared her desire for him, puts him in a situation in which he must acknowledge his desire for her if his fantasy is not to be completely thwarted.

The movie screen, the Wall of Jericho separating this woman from *us*, automatically vouchsafes that we are not in this man's situation (or this woman's, for that matter). The screen is not a barrier that can be crossed, or sidestepped; our displacement from the world on film is automatically assured. Viewing *It Happened One Night*, it is not *possible* for us to marry our fantasies to the world framed by the movie screen. Nor is it possible for us to *fail* to do so. That is why movies are "reliefs from private fantasy and its responsibilities," and why, given that we have become displaced, have displaced ourselves, from our natural habitation within the world, movies seem more natural than reality to us.

When Cavell adds that movies are reliefs "from the fact that the world is *already* drawn by fantasy," he is reiterating this point (102). The "fact" Cavell has in mind is that reality, as we are capable of knowing it (grasping it, seeing it), is not objectively given to us, but has already been "filtered through a normal stage of fantasy," as Chapter 13 puts it. In *It Happened One Night*, for example, the Gable character's perception is "filtered" through his longing to find the *one* woman he is seeking, the woman of his fantasy. However he tries to keep his fantasy hidden from the world, reality bears the mark of his fantasy; in every situation in which he finds himself, he is reminded of his failure to fulfil his responsibilities toward his desire, his failure to marry his fantasy to the world.

That there *is* no world apart from the one existing world is one of Cavell's bedrock philosophical principles. It is no less a Cavellian principle that there is no world apart from fantasy. The world drawn by fantasy is not a world separate from the real world; fantasy and reality are aspects of the one existing world, much as the duck and the rabbit (in Wittgenstein's famous example from Part II of *Philosophical Investigations*) are aspects of the one figure which together they constitute. That is why Cavell can write, in Chapter 13, "It is a poor idea of fantasy which takes it to be a world apart from reality, a world clearly showing its unreality," implying that fantasy and reality are really one, and then immediately add, "Fantasy is precisely what reality can be confused with," implying that fantasy and reality are really separate.

Movies are "reliefs from the fact that the world is *already* drawn by fantasy" for the simple reason that the world on film is *not* drawn by fantasy. The world on film is not drawn at all. On film, the world is *automatically* re-created, and that, again, is why movies seem more natural than reality to us.

If it is not because movies are escapes into fantasy that they seem more natural than reality to us, it is also "not because they are dreams," Cavell argues, "but because they permit the self to be awakened, so that we may stop withdrawing our longings further inside ourselves" (102).

Movies are not dreams any more than they are escapes into fantasy. Viewing a movie, we are not dreaming. The world on film, the world framed by the movie screen, is real. When dreaming, we are asleep; our eyes are closed. Movies not only require us literally to keep our eyes open, they enable "the self to be awakened" beyond the mode of perception we ordinarily think of as wakeful. Movies awaken us *from* the mode of perception that has come to seem natural to us, the mode of perception in which, in order to view the world unseen, we look out at the world "from behind the self" and make our fantasies invisible, or, rather, deny that their visible mark is to be found in the world they have already drawn.

179

Wittgenstein's duck/rabbit.

Movies permit the self to be awakened from a mode of perception closer to dreaming than to wakefulness. They "convince us of the world's reality in the only way we have to be convinced," Cavell goes on, "without learning to bring the world closer to the heart's desire (which in practice now means learning to stop altering it illegitimately, against itself): by taking views of it" (102). Movies awaken us to the world's reality and thereby awaken us to the reality of our unnatural condition, a condition in which we have become displaced, have come to displace ourselves, from our natural habitation within the world. Because our unnatural condition is that we have come to feel that our only way of establishing connection with the world is by viewing, and because it is *by viewing* that we are awakened by movies, viewing movies cannot free us from our unnatural condition, cannot put us in a position to marry our fantasies to the world, as we long to do. Movies cannot "bring the world closer to the heart's

180

desire." Movies can only awaken us to the fact that we long to stop—we must stop—altering the world "illegitimately, against itself."

■ ■

Before poetry, music, and painting entered the modernist environment, the traditional media of those arts allowed given works to tap naturally the power of their medium. The power of a sonnet, a rondo, or a portrait was "its power to stand in for the form it took and thence to invoke the power of the medium," to invoke the art of poetry or music or painting as such (103).

"Modernism signifies not that the powers of the arts are exhausted," Cavell argues, but, on the contrary, that

> it has become the immediate task of the artist to achieve in his art the muse of the art itself—to declare, from itself, the art as a whole for which it speaks, to become a present of that art. . . . [T]he task is no longer to produce another instance of an art but a new medium within it. . . . In such a predicament, media are not given *a priori*. The failure to establish a medium is a new depth . . . of artistic failure. (103)

In contrast to poetry, music, and painting, the traditional media of movies until recently enabled filmmakers to tap naturally into the power of the film medium itself. Because it is by virtue of the automatism of photography that moving pictures satisfy our wish for the world re-created in its own image, the power of the film medium can be said to be the power of its automatism. To say that until recently movies have remained traditional is thus to say that until recently film retained "its natural relation to its traditions of automatism" (103).

Cavell notes that, since he is "intent upon keeping these levels of artistic fact separate," it may seem perverse of him "to use the concept of automatism . . . also in the description of film's physical basis" (105). It is, indeed, confusing to think of automatism as a feature of the physical basis of the film medium and at the same time to call the diverse media of film "automatisms." And yet, as Cavell argues, the confusion is not caused by applying one concept in the two places. It is caused, rather, by "precisely the fact that this concept is justified in both places."

What causes confusion, Cavell suggests, "has to do with the identity of the art of film itself," with the fact that the automatism of photography *is* a feature of its physical basis (105). Whatever the art, it is confusing to think about the relationship between that art's physical basis and the diverse media that have given significance to features of that basis. That is why, although he is "trying to free the idea of a medium from its confinement . . . to the physical basis of various arts," Cavell insists on using the word "medium" to "name those bases as well as to characterize modes of achievement within the arts." Here, too, confusion is caused "by precisely the fact that this concept is justified in both places. And it will not be dispelled by redefining or substituting some labels" (105).

The relationship between an art's physical basis and the diverse media that give significance to features of that basis is confusing, and this fact has implications that are at once historical and ontological. Modernist art may be thought of as "an investigation of this confusion, or of the complexities of this fact," Cavell maintains (106). The fate of modernist art is precisely that "its awareness and responsibility for the physical basis of its art compel it at once to assert and deny the control of its art by that basis" (105). In a modernist art, the concepts of style and genre lack clear application; the concept of a medium seems to denote the physical materials of the art as such. But what *is* "the medium of painting or poetry or music as such?" In addressing this question, "one of two responses seems forced upon us," Cavell argues, "and neither is an answer to the question."

The first response is that "the medium of music as such is sound as such; the medium of painting is paint as such, etc." (106). One problem with this formulation is that it seems to imply "that all sound is music, all areas of color are paintings." To human beings, however, not all sound *is* music; not all areas of color *are* paintings. Saying "The medium of music is sound," or "The medium of painting is paint," is to say nothing about music or painting *as an art*. If we found all sounds as expressive as music and all areas of color as expressive as paintings, we could forgo music and painting "in favor of the natural, or contingent." But for human beings, sounds and colors only have the significance we give them. The "medium of an art as such" *is* the medium of an *art* only insofar as it provides a physical basis for human beings to give significance, to "make sense."

This idea uncovers a deep connection between the first and second halves of Chapter 14. Just as reality and the world drawn by fantasy are not separate worlds but aspects of the one existing world, the medium of an art cannot be separated from the possibilities for making sense for which it provides the physical basis. That is why it is no answer to the question "What is the medium of painting as such?" to say "The medium of painting is paint." Apart from the ways painting gives paint significance, paint is not the medium of an art at all. No art's existence is *physically* assured.

A second response to the question "What *is* the medium of painting or poetry or music as such?" is: "Nothing is *the* medium of, say, painting as such" (107). A medium of painting is "whatever way or ways paint is managed so as to create objects we accept as paintings."

This, too, is no answer to the question, Cavell argues. Every art has a singular mode of existence, and nothing exists in the world without a physical basis. No art's existence as an art is physically assured, but no art can exist apart from its physical basis, either. There is no art of painting apart from the ways artists discover to make meaningful objects in paint. But there can be no meaningful objects in paint without paint.

In the epigrammatic line "Only an art can define its media" (107), Cavell finds an elegant way to say, all at once, that an art's media can only be defined by that art; that nothing but an art has the capacity to define its own media; and that defining its own media calls for the magic, or spiritual achievement, of an art (as opposed, for example, to a science).

"A modernist art," Cavell argues, "investigating its own physical basis, searching out its own conditions of existence, rediscovers the fact that its existence as an art is not physically assured" (107). In accepting this fact, modernist art "gracefully accepts our condemnation to meaning." By characterizing us as "condemned to meaning," Cavell means that we have no way of getting through to others except by making ourselves understood. We have no way of making ourselves understood except by making sense. We have no way of making sense except by expressing ourselves in a particular way, that is, in a particular medium, a medium with a particular physical basis. We have no way of expressing ourselves except in a medium we are capable of acknowledging as our own ("To discover ways of making sense is always a matter of the relation of an artist to his art, each discovering the other"). And we have no way of not expressing ourselves at all ("expressionlessness is not a reprieve from meaning, but a particular mode of it" [107]).

Every medium of every art has a physical basis, but the existence of a medium of art is not physically assured; it must be achieved. Cavell understands these conditions of the existence of art to reflect conditions of our existence as human beings, as "separate creatures of sense and soul." Human existence has a physical basis; we could not be human unless we were in the world, embodied, subject to physical conditions. And yet our existence *as* human is not physically assured; our humanity, too, must be achieved. Achieving a human existence requires that we achieve presentness, that we reach this world and attain selfhood. Hence we are yet again returned to the quintessentially Cavellian principle, "Apart from the wish for selfhood (hence the always simultaneous granting of otherness as well), I do not understand the value of art." A medium of art is a particular way people have discovered for satisfying this wish.

Cavell concludes Chapter 14 by offering three specific justifications for calling artistic media "automatisms":

> First . . . a medium . . . generates new instances: not merely makes them possible, but calls for them, as if to attest that what has been discovered is indeed something more than a single work could convey. Second, the notion of automatism codes the experience of the work of art as "happening of itself." In a tradition, the great figure knows best how to activate its automatisms. . . . In a modernist situation . . . your work is all your own, there is no longer a natural relation between your work and its results, you are *looking* for what works (happens of itself). . . . A third impulse in calling the creation of a medium the creation of an automatism is to register the sense that the point of this effort is to free me not merely from my confinement in automatisms that I can no longer acknowledge as mine . . . but to free the object from me, to give new ground for its *autonomy*. (107–8)

Creating a work of art in a medium we can acknowledge as our own is a way for us to reach this world and attain selfhood. Such an object is fully in the world, but is also an expression of our subjectivity. Making an object in a medium we can no longer acknowledge as our own, however, is not a way to declare ourselves, or to get through to others. Such an object confines us, because it is an expression of the isolation we wish to overcome, an expression of our lack of self. An expression of our lack of presentness, it, too, lacks presentness. Confining us, it is confined by us. It does not grant us selfhood, and we do not grant it autonomy.

Chapter 14 is written primarily in the first person plural. In this closing paragraph the prose shifts. Explaining his reason for calling artistic media "automatisms," Cavell alternates between writing in the third person about the traditional artist ("The automatisms of a tradition are given to the traditional artist, prior to any instance he adds to it" [107]) and writing in the second person about the modernist artist ("Only after the fact will the muse come to bless your work, or not" [107]). The sentences in the second person are noncommittal on the relationship of the author and us to the modernist artist. The sentences in the third person, while noncommittal on our relationship to the traditional artist (thus enabling the passage to remain noncommittal on our relationship to the modernist artist), dissociate the author from the traditional artist.

When Cavell gives his third reason for calling artistic media "automatisms," his prose shifts to the first person singular ("the point of this effort is to free me not merely from my confinement in automatisms that

I can no longer acknowledge as mine . . . but to free the object from me"). Rhetorically, these culminating sentences of Chapter 14 are no longer concerned with soliciting our agreement. Whether or not we identify with the figure of the modernist artist, these sentences declare Cavell's identification with that figure, declare that he is writing from *within* the modernist situation.

In invoking "the point of this effort," Cavell is referring in general to the effort of modernist artists to create new automatisms, new media of their art. He is also referring specifically to his own effort in writing *The World Viewed*. *The World Viewed* is not an instance of a traditional medium of philosophy. To discover a way to thinking philosophically about his experience of movies, about the movies in his experience, Cavell undertakes to create, within philosophy, a new medium that he can make his own. If *The World Viewed* fails to establish such a medium, its failure is absolute.

In the Preface, composed upon the completion of the body of the book, Cavell writes, "To account for the motive in writing this book may be the most accurate description of its motive." The culminating sentences of Chapter 14 provide a partial account of this motive: *The World Viewed* is written at once to free Cavell from his confinement in automatisms of philosophy he can no longer acknowledge as his (the analytical journal article, for example) and "to free the object" from him, to give "new ground for its autonomy." The "object" this line invokes is *The World Viewed* itself. The line also invokes the objects that are the subjects of *The World Viewed*, the movies in Cavell's experience, memories of which are strand over strand with memories of his life.

Chapter 15: "Excursus: Some Modernist Painting"

In Chapter 15, Cavell continues to develop the concept of "automatism" in preparation for returning to his questions about the possibilities for modernism in film. In this chapter, specifically, he goes more deeply into what Chapter 2 refers to as "the recent major painting which [Michael Fried] describes as objects of *presentness*" (23). Chapter 15 reflects on what such modernist painting finds it necessary to do, and to be faithful to, in order to maintain its conviction in its own power to establish connection with reality by, as Chapter 2 puts it, "permitting us presentness to ourselves, apart from which there is no hope for a world" (22–23).

Cavell does not expect simply to apply this example to film, as if modernist film has to do the same thing modernist painting has to do. As

Chapter 14 argues, the different arts do not do the same thing in different ways, they are different ontologically; they have different modes of existence. Cavell's hope, in reflecting on these "objects of presentness," is that these examples of modernist painting might help provide a *perspective* for thinking about the possibilities of modernism in the art of film.

In *Dada, Surrealism and Their Heritage*, William Rubin argues that Jackson Pollock took from Surrealism not a manner but an idea, the idea of automatism. Cavell responds to Rubin's claim:

> The surrealists looked for automatisms which would create images; Pollock looked for an automatism with which to create paintings. . . . Using automatism to create paintings is what painters have always done. In order that any new automatism he found might create paintings, he had newly to consider what constitutes a painting (*what* it was painters have always done, that is, made) and in particular to discover what would give any automatism of his the significance of painting. (108)

It is inapt to call Pollock's major work "action painting," Cavell argues, because "the 'action' in question was a discovery of Pollock's that precisely *evaded* the traditional actions of painters, which he had found no longer made paintings" (108).

Was Pollock's discovery his oft-cited "all-over line"? But that would have been no discovery at all had not *his* all-over line produced works we accepted as painting. "The question ought therefore to be: Since it made paintings, what does his all-over line discover? One fact of painting it discovered is . . . not exactly that a painting is flat, but that its flatness, together with its being of limited extent, means that it is *totally there*, wholly open to you, absolutely in front of your senses, of your eyes, as no other form of art is" (109).

When "a painter discovers, by painting, something true of all paintings"—for example, that a painting is "totally there," totally up front— it is not like "a case of something hidden in unconsciousness becoming conscious." Rather, Cavell maintains, it is like "something hidden in consciousness declaring itself. The mode is revelation. I follow Michael Fried in speaking of this fact of modernist painting as an *acknowledging* of its conditions. Any painting may teach you what is true of all paintings. A modernist painting teaches you this *by* acknowledgment" (109).

Cavell speaks of "following" Fried in applying to modernist painting the concept "acknowledgment." As he points out in a footnote, though, that concept first showed its significance for him independently of Fried's work, in thinking about our knowledge of other minds in "Knowing and Acknowledging," one of the essays in *Must We Mean What We Say?* Al-

186

though they first applied the concept in very different places, Cavell notes, in both Fried's writing and his own "the concept of acknowledgment is immediately related to issues of presentness, and of theatricality, in aesthetic, epistemological, and theological contexts" (*WV,* 110n). This confluence strikes Cavell as a revealing fact about acknowledgment. That this concept is justified in thinking about our knowledge of minds and about works of art is, in turn, a revealing fact about the human mind, and about art.

In "Knowing and Acknowledging," Cavell argues that an acknowledgment calls for an acknowledgment in response. If we do not respond by acknowledging an acknowledgment *as* an acknowledgment, we are withholding that acknowledgment. To say that a modernist painting teaches *by* acknowledgment entails, then, that our response to it takes the form of acknowledging it as an acknowledgment, or else withholding that acknowledgment. Since what is in question is a modernist painting's acknowledgment of the conditions of painting, either we acknowledge that it satisfies those conditions, or else we withhold that acknowledgment. In other words, our response takes the form of accepting, or else rejecting, its claim *to be* a painting.

In ordinary cases of acknowledgment, one acknowledges something one knows to be true of oneself. Then how can a painting speak for all paintings in its acknowledgment of the conditions of painting? "That is where the art comes in," Cavell artfully observes. For a painting to perform an acknowledgment on behalf of all paintings calls for art's spiritual achievement, or magic. When he adds, "And there have always been some men who have been able to acknowledge something that other men accept as true also of them, or that they have to deny," another feature of his understanding of art also becomes clear (110). Because a medium of art provides ways for human beings to make sense, whenever a work of art performs an acknowledgment, and whenever that acknowledgment is itself acknowledged, it is also an instance of a human being performing, and accepting, an acknowledgment. Thus a modernist painting acknowledges not only "what paintings are, but what the painting of them is. At some point the work must be done, given over, the object declared separate from its maker, autonomous" (111).

A modernist painting's acknowledgment of its separateness from its creator is also the artist's acknowledgment of the autonomy of the work he or she has created. The painting's acknowledgment of the conditions of painting is also the artist's acknowledgment that the created object satisfies those conditions, that the artist experiences it *as* a painting. For us to accept this acknowledgment—at once the painting's and the artist's—

is to acknowledge that we, too, experience the object as a painting, hence as a work of art.

Part of Cavell's implication is that art has always been a matter of acknowledgments performed on behalf of others as well as oneself. For example, there have always been painters who acknowledge—whose paintings acknowledge—not the conditions of all paintings, perhaps, but conditions other human beings have had to deny, or else accept as also true of themselves.

There have been figures from religion or politics, too (Martin Luther, Lincoln, and Gandhi come to mind), who have mastered the art of acknowledging things as true for other human beings as well as themselves. There have been artful philosophers who fit this description as well (Kierkegaard, Emerson, Thoreau, Nietzsche, Wittgenstein, Austin, Cavell). And the fact that it is possible for one human being to acknowledge something other human beings have to accept as true of them, or else deny, is the premise of ordinary language philosophy, the philosophical procedures Cavell at once embraced and transformed in *Must We Mean What We Say?* by bringing them to an explicit self-consciousness. A central aspiration of the writing of *The World Viewed* is to acknowledge something other human beings have to deny or accept as true of them, too. (That is where the art comes in.)

For human beings, coming to an understanding is always a matter of acknowledgment. With an echo of Heidegger, Cavell puts it this way: "Acknowledgment is the home of knowledge" (110). For Cavell, art is revelation; it is revelation because it is acknowledgment; being acknowledgment, it is knowledge, of itself and of its world. Art has always revealed acknowledgment to be a necessity of human existence. Cavell speaks of modernist art as "reasserting" this necessity, adding that it is a fact "the remainder of culture is at pains to forget." The necessity of acknowledgment has become hidden in our culture. Thus it is empty, if comforting, "to speak now of modernism as the activity of an *avant-garde*," Cavell argues. That is to envision a conflict between "a coherent culture and a declared and massed enemy; when in fact the case is more like an effort, along blocked paths and hysterical turnings; to hang on to a thread that leads from a lost center to a world lost" (110).

With this formulation, the chapter segues back to its initial reflections on the concept of "total thereness." (It is striking that the line that prompts this transition—"a thread that leads from a lost center to a world lost"—reads precisely like a characterization of the "all-over line" that is the medium Jackson Pollock discovered for acknowledging "total thereness" as a condition of painting. It is as if in casting this line Cavell is reminding us, reminding himself, of his writing's own overall line—all-over line?—of thought. Then is it a feature of Cavell's new medium of philosophy that it, too, can be characterized as "an effort, along blocked paths and hysterical turnings to hang on to a thread that leads from a lost center to a world lost"?) Post-Pollock painting, Cavell points out, employs diverse ways of "acknowledging the condition of painting as total thereness." For example, a painting may acknowledge "its frontedness, or its finitude, or its specific thereness—that is, its presentness; and your accepting it will accordingly mean acknowledging *your* frontedness, or directionality, or verticality toward its world, or any world—or your presentness, in its aspect of absolute hereness and nowness" (110).

Among these possibilities of painting—not particular forms that paintings may take, but particular features of their condition that they may acknowledge—Cavell singles out one quality he describes as "openness achieved through instantaneousness." Speaking of openness achieved through instantaneousness is "a way of characterizing the candid," Cavell observes, adding that the candid has a reverse feature as well, that it must occur "independently of me or any audience, that it must be complete without me, in that sense *closed* to me. This is why candidness in acting was achieved by the actor's complete concentration within the character, absolutely denying any control of my awareness upon him" (111).

It is a condition of all painting, in other words, that a painting is at once completely open and completely closed. For Cavell, it is Morris Louis's work, especially the "Unfurled" series, that most palpably declares this quality of candidness.

> The singular candidness in Louis's Unfurleds has to do with the vast expanse of canvas he has, in candor, left white; not with the sheer fact that it is blank but with the effect upon that blankness of the side falls of colors, which bring the vastness to uncanny incandescence. In achieving these works without the trace of hands or wrists or arms, without muscle—the idea realizing itself—an automatism of canvas and paint . . . is set in motion, admitting an overpowering beauty. I do not wish to exaggerate: only *Sigma* strikes me as of overpowering beauty among the Unfurleds I have seen, though all are beautiful. . . . But to speak of an automatism which admits a sometimes overpowering beauty is a way of characterizing nature. (113)

On the basis of this breathtaking last insight, Cavell argues that works such as Louis's Unfurleds "achieve in unforeseen paths an old wish of romanticism" by imitating "not the *look* of nature, but its conditions, the possibilities of knowing nature at all and of locating ourselves in a world." "For an old romanticist, these conditions would have presented themselves

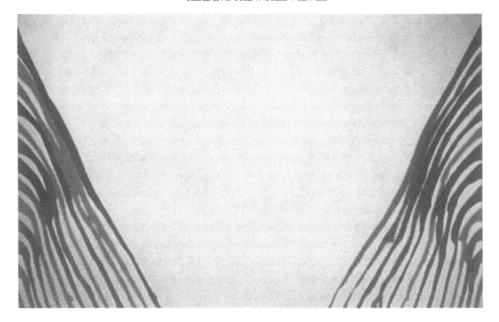

An overpowering beauty. Morris Louis, *Sigma.*

as nature's power of destruction or healing, or its fertility. For the work of the modernists I have in mind, the conditions present themselves as nature's autonomy, self-sufficiency, laws unto themselves. ('Not *how* the world is, but *that* it is, is the Mystical.')" (113).

Cavell follows this quotation of a Wittgenstein epigram with a paragraph that consists of a series of epigrammatic lines of his own, worthy of Thoreau in their seamless joining of poetry and logic, which affirm and embrace the new romanticism, the new faith in nature, of these modernist paintings. Cavell's paragraph itself attains an overpowering beauty, at least at times, as do any number of passages in *The World Viewed* that affirm the aspirations of modernist art. That Cavell chooses such junctures to reveal that his medium of philosophy, too, "admits a sometimes overpowering beauty" underscores that his characterizations of modernist art are also characterizations of his own writing, declarations of faith in its nature-like power to enable us to "locate ourselves in a world" (113).

"This is not a return *to* nature," the paragraph begins, "but the return *of* it," the "release of nature from our private holds." It reasserts that however we may

> choose to parcel or not to parcel nature among ourselves, nature is held—we are held by it—only in common. Its declaration of my absence and of

190

nature's survival of me puts me in mind of origins, and shows me that I am astray. It faces me, draws my limits, and discovers my scale; it fronts me, with whatever wall at my back, and gives me horizon and gravity. It reasserts that, in whatever locale I find myself, I am to locate myself. . . . The faith of this romanticism, overcoming the old, is that we can still be moved to move, that we are free, if we will, to step upon our transport, that nature's absence—or its presence merely to sentiment or mood—is only the history of our turnings from it, in distraction or denial, through history or industry, with words or works. (113–14)

In modernist painting there is no representation of nature, but this does not mean that nature is absent. After all, Cavell astutely observes, "it is not as though we any longer trust or ought so fondly to trust our representations that the absence of them must mean to us the absence of the things represented." Modernist painting declares that the making of representations *of* the world had also become the making of representations *to* the world. (In an elegant Austinian turn, Cavell lists a few of the "causes" there have been "for painting the world": "to appeal, protest, state, claim, assert, judge, comment, notice, witness, accuse, praise, interrogate, pledge, remember, behold" [114].)

That representations *of* the world are also representations *to* the world does not mean, though, that "nature can never really be represented." That would be like saying that "people can never be represented because their representatives are other people." "In both cases faithfulness is required, and objectivity: then the questions are what you are being faithful to, or failing to be faithful to; and on behalf of whom, and to what it is, you appeal and protest; and why and when an objective representation, a likeness, fails to capture your interest in an object or an issue" (115).

There is more than an analogy, Cavell believes, linking representation in painting with representation in politics. It is no accident—such matters are never accidents, in his view—that the concept of representation is applied in both places; it is *justified* in both places. In Cavell's understanding, America's fate, the fate of America's experiment in representative democracy, is bound up with the fate of representation in painting.

At a point in the nineteenth century, Cavell suggests—at the historical moment Thoreau was declaring the American democracy to be in crisis, in fact—painters found that painting's "appeals and protests" had come to be "made on behalf of nobody, to nothing" (115). Nature could no longer be represented because our *distance* from nature could no longer be represented. Our representations had come to distance us from the world, to turn us from it, because the perspective of representation itself

191

"places nature before or away from us, and falsifies our knowledge that we are lost to nature, are absent from it, cannot face it." Perhaps an art that reveals without representation may give us perspective by showing us, for example, "that a painting must be viewed alone, from the one place one occupies at any given time—an acknowledgment not directly that one must view things for oneself, but that one must take them one at a time" (115).

That one must take things one at a time, Cavell suggests, is the meaning of the fact that in the modernist paintings of Pollock, Louis, Noland, Stella, and Olitski "a new medium establishes and is established by a series. Each instance of the medium is an absolute realization of it; each totally eclipses the others" (115).

To speak of the inevitability of a Bach fugue is to praise the particular way Bach worked the theme out; we know it "might have worked out differently, not merely in the sense that other fugues might have been written on the subject, but that *this* one might be more or less otherwise than it is" (115). In contrast to works in a traditional artistic medium, *any* change in a Pollock all-over line painting, a Louis stripe, a Noland chevron, or a Stella Z-form would simply create a new painting.

> If one speaks of a given instance as inevitable, that is no longer a term of praise, but a statement of its existence. These are works every one of whose properties is essential to them. This is the definition of a Leibnizian monad. Like a monad, like the world there is, the only fact about these paintings that does not follow analytically from a complete idea of them is that they exist in space and time. Existence in this world, like the existence of the world itself, is the only contingent fact about them. They are themselves, I feel like saying, contingencies, realizations. (115–16)

Instances of such media are contingencies, realizations, realizations *of* contingency, because nothing but our acceptance of an instance determines whether its series is worth realizing, or how far it is worth it to go on in generating instances. "[W]hen we find that a series is exhausted, it is absolutely past, over. As instances, they declare the evanescence of existence in space and time. (Literal or material objects do not declare evanescence, however transitory they or their arrangement may be. Metaphysically, a pyramid is as evanescent as wrappings are, or as a flash of neon.)" (116).

Cavell is well aware that there are people who deny that any object "the actual making of which is so unimportant could conceivably bear the major importance we have attached to works of art" (116). These paintings "look as if they might as well have been made instantaneously, and that their use should take no longer. But the fact about an instance, when it happens, is that it poses a permanent beauty, if we are capable of it."

With this last remark Cavell begins a meditation on the significance of beauty in modernist painting that is, not coincidentally, one of *The World Viewed*'s most beautiful passages. An instance, Cavell says, "poses a permanent beauty" *when it happens*, that is, when the *instance* happens (if it happens to be a beautiful one). However, an instance happens only "if we are capable of it"—capable of accepting it *as* an instance of a series that establishes and is established by a medium of the art of painting. *What* happens when an instance happens (if it happens to be beautiful) is that it "poses a permanent beauty."

Cavell's next line ("That *this* simultaneity should proffer beauty is a declaration about beauty . . ." [116]) invites us retroactively to read the word "poses" (in "poses a permanent beauty") in its sense of "posits" or "proffers." But why choose the evocative word "poses" if not also to intimate that an instance poses a beauty in the sense that a traditional painter or still photographer poses a subject? (A painting's nature, Cavell has argued, is to be at once completely open and completely closed. Is it any wonder that its candor is also a pose?) In the case of the beauty that an instance poses, though, there is this striking feature: It is the instance itself that simultaneously poses the beauty and is the beauty posed.

Apart from the contingency of this instance's happening, which is itself contingent on our accepting it *as* an instance, the beauty posed by an instance has no realization—no existence in space and time—at all. *This* particular beauty is realized in no other instance. Yet the realization of this instance is precisely the realization of the contingency of its existence. This realization *is* the beauty the instance poses.

Thus Cavell insists, however paradoxical it may sound, that the beauty an instance poses (when it happens, if we are capable of it) is a *permanent* beauty. The beauty it poses is an essential feature of such an instance; that it happens to exist, that it is in space and time, is a mere contingency. Like a Leibnizian monad, like the world as a whole, the instance is not literally *in* space and time; evanescence is not essential to it. That is why it is capable of *declaring* the evanescence of existence in space and time as no "literal" or "material" object can.

> That *this* simultaneity should proffer beauty is a declaration about beauty: that it is no more temporary than the world is; that there is no physical assurance of its permanence; that it is momentary only the way time is, a regime of moments; and that no moment is to dictate its significance to us, if we are to claim autonomy, to become free. Acceptance of such objects achieves the

absolute acceptance of the moment, by defeating the sway of the momentous. It is an ambition worthy of the highest art. (116)

To accept this object *as* an instance of a series that establishes and is established by a medium of the art of painting is at once to acknowledge its significance and to acknowledge that this significance is not dictated to us. It is to acknowledge that we are, in this instance, free. But since every instance excludes every other, and since no instance makes up for another, our freedom is born of loss.

> Nothing is of greater moment than the knowledge that the choice of one moment excludes another, that no moment makes up for another, that the significance of one moment is the cost of what it forgoes. That is refinement. Beauty and significance, except in youth, are born of loss. But otherwise everything is lost. . . . The only return on becoming adult, the only justice in forgoing that world of possibility, is the reception of actuality—the pain and balm in the truth of the only world: that it exists, and I in it. (117)

Thus this meditation on beauty culminates, appropriately, with Cavell's revision—modernist painting's revision—of the Cartesian "*Cogito ergo sum*" ("I think, therefore I am"). Descartes believed that on the basis of the *cogito* he could prove, beyond the possibility of doubt, that the world exists. For Cavell, the problem in our relationship to the world is not that we lack certainty of its existence; what is lacking is not a matter of certainty, it is a matter of acknowledgment. To accept this object *as* an instance of a series that establishes and is established by a medium of the art of painting, to acknowledge the permanent beauty it poses (if it poses beauty), is to acknowledge that the world exists and that we exist in it. "In its absolute difference and absolute connection with others, each instance of a series maintains the haecceity (the sheer that-ness) of a material object, without the need of its substance. . . . I must respond to it, if I am to know it, by acknowledging my own haecceity" (117).

Roughly, what Cavell is here calling "haecceity" is what elsewhere he calls "presentness." So to accept an instance as an instance is to acknowledge its presentness, its acknowledgment that presentness is a condition of all painting. To acknowledge its presentness, we must respond to this instance by acknowledging our own presentness. That is why, in accepting this instance *as* an instance, we are acknowledging the existence of the world and of ourselves in it. This is the crucial point Cavell teases into the splendidly paradoxical-sounding revision of the Cartesian *cogito*, "My existence is inescapable from my presentness" (117).

■ ■

After "the failure of representations to depict our conviction and connect-edness with the world," these paintings "retain the power of art." They "overcome the representativeness which came between our reality and our art" by

> abstracting us from the recognitions and engagements and complicities and privileged appeals and protests which distracted us from one another and from the world we have constructed. . . . Not catching our attention yet again, but forming it again. Giving us again the capacity for appeal and for protest, for contemplation and for knowledge and praise, by drawing us back from private and empty assertion. These works exist as abstracts of intimacy—declaring our common capacity and need for presentness. . . . They represent existence without assertion, authority without authorization; truth without claim, which you can walk in. It is out of such a vision that Thoreau in *Walden* ("The Pond in Winter") speaks of nature as silent. (117–18)

These modernist paintings are born of our loss of our natural habitation within the world. They reawaken, and satisfy in the abstract, our longing for "clear separateness and singleness and connection, for horizons and uprightness and frontedness, for the simultaneity of a world, for openness and resolution" (118). They pose permanent beauties, but they remain abstractions. The perspective they give us, apart from *these* instances, has not, at least as yet, brought us—brought America, brought the world—closer to our heart's desire. "Is the power of representation otherwise irretrievable? Is there no way to declare again the content of nature, not merely its conditions; to speak again from one's plight into the heart of a known community of which one is a known member, not merely to speak of the terms on which any human existence is given?" (118).

These are fateful questions, and Cavell does not claim to answer them here. He responds to them by quoting two more questions as hauntingly posed by Thoreau. These questions enable Chapter 15 to close on a note of muted, yet fervent, hope. " 'Who knows what the human body would expand and flow out to under a more genial heaven?' 'Who knows what sort of life would result if we had attained to purity?' " (118).

VII

■ ■ ■ ■

Chapters 16–18:
Film and Theatricality

AT THIS POINT in *The World Viewed*, it remains a standing question how film can for so long have avoided the fate of modernism, for so long maintained its continuities of audiences and genres without assuming the serious burden of justifying its existence as an art. Apart from the wish for selfhood (hence the always simultaneous granting of otherness as well), art is merely exhibition, in Cavell's view. Then the question of how film for so long avoided modernism is inseparable from the question of how the traditional media of movies for so long appeared to satisfy our wish for selfhood.

In Chapter 16, Cavell gives a deceptively simple answer to this standing question, one which leads to the thought that we now have a new sense of film, a sense that movies now need to acknowledge something about their making.

Chapter 17 directly addresses two of *The World Viewed*'s central questions: How, specifically, are movies questioning themselves, and what specifically requires acknowledgment in their making?

Chapter 18, the book's penultimate chapter, begins by announcing that in it Cavell is collecting some uses of the devices or techniques that it has become fashionable to use in ways that betray film's promise to allow the world to exhibit itself. The thrust of Chapter 18 is that these devices also *can* be used to keep faith with film's promise. Cavell uses these examples to illustrate some of the general principles about art and language, explicitly articulated in *Must We Mean What We Say?*, that underwrite *The World Viewed*. He also uses those general principles to illuminate particular aesthetic possibilities specific to film.

Chapter 16: "Exhibition and Self-Reference"

In Cavell's understanding, the wish for selfhood is inseparable from the wish for presentness. Chapter 16 argues that modernism's "quest for presentness . . . arises with the growing autonomy of art (from religious and political and class service)." That quest "is set by the increasing nakedness of exhibition as the condition for viewing a work of art." Increasingly, *all* artists can do with their works is to exhibit them. To the extent that "the fact of exhibition takes precedence over the quality and meaning of the object exhibited," art forgoes "all hope for acknowledgment by and of the self" (120).

An art in such a condition cannot justify its existence without *overcoming* this "shadowing of seriousness with exhibition." Modernist painting, for example, had to learn to "close the remove of our vision from its object, to stand the self within the self again so that it may bear again the world's gaze," as Cavell evocatively puts it, summing up these facts by saying that painting, like religion, had to "learn to defeat theater" (120–21). Thus the modernist paintings Chapter 15 cites establish their right to be exhibited and viewed as examples of the *art* of painting by candidly declaring their total presentness and acknowledging it as a condition of all painting.

This line of thought enables Cavell to give a deceptively simple answer to his standing question of how film can have avoided modernism for so long. Film was able to avoid modernism's "perplexities of consciousness, its absolute condemnation to seriousness," because it avoided the "shadowing of seriousness by exhibition" that in arts like painting prompted the emergence of modernism in the first place (122). Film was able to avoid this because successions of automatic world projections are quite simply not exhibited. Unlike paintings, movies are "distributed and screened and viewed," which is why film never had to learn to defeat the theatricality inherent in exhibition. Movies do not have to "establish presentness to and of the world: the world is there. They do not have to deny or confront their audiences: they are screened. And they do not have to defeat or declare the artist's presence: the object was always out of his hands" (118).

On the other hand, paintings are capable of defeating theater by declaring their total presentness, but film cannot defeat theater that way. Movies are not objects capable of declaring their total presentness because, unlike paintings, they are quite simply not totally present (the world is present *in* them), and because movies are not objects at all. Movies are quite simply not representations either. The modernist paintings cited in Chapter 15 achieve an art that reveals without representation and thereby overcomes the theatricality inherent in representation. For media based upon successions of automatic world projections, revealing without representation is not an artistic achievement. Film automatically overcomes the theatricality inherent in representation, just as it automatically overcomes the theatricality inherent in exhibition.

Film also automatically overcomes what in Chapter 13 Cavell calls the "inherent theatricality of the (still) photograph." Captured unaware, frozen in poses beyond our or their control, the subjects of still photographs are denied spontaneity. Still photographs dramatize their subjects, invest them with depth, by imposing a "foreign animation"—a life not their own—on their faces and bodies. ("Artistry here," Cavell shrewdly notes, "must come to terms with this condition, exploit this new assertion of theatrical depth, explore the condition of capture itself—in order to discover what will register as candor and what instantaneousness can reveal of character and of the relation of character to its locale.") Movies do not impose a "foreign animation" on their subjects. Movies grant their subjects dramatic life, grant them depth and individuality, by an animation that *is* their own. "In motion, the photographic subject is released again," as Cavell puts it (adding, suggestively, "or the viewer is released, in the face of a presenting of the past, from the links of nostalgia" [119]).

As earlier chapters of *The World Viewed* have amply made clear, Cavell does not believe that movies are altogether released from theatricality, however. In film, another region of theatricality "overtakes the image: the presenting of the past world becomes a presentation of it. Instead of being caught in a pose, the subject is cast in a type. The maker of films has then to find media within which types can project the world's presentness" (119).

In Chapter 17, Cavell will argue that now that we are losing conviction in the traditional media of movies, film's presenting of the past world is being overtaken by theatricality in a new way. His point here is to reiterate that movies have always been theatrical. Movies traditionally relied on theater by casting their human subjects as—revealing them to be—types. The types around which the traditional media of movies revolve, individuals present in the projected world and thus able to "project the world's presentness," have their own ways of taking reality theatrically. That their modes of theatricality are internal to their ways of being in the world does not make them any less theatrical.

198

Traditional movies, which rely on the inherent theatricality of types, are no less theatrical than representational paintings or still photographs, in other words. They simply rely on theatricality in different ways, rely on different modes of theatricality. If our recent loss of conviction in the traditional media of movies is a loss of conviction in the types around which these media revolve, as Chapter 13 argues, our loss of conviction in these types is also a loss of conviction in their modes of theatricality, the forms of drama they once appeared naturally to incarnate.

The fact that traditional movies rely on types in projecting the presentness of the world reminds us, first, that film enables the presentness of the world *to be* projected. Movies do not have to establish the world's presentness, the way painting does: The world is simply there. Second, it reminds us that projection is the condition of the presentness of the world on film. In movies, the world's presentness can only be projected; it cannot be established.

This latter fact brings home to us that movies, in Cavell's punning formulation, take "our very distance and powerlessness over the world as the condition of the world's natural appearance" (119). Because we are displaced from it, because we are powerless to control it, the world on film can seem both to appear *naturally* (we do not question its existence) and to appear *natural* (as it is in itself, candid). Film promises "the exhibition of the world in itself. This is its promise of candor: that what it reveals is entirely what is revealed to it, that nothing revealed by the world in its presence is lost" (119).

In "More of *The World Viewed*," Cavell seems to misremember this passage when he refers to it as being about "the fate of the camera as revealing all and only what is revealed to it" (*WV*, 184). The subject of these sentences is film, not the camera, and the passage speaks about film's promise, not its fate. What accounts for this slip in "More of *The World Viewed*," perhaps, is the fact that in the original passage there is a shift of subject that its wording does not explicitly register. In "It promises the exhibition of the world in itself" and "This is its promise of candor," film— the medium of film, the material basis of the media of movies—is the "it." But what film reveals is everything that was revealed to the camera. The camera is the "it" in whose presence nothing revealed by the world is lost.

The camera is only a machine that does all and only what it is made to do. In Cavell's understanding, revealing what is revealed to it is not the camera's promise (a machine is not capable of making, or breaking, promises), but the camera's fate, what it cannot but do (when it is made to do it). As "More of *The World Viewed*" makes explicit, the fate of the camera (mythologically, as it were) is twofold. First, the camera "has no choice either over what is revealed to it nor over what it reveals." Second (and herein lies the camera's mystery), "you cannot know what you have made the camera do, what is revealed to it, until its results have appeared" (*WV,* 184).

By contrast, Cavell understands the exhibition of the world in itself to be, not the fate of the medium of film, but its promise. Of course, for candor to be film's promise, it must be within film's power *not* to be candid (there is no such thing as a promise that cannot be broken). Film's power to break its promise of candor, its power to theatricalize reality no less than its promise to exhibit the world as it candidly is, resides in the fate of the camera to reveal what is revealed to it. Indeed, as we have seen, Cavell believes the world presented by traditional movies, reality as it candidly reveals itself on film, has always been reality dramatized. Hence the presenting itself has always been theatrical ("The presenting of the past world becomes a presentation of it"). But now film is being overtaken by a new theatricalizing of its images, a theatricality that calls into question film's continued existence as an art.

All this is perplexing. So it is not surprising that Cavell voices his perplexity by posing to himself a perplexing question: "Am I saying that everything revealed by film is true?" (120).

To be sure, Cavell *is* claiming that everything revealed by film has been revealed to the camera, revealed by the world in the camera's presence. And there is no such thing as a revelation that is not true (if it is not true, it is not truly a revelation, not a true revelation). Thus, Cavell can hardly deny that everything revealed on film is true. He also can hardly deny that there are obscurities, mysteries, in this truth. (It is obscure, for example, what is to *count* as a revelation.) So Cavell, in Wittgensteinian fashion, continues to act as his own interlocutor by posing to himself another perplexing question: "Then why, say, does Steichen take a thousand various pictures of the same cup and saucer?" (120).

Cavell knows full well that there are significant differences between still photography (which is inherently theatrical) and film (which overcomes the inherent theatricality of still photographs only to be overtaken by theatricality in a different way). He also knows that there are significant differences between the questions "Is everything revealed by still photography true?" and "Is everything revealed by film true?" (For example, everything revealed about their subject by still photographs of Humphrey Bogart is true about that flesh-and-blood human being—about Humphrey Bogart as he *was,* that is—while everything revealed by Bogart movies about their star is true about a mythical type who is and is not—and never simply was—the flesh-and-blood Humphrey Bogart.) Yet Cavell's question about Edward Steichen's exercise is no non-sequitur. The still camera does share the fate of the movie camera to reveal what is revealed to it, and Steichen's still photographs of one cup and saucer do promise the exhibition of the world in itself.

"More of *The World Viewed*" amplifies on Steichen's exercise. Each shot "has a different physiognomy," Cavell notes. "But do what he will—change lenses, use different film or filters, vary the lighting, the angle, the distance—it is still the same cup and saucer. Therein lies the fascination of the thing of photography"—the fascination of things as they appear in photographs; the fascination of the thing called "photography"—"like the fascination in faces. The art of the thing"—photography's "art of the thing"; the art of the thing called "photography"—"lies in the capacity for finding what will cause what, and for finding what is wanted" (*WV*, 186).

One truth revealed in Steichen's myriad photographs of one cup and saucer is the subject's capacity to reveal so many "faces" to the camera. As Cavell puts it, Steichen "will not assume that we know beforehand how few or many revelations the truth will take, or how any may be made" (120). A photographic subject is in principle capable of any number of revelations; we can never be certain that it has been *completely* revealed, that no further revelations can be forthcoming. Nonetheless, at some point Steichen finally stops shooting the cup and saucer, finally is satisfied that "the truth" about this subject has been revealed. Cavell's point is, first, that the photographer insists on the right to judge for himself when a subject has been fully revealed, revealed to his satisfaction, a judgment he can make only in view of the photographs he has already taken. Second, that each time a photographer takes a new shot, he has no way of knowing beforehand—before viewing the resulting photograph, that is—what new revelation, if any, the shot is fated to make (again: "You cannot know what you have made the camera do, what is revealed to it, until its results have appeared"). As Cavell puts it in "More of *The World Viewed*,"

> The mysteriousness of the photograph lies not in the machinery which produces it, but in the unfathomable abyss between what it captures (its subject) and what is captured for us (*this* fixing of the subject), the metaphysical wait between exposure and exhibition, the absolute authority or finality of the fixed image. . . . Film turns our epistemological convictions inside out: reality is known before its appearances are known. (185)

Steichen can no more know beforehand how many shots it will take to reveal in full this cup and saucer's powers of revelation, or what, if anything, *this* shot will reveal, than Morris Louis can know beforehand how many instances it will take for the Unfurled series to be exhausted, or what particular beauty, if any, *this* instance will pose. Hence from these artists' very different projects Cavell draws essentially the same philosophical moral. Chapter 15 puts it this way: "No moment is to dictate its significance to us, if we are to claim autonomy, to become free." Chapter 16 words it only slightly differently: "The world has to be told not to dictate what we are to say about it, or when we have something to say, or from what angle and in what light and for how long" (120).

Again, the revelations in Steichen's photographs are not dictated *to* Steichen *by* the cup and saucer. Neither does Steichen dictate *to* the cup and saucer what revelations, if any, they are to make. What is revealed in these photographs is what this cup and saucer have revealed to the camera; in the photographs, the cup and saucer speak for themselves, reveal their own powers of revelation. Yet it is only the resulting photographs that are capable of revealing, to Steichen or to us, what this subject is capable of revealing to the camera. What is revealed *in* these photographs is also what is revealed *by* them, in other words. In these photographs, by these photographs, a medium's powers of revelation, too, are revealed. But it is the photographer who has chosen this subject, lens, and film stock, chosen to shoot from these angles, in these lighting conditions, at these exposures and shutter speeds. In—by—these photographs, Steichen is also spoken for. That is, he acknowledges their medium as his own. (He is, after all, one of its presiding geniuses.)

■ ■

For modern human beings like us, the achievement of freedom is still possible, but to be free we must *claim* our freedom, must *claim* our right to speak in our own voice, neither dictating to the world nor dictated by it. This is one of Cavell's bedrock philosophical principles. In Chapter 15, he speaks of the modernist painting that affirms this principle as thereby exemplifying a new romanticism. Perhaps we may extend this term to Cavell's modernist practice of philosophy, too, which aspires at once to inherit and to overcome a romantic tradition whose own aspiration is to inherit and overcome the history of Western philosophy and art out of which it emerged. That *The World Viewed* aspires at once to inherit and overcome traditional romanticism is the key to Cavell's virtuoso segue from his remarks about the Steichen project to the passage that follows, one of his inimitable sweeping summations of the history of Western thought:

> Descartes finds the possibility of error in the will's freedom to overreach our position; freedom is the price, and sets the task, of knowledge. A few years later, Milton found the possibility of error to be the price, and to set the task, of freedom. By the end of the next century, Kant's problem was not to check the will within God's ordinance, but to keep nature from swamping it. Hegel wished to ride it on the back of history. Romantics still shift between paralysis and omnipotence. (120)

The unstated implication of this grand passage is that Cavell's own practice of philosophy—in its refusal of knowledge that is not a mode of acknowledgment, its insistence that selfhood cannot be achieved apart from the simultaneous acknowledgment of otherness, its affirmation that self and world must not dictate to each other—exemplifies the new romanticism. At one level, the passage embeds a claim about the writing of *The World Viewed* itself, a claim that resonates deeply with one of the book's central claims about film, most explicitly stated in "More of *The World Viewed*" in a line we have already had reason to quote: "Film turns our epistemological convictions inside out: Reality is known before its appearances are known."

Acknowledging its romanticism, *The World Viewed* also confesses a doubt. If its claim to overcome (and not merely inherit) traditional romanticism is denied, the writing of *The World Viewed* will be condemned to the traditional romantic's fate of shifting desperately between paralysis and omnipotence. Thus the writing of *The World Viewed* mirrors what Chapter 17 will speak of as film's "growing doubt of its ability to allow the world as a whole to exhibit itself."

■ ■

As Cavell insists, movies are not exhibited, they are distributed and screened and viewed. What is presented *in* movies, by movies—at least, this is film's promise—is the world in itself—"*That* thing *now*, in the frame of nature, the world moving in the branch." When Cavell adds, "We are told that people seeing the first moving pictures were amazed . . . as if by the novelty," his surprising implication is that the amazement moving pictures originally engendered had nothing to do with novelty. Indeed, there was nothing novel about workers leaving factories, say, or trains pulling into stations. "The world moving in the branch" has always been readily available for us to view. It has always been open to human beings

203

to attend to, take an interest in, our experience of "that thing now, in the frame of nature." Thus if movies have been losing their power to amaze us, as Cavell believes they have, "it is not novelty that has worn off, but our interest in our own experience" (122).

> Movies *can* still "work their original fortune." That is why most good movies are still largely traditional—but not all good movies, and the traditions are borne uneasily. Our sudden storms of flash insets and freeze frames and slow-motion and telescope-lens shots and fast cuts and negative printing and blurred focusings . . . are responses to an altered sense of film, a sense that film has brought itself into question and must be questioned and openly confessed. (122–23)

And it is around this point that Cavell is led to pose two of *The World Viewed*'s central questions: "How, specifically, are movies questioning themselves, and what specifically requires acknowledgment in their making?" Chapter 17 will begin to answer these questions. The remainder of Chapter 16 approaches them indirectly by examining what Cavell calls a "habitual answer," one he finds wanting. That answer begins with the idea that "the way for a work to acknowledge itself is to refer to itself" (123).

Cavell recognizes that there is something valid in the notion of self-reference in this context, namely its recognition that "the artist's self-consciousness has come between his conviction and his work, between himself and the conventions (automatisms) he relied upon, forcing him to justify his works even as he performs them" (123). Yet he remarks, with barely restrained contempt, that "stranded upon" this notion Mallarmé and Joyce Kilmer are indistinguishable. And there is a "specific emptiness" to the idea that movies can acknowledge our "altered sense of film" simply by performing self-referential gestures. "The specific emptiness of the notion here is its forgetfulness of film's early capacities for self-reference, both by alluding to other movies and by calling attention to the camera at hand" (124).

Reiterating a point made in the Preface, Cavell's intuition is that the capacity for self-reference is *internal* to the traditional media of movies. This means that "the allusions to Hollywood films in the films of French New Wave directors are not simple acts of piety toward a tradition they admire, but claims to be a continuation of that tradition" (124). It also means that self-reference is not in itself an acknowledgment of our "altered sense of film," our sense that film has now brought itself into question and must be questioned and openly confessed.

Indeed, self-referential gestures may or may not be acknowledgments at all. If you are acknowledging that you have not done what

204

you promised you would do, you would say, or begin by saying, something like "I know I promised. . . ." As Cavell observes, the general form of an acknowledgment is "I know I [promised, am withdrawn, let you down . . .]" (123). In such a formulation, the "I" does not *refer* to the self. For "an acknowledgment is an act of the self (if it is one of recognition, then it is not like recognizing a place but like recognizing a government)." An acknowledgment cannot be performed "apart from an admission of the existence of others (denial of which made the acknowledgment necessary) or apart from an expression of one's aliveness to that denial (the revelation in acknowledgment)." From these facts, Cavell draws the conclusion that "self-reference is no more an assurance of candor in movies than in any other human undertaking." Apart from acknowledgment—"apart from an admission of the existence of others (denial of which made the acknowledgment necessary) or apart from an expression of one's aliveness to that denial (the revelation in acknowledgment)"—self-reference in art, like art itself, has no value. Apart from acknowledgment, self-referential gestures are mere exhibitions of the self (123–24).

As Cavell points out, it is a striking feature of self-referential instances in traditional movies that their effect is comic. He cites, for example, "Katharine Hepburn in *The Philadelphia Story* walking abstractedly through a room, cradling a sheaf of long-stemmed flowers, saying aloud to no one in particular, 'The calla lilies are in bloom again' (see *Stage Door*)." He also cites "Cary Grant's response, upon being introduced to Ralph Bellamy in *His Girl Friday*, 'Haven't we met someplace before?' (they had, in the same juxtaposition of roles, a couple of years earlier in *The Awful Truth*)" (125).[32] This feature is confirmed, Cavell argues, by "extendedly reflexive" movies like W. C. Fields's *Never Give a Sucker an Even Break* and Buster Keaton's *Sherlock, Jr.* Chapter 16 ends with a set of remarks about the "comedy of self-reference" these films exemplify.

Earlier in Chapter 16, Cavell argued that vaudeville, rather than assuming the modernist burden of overcoming the condition of theatrical performance "in which the fact of exhibition takes precedence over the quality and meaning of the thing exhibited," makes that condition laughable (122). These extendedly reflexive film comedies—not coincidentally created by former vaudevillians —likewise do not assume modernism's "burden of seriousness." Rather than trying to prove film's capacity for seriousness, they satirize the condition of movies—our condition, as movies reveal it—that "we are at the mercy of what the medium captures of us, and of what it chooses, or refuses, to hold for us" (126).

For example, in the "virtuoso passage in which Keaton dreams of himself as the great sleuth repeatedly undone by shifting scene placements," the comedy arises "first from a transgression of . . . conditions upon which coherent narration in film has depended. Beyond that, reversing the old idea that laughter is a burst of danger miraculously escaped, *Sherlock, Jr.* [projects] dangers which the new art miraculously creates" (125). Keaton uses "the fact that in film anything can follow anything, and any place any other place," to show "our lack of control over both fantasy and reality—above all, our helplessness to align them."

In *Never Give a Sucker an Even Break*, "at some point in the back-and-forth between Fields's reading of his script to Franklin Pangborn and the projected visualizations of it," it dawns on us "that what Fields has in his hands is the whole film we are seeing, including his readings and Pangborn's heavenly exasperations" (125). That is, Fields uses the fact that we are suckers for movies, that "there is nothing beyond the power of film to make us accept," to show that suckerhood is our general condition. In satirizing the fact that we are suckers for movies, these comedies of self-reference satirize "the effort to escape the self by viewing it," Cavell argues. They mock the idea that "there is a position from which to rest assured once and for all of the truth of your views" (126). They make laughable the notion that film can prove its seriousness simply by referring to itself.

If movies stop playing us for suckers, how can they declare their seriousness? How can movies acknowledge our "altered sense of film," our sense that "film has brought itself into question and must be questioned and openly confessed"? (123). And "how, specifically, are movies questioning themselves, and what specifically requires acknowledgment in their making?" Chapter 17 undertakes to answer these questions directly.

Chapter 17: "The Camera's Implication"

"One can feel," Chapter 17 begins, "that there is always a camera left out of the picture: the one working now" (126). At any ordinary moment of movie-viewing, it would seem, a camera *is* left out of the picture—the camera whose view this projected image is. It is possible to imagine another projected image which includes that camera, but unless that image includes the reflection in a mirror of the camera "working now," it would seem that it, too, leaves a camera out. What would indicate, in any case, that the camera in the mirror is the camera whose view we are viewing?—Hence the "always" in the formulation "One can feel that there is always a camera left out of the picture."

Cavell's next sentence—"When my limitation to myself feels like a limitation of myself, it seems that I am always leaving something unsaid; as it were, the saying is left out"—stakes out an analogy, central to the chapter, between one's relationship to one's words and the camera's relationship to its subject (126).

Whenever one says anything, one can feel that one is leaving something unsaid: the saying itself, as it were—one's saying of these words, now, for one's own private reasons. "I want my words to *happen* to me," Cavell writes (126). But one has to *say* everything one says; one is limited to oneself in one's use of language. The feeling that one is always leaving something—the crucial thing—unsaid arises when one's limitation *to* oneself feels like a limitation *of* oneself. It is then that one feels doomed to insincerity, that "human existence is metaphysically dishonest." Analogously, Cavell implies, one feels that movies are always leaving a camera out of the picture on occasions when the camera's limitation to itself—to its view of its subject—feels like a limitation *of* the camera. On such occasions, film's ontology seems to doom it to insincerity, too.

The camera's subject is in the world, of the world; whatever is in its frame at any given moment, the camera's subject is always also the world as a whole. When Cavell sums up the underlying analogy by saying "The camera is outside its subject as I am outside my language," a thrust of his formulation is that one's language and the camera's subject—the world— are *wholes* (127).

Every word one says has meanings known to all who understand one's language. Yet what one word means cannot be separated—logically, grammatically—from the meanings of all the words of one's language. That one is outside one's language means that one is outside, separate from, the words one says at any particular moment. It also means that one is outside one's language as a whole, that one's language *is* a whole, separate from oneself, complete unto itself, complete without oneself in it.

To make an assertion about something in the world is also to make an assertion about the world as a whole; to make an assertion *about* the world is to make an assertion *of* the world. To be outside one's language means to be outside the world of one's assertion. And it means that saying one's words places them in the world, where they may be shared by others who understand the public meaning of one's words.

Although the words of one's language have public meanings, one attaches private meanings to words by saying them. That one is outside one's language is what makes it possible to speak insincerely, without acknowledging one's private reasons for saying those words on that occasion.

It is also what makes candor possible—what enables one to *mean* one's words, to allow the words one says to acknowledge one's private reasons for saying them. As Cavell succinctly puts it, "The abyss of ready insincerity is fixed, but that is what makes truthfulness possible—and virtuous" (127). One's limitation to oneself in one's use of language is *not* a limitation of oneself, or of one's language; it is a condition of the possibility of one's using language at all. One sometimes feels that everything one says leaves something crucial unsaid, yet human existence is *not* metaphysically dishonest.

The camera is a machine. By itself, it is not capable of asserting anything, but it is capable of being *used* to make assertions about the world, to allow the world to assert itself. More precisely, it is capable of being used to make revelations about the world, to allow the world to reveal itself. That the camera is outside its subject means it is outside, separate from, the persons or things in its frame at any given moment. It also means the camera is outside the world on film as a whole, that the world that reveals itself on film is separate from the camera. The camera occupies a position outside the world on film; the world that reveals itself on film, that reveals itself to *be* the camera's subject, is complete unto itself, complete without the camera in it.

The camera's position, Chapter 16 argues, is not one from which one can rest assured of the truth of one's views. And yet, insofar as the camera *is* outside its subject, insofar as it *does* occupy a position outside the world on film, the camera's views cannot but be truthful (as, in effect, Chapter 16 also argues). The camera can also be used untruthfully, as it were, but only when it is used in a way that fails to keep film's promise to allow the world to reveal itself; fails to acknowledge that its subject is a subject, that the world is capable of revealing itself on film; fails to allow there to *be* a world on film, a world complete without the camera in it. When the camera is used in a way that allows film to keep its promise to reveal the world in itself, the camera is not left out of the picture. The "picture" is complete without the camera in it.

That one is outside one's language is not a state of affairs that could be otherwise. It is a condition of the possibility of using language at all, as we have said. That the camera is outside its world is a condition of film's existence as an art, a condition of the media of movies. Film is no more metaphysically dishonest than language is. For film, as for language, "The abyss of ready insincerity is fixed, but that is what makes truthfulness possible—and virtuous."

One wants one's words simply to happen to one, but when one says one's words, one is responsible to—responsible for—one's private reasons for saying just those words just then. The revelations presented on film simply happen to the camera—but only if the filmmaker uses the camera in ways that allow the exhibition of the world in itself to happen. Film, like language, has a public aspect. But filmmakers have their private reasons— their reasons for allowing, or not allowing, the world to reveal itself on film. For film as for language "publicness is a shared responsibility; if what we share is superficial, that is also our responsibility" (127). Filmmakers are not responsible for the ways we view. They *are* responsible for the private meanings they attach to the world by allowing it to exhibit itself.

Cavell notes that such issues of responsibility "arise most explicitly in documentary films," but that "the distinction between documenting and narrating blurs here as elsewhere." The documentary filmmaker, the passage continues, naturally

> feels the impulse to make his presence known to his audience, as if to justify his intrusion upon his subject. But this is a guilty impulse, produced, it may be, by the filmmaker's denial of the only thing that really matters: that the subject be allowed to reveal itself. The denial may be in spirit or in fact an unwillingness to see what is revealed or an inability to wait for its revelation. (127)

It is insofar as it fulfills its promise to allow the world to reveal itself, of course, that film blurs the "distinction between documenting and narrating." Allowing film to keep that promise is the "only thing that really matters," in Cavell's view. A filmmaker cannot justify intruding upon his subject by declaring the camera's presence to the audience, for it is only insofar as the filmmaker fails to allow the subject to reveal itself that there is an "intrusion" to justify.

A subject's revelations to the camera are also revelations of—by—the camera. This means that whenever it is allowed to do its work of allowing the world to reveal itself, the camera reveals itself as well. Only by revealing itself *in* its work can the camera *do* its work.

To allow a subject to reveal itself to the camera, the filmmaker must allow that subject complete freedom to make any and all revelations about itself, freedom to reveal itself completely. The filmmaker must allow the camera, too, complete freedom to reveal itself, freedom to reveal itself completely. "The only justification for the knowledge of others is the willingness for complete knowledge," Cavell writes. "That is the justice of knowledge. Your position in this is no more localizable beforehand than the knowledge itself is" (128–29). You cannot be willing to know another human being without being willing to know that other completely; you cannot be willing to know that other completely without being willing to know his or her relationship to you; you cannot be willing to know another's relationship to you without being willing to know your relationship to that other; you cannot be willing to know your relationship to another without being willing to know yourself completely.

"If the presence of the camera is to be made known, it has to be acknowledged in the work it does," Cavell goes on, his formulation implying at once that the camera's work is *what* has to be acknowledged and that it has to be acknowledged *by* the work the camera does, by the shown film itself. "This is the seriousness of all the shakings and turnings and zoomings and reinings and unkind cuts to which it has lately been impelled. But then why isn't the projected image itself a sufficient acknowledgment? Surely we are not in doubt that it comes by way of a camera" (128).

We are ordinarily *not* in doubt that the projected image "comes by way of a camera." If we really doubted this, how could any number of "shakings and turnings and zoomings and reinings and unkind cuts" make us certain? Indeed, as Cavell shrewdly argues, the projected image itself is ordinarily the most complete *possible* evidence of the camera's presence.

It is another question whether the projected image makes the camera's presence known, makes the camera itself known, makes known what is present when the camera is present. In Cavell's understanding, whether a projected image makes the camera's presence known hinges on whether it is an adequate acknowledgment *by* the camera of the work *of* the camera.

What is an adequate acknowledgment?

> Knowing your claim to an acknowledgment from me, I may be baffled by the demand you make for some special voicing of the acknowledgment. . . . Why am I called upon to *do* something, to say specific things that will add up to an explicit revelation? Because what is to be acknowledged is always something specifically done or not done; the exact instance of my denial of you. The particular hurt or crudity or selfishness or needfulness or hatred or longing that separates us must be given leave to declare our separateness, hence the possibility of our connection. It is balm but it must still touch the wound. (128)

If we now have a new sense of film, as *The World Viewed* claims, a sense that movies now need to acknowledge something about their making, that "something" cannot be the mere fact of the camera's presence. That is why it is not enough for the camera to tip its hand. Movies now have to acknowledge something about what the camera's presence comes to, what the camera is, the mysterious work it does.

"Mere declaration of your presence is specifically called for in cases of physical concealment or emotional withdrawal," Cavell reminds us. When he then poses the question "Is that the state the camera now finds itself in—concealed, or withdrawn?" his implied answer is negative (129–30).

—The camera is *not* ordinarily concealed from us. Again, the shown film itself is ordinarily the most complete possible evidence of the camera's presence at the time of filming. And at the time of projection, although the camera is not ordinarily in our presence, neither is it concealed from us.

—Nor is the camera ordinarily concealed from its subjects. To be sure, they cannot know what revelations the camera will make about them. Even if, while filming, you "project what you're taking on a screen in full view of your subjects so that they can see and respond to the image as it is taken from them," they cannot know what their responses will reveal (130). True, Cavell goes on to invoke the idea that what is unknown to the camera's subjects is "the secret of the camera's presence, the foreign animation it imposes upon them" (130). He is only entertaining this formulation, however, not endorsing it. He cannot be endorsing it, first, because although the camera's fate of revealing all and only what is revealed to it—hence of concealing all and only what is concealed from it, it might be added—makes its work mysterious, that mystery is not a secret concealed from its subjects, not something the camera is capable of revealing by declaring its presence. Second, the camera imposes a foreign animation on its subjects only insofar as the filmmaker fails to allow those persons or things to reveal themselves to the camera. Such a failure to allow the camera to do the work that is the "only thing that really matters" can no more be justified or redressed by declaring the camera's presence to its subjects than by declaring it to the audience.

—The camera also has not become emotionally or spiritually withdrawn. It is only a dumb machine; it has no emotions of its own, no "spirit," *to* withdraw. If withdrawal were its condition, merely declaring its presence would not make it any less withdrawn, in any case. For that, the camera would have to overcome its withdrawal, to "swing into life," as Cavell puts it (130). What can it mean for the camera to "swing into life" except for it to declare its presence in the work it does?

It is a condition of the use of language that one "cannot in general merely say something" but must say some specific thing, and that "there will be a reason for saying just that just then." The camera, too, cannot declare itself in general. For its presence to be acknowledged in the work it does, the camera must give—be given—"at least the illusion of saying something"—of declaring something particular about these subjects, about their world—hence of having "a reason for saying just that just then" (128–29).

211

Cavell cites, as an example, "the long, slow swings Godard maintains for the conversation piece in *Contempt*" (129). These are "clearly enough an acknowledgment of the camera's presence," he argues, "but by that fact they are also a statement from the camera about its subjects, about their simultaneous distance and connection, about the sweeping desert of weary familiarity." In other words, these long, slow swings of the camera would not be *acknowledgments* of the camera's presence unless they made some particular revelation—not necessarily this one—about these subjects, about the world.

Cavell goes on to consider a second illustration of the principle that for the camera's presence to be made known it must at least seem to declare something particular about its subjects and their world. "It is sometimes said," the passage begins,

> it is natural to suppose, that the camera is an extension of the eye. Then it ought to follow that if you place the camera at the physical point of view of a character, it will objectively reveal what the character is viewing. But the fact is, if we have been given the idea that the camera is placed so that what we see is what the character sees *as he sees it*, then what is shown to us is not just something seen but a specific *mood* in which it is seen. (129)

What one views cannot be separated from the mood in which one views, from the private feelings one attaches to one's views ("The world is already drawn by fantasy"). This means that one's point of view is never simply the placement and angle, the physical location, of one's eyes. One is not outside one's view the way one is outside one's language, or the way the camera is outside its subjects and their world. In Stanley Kubrick's *Paths of Glory*, for example, "we watch Kirk Douglas walking through the trenches lined with the men under his command, whom he, under orders, is about to order into what he knows is a doomed attack. When the camera then moves to a place behind his eyes . . . we are given a vision constricted by his mood of numb and helpless rage" (129).

By presenting what the protagonist sees the way he sees it, Kubrick is using the camera to declare something about this man: His vision is "constricted by his mood of numb and helpless rage." He is viewing as if his point of view *were* simply the physical location of his eyes, as if he were only a dumb machine. But viewing as if he had no mood *manifests* his mood. He is *dissociating* his viewing from his feelings.

Dissociating viewing from feeling is something human beings do, an act they perform on particular occasions—for example, when they are in a mood to deny their existence in the world, as this man is. By viewing the world this way, he is confirming, despite himself, precisely what he is in a

Kubrick's protagonist (Kirk Douglas); his constricted vision (*Paths of Glory*).

mood to deny, precisely what it is that the camera is declaring about him, that he is in the world, not outside it.

The protagonist is not on view at the moment the camera declares that he is in the mood to deny that he is in the world. The camera makes this declaration about him by declaring something about what is on view at this moment. In turn, that declaration is made not by a view that is rendered expressive of his feelings, but by a view rendered feeling-less, devoid of expression. In the protagonist's view, the world appears as if it were a mere object, not a subject capable of revealing itself; the world appears as if it were not drawn by fantasy, as if it were not a world at all.

For this example to illustrate the principle that the camera can only declare itself by at least appearing to declare something about its subjects, however, it must be that the camera is also declaring something about itself at this moment. Indeed, this is the case: It is declaring that the protagonist's view is not, cannot be, the camera's own. The moral is "not merely that the camera will have its assertion, but that a narrator cannot cede his position to his protagonist, and, more specifically, that the protagonist's point of view is not the same as the placement and angle of the camera which records it" (129).

By viewing the world as if he were a dumb machine, the protagonist is confirming that he has a point of view not reducible to the physical placement and angle of his eyes, that he has—that he is—a self. The camera *is* a dumb machine. It is not capable of dissociating viewing from feeling, for it has no feelings *to* dissociate from its views of the world. It takes a self to deny itself, but the camera has no self to deny; it is no self capable of denying itself. By using it in a way that dissociates its view from the protagonist's, Kubrick is using the camera to declare that it is outside the world on film in a way the film's protagonist cannot be. The world on film is the camera's subject. The camera is outside its subject.

Therein resides Cavell's answer to his question as to what it is that movies now have to acknowledge: "The questions and concepts I have been led to admit in the course of my remarks all prepare for an idea that the camera must now, in candor, acknowledge not its being present in the world but its being outside its world" (130).

The camera exists in the one existing world. But the camera is outside "its" world—it does not exist in the world that reveals itself on film, the world that differs from the existing world solely by not existing. That the camera is outside the world on film has always been a condition of film's promise to let the world exhibit itself. Movies can no longer take that condition for granted.

With the draining from the original myths of film of their power to hold our conviction in film's characters, with the loss of conviction in film's capacity to carry the world's presence, "the screen no longer naturally holds a coherent world *from* which I am absent" (130). Our mechanical absence no longer assures the world's presence to us. It is still possible for film to hold a "coherent world"—a world complete without our existence in it, or the camera's. But the traditional automatisms of movies no longer assure this. It no longer happens *naturally*.

It is no longer natural for the world as a whole to exhibit itself to the camera, for the camera to allow the exhibition of the world in itself. It is no longer natural for the camera to occupy a position outside the world on film, not because its work now places it inside—that cannot be—but because it is no longer natural for the camera to do the mysterious work that once came naturally to it. The world no longer naturally appears—or appears natural—on film. The camera's presence no longer assures the presence, on film, of anything we can call a world.

Naturalness, candor, has been withdrawing—nature itself has been withdrawing—from film. But "nature's absence," as Chapter 15 puts it, "is only the history of our turnings from it." If nature increasingly has been turning away from film, film increasingly has been turning away from nature, indeed, from its own nature. What Cavell calls "film's growing doubt of its ability to allow the world to exhibit itself" has led to a "new theatricalizing of its images" (132). Increasingly, film has taken over the task of exhibition, betraying its nature.

> The conventions upon which film relied have come to seem conspiracies: close-up, which used to admit the mysteriousness of the human face, now winks a penny-ante explanation at us. Hitchcock parodies this with the long final close shot of Tony Perkins in *Psycho*, making a mystery of himself. As its final vulgarization, my choice is the point in *Ship of Fools* at which, in response to the jocular line "What can Hitler do? Kill all the Jews in Germany?" Kramer's camera pushes into the dwarf's face, which . . . is supposed to register at a glance an explicit vision and comprehension of the following decade of German history. (131–32)

When he uses the camera to assert that the dwarf possesses a "vision and comprehension" his face fails to reveal, Stanley Kramer is, indeed, using the camera to theatricalize its subject, to impose a foreign animation instead of allowing the subject to reveal itself. In using the camera to deny its subject in this way—to deny he is a subject—Kramer is using the camera to deny the subject's world as well—to deny that there *is* a world on film complete without the camera's presence. By contrast, when at the end of *Psycho* Alfred Hitchcock frames a close-up of Tony Perkins "making

215

a mystery of himself," he is using the camera to acknowledge a sense of withdrawing candor (131). Hitchcock is using the camera to parody (in advance) the "new theatricality" of films like *Ship of Fools*, to mock such betrayals of film's nature, to deny such denials of the "only thing that really matters."

The lesson Cavell draws is that traditional devices such as the close-up, which have increasingly been used in ways that betray film's promise of the exhibition of the world in itself, can still keep faith with that promise. That is true as well of the untraditional devices movies have increasingly been employing. As Chapter 18 undertakes to demonstrate, those devices can be used in ways that acknowledge, as well as ways that deny, our new sense of film—our sense of withdrawing candor, our sense that the screen no longer naturally holds a world from which we and the camera are absent.

■ ■

As we have noted, the analogy summed up by the equation "The camera is outside its subject as I am outside my language" is central to the argument of Chapter 17. Indeed, the chapter seems to contain one set of remarks about the camera/subject side of this equation and a separate set of remarks about the I/language side. Yet the thrust of the chapter is that these sets of remarks are not, cannot be, separate. Obviously, the sentence "The camera is outside its subject as I am outside my language" joins together these two sets of remarks. So, too—if less obviously—does the sentence "The questions and concepts I have been led to admit in the course of my remarks all prepare for an idea that the camera must now, in candor, acknowledge not its being present in the world but its being outside its world."

Self-evidently, this latter formulation culminates the chapter's remarks about the camera. It equally culminates the chapter's remarks about language, but that is only evident if one reads those remarks—at one level about the conditions of anyone's use of language—as also specifically about Cavell's use of language, of which a paradigm is *The World Viewed* itself.

In Chapter 14, we observed, a simple shift to the first person signals Cavell's declaration, crucial to the chapter as a whole, that *The World Viewed* is written from within the modernist situation. That Chapter 17, too, is concerned with declaring something about the writing of *The World Viewed* is signaled by its opening sentences. In the transition from "One can feel that there is always a camera left out of the picture: the one

216

working now" to "When my limitation to myself feels like a limitation of myself, it seems that I am always leaving something unsaid; as it were, the saying," the shift from camera to language is marked by a shift from third to first person. Throughout the chapter, the pattern is consistent: Every remark about the camera is in the third or second person, every remark about language in the first person.

Chapter 15 makes the point that there have always been some people able to "acknowledge something other human beings have to deny or accept as true of them, too." Our reading of that chapter reminds us that Cavell is one of those people, that it is a central aspiration of his writing to acknowledge things that others have to acknowledge or else deny. This point is borne out by Chapter 17's remarks about the camera. By saying "One can feel that there is always a camera left out of the picture: the one working now," for example, Cavell is acknowledging that he, personally, has had that feeling. He is also acknowledging this on our behalf, challenging us to admit that what is true for him, in this case, is true for us as well.

Chapter 17's remarks about language—for example, "When my limitation to myself feels like a limitation of myself, it seems that I am always leaving something unsaid; as it were, the saying"—can also be read as Cavell's acknowledgments of things he holds to be true for others, not just himself. Indeed, in our discussion up to this point, this is precisely how we read them. Our "I" is not Cavell's "I," so we did not use "I" in paraphrasing those remarks, which are written in the first person. Had we used "he," the paraphrases would have seemed to deny the public dimension of Cavell's language. So we opted for the impersonal "one," with the consequence that the paraphrases consistently fail to register the *private* dimension of the chapter's reflections on language, the private meanings Cavell's "saying" of these words attaches to them, his private reasons for writing just those words, just then. Before taking leave of Chapter 17, it is incumbent on us to redress this omission.

In doing so, let us begin by reconsidering the chapter's initial first-person remark: "When my limitation to myself feels like a limitation of myself, it seems that I am always leaving something unsaid: the saying itself." Read as a remark about the writing of *The World Viewed*, it is akin to a confession—it confesses, first, Cavell's feeling that his self is endlessly present in his writing; second, his feeling on occasion that this is a limitation of himself, a limitation of his writing; third, his feeling, on such occasions, that *The World Viewed* is always leaving its "saying," that is, its writing, "unsaid."

217

To read this sentence as a remark about *The World Viewed*, in other words, is to read it as registering a doubt that this writing is capable of acknowledging its own "saying." "Declaring its motivation," as our discussion of Chapter 16 puts it, "the writing of *The World Viewed* is also confessing a doubt about itself." In confessing such a doubt, the sentence does *not* leave its "saying" unsaid; it also overcomes the doubt it confesses, overcomes it *by* acknowledging its own "saying." And all the chapter's remarks in the first person can be read as confessing self-doubts they overcome by acknowledgment.

The chapter's most extended meditation on the concept of acknowledgment—the passage that begins "Knowing your claim to an acknowledgment from me, I may be baffled by the demand you make for some special voicing of the acknowledgment . . ." (128)—is in the first person, hence invites being read as, at one level, about the writing of *The World Viewed* itself. Cavell follows this passage by reprising the question "What is it the movie's turn to acknowledge?" rather than by posing the more obvious question "What is it my turn [*The World Viewed*'s turn] to acknowledge?" Thus it might appear that for private reasons he is suppressing the latter question. Rather, he is acknowledging that *The World Viewed* has already been engaged in answering this question about itself—answering it *by* acknowledgment, by acknowledging what it is this writing's turn to acknowledge.

That one is outside one's language is a condition of anyone's use of language. Yet in writing his little book about movies, Cavell finds himself no longer able to take this condition for granted. *The World Viewed* is written from within the modernist situation, as Chapter 14 declares. This means that its writing aspires at once to free Cavell from automatisms he can no longer acknowledge as his and to free *The World Viewed* from him, to give "new ground for its autonomy."

To be outside the language of *The World Viewed* is an *aspiration* of its writing, in other words. For the book to achieve such a position, it is not enough for its writing merely to refer to itself; what is called for is an acknowledgment. What the writing of *The World Viewed* must acknowledge about itself, specifically, is at once that its author is capable of acknowledging its language as his, and that he is outside its—his—language, that *The World Viewed* is autonomous.

In Chapter 17, *The World Viewed* undertakes to answer the questions "How, specifically, are movies questioning themselves, and what specifically requires acknowledgment in their making?" Now it is possible for us to add: *The World Viewed* undertakes to answer these questions by questioning itself, by acknowledging what it is that specifically requires acknowledgment in its writing. Hence the aptness of the wording of Cavell's climactic announcement: "The questions and concepts I have been led to admit in the course of my remarks all prepare for an idea that the camera must now, in candor, acknowledge not its being present in the world but its being outside its world."

Cavell's words are literally saying: In response to film's growing doubt of its capacity to exhibit the world in itself, the camera must now be used in a way that candidly acknowledges that doubt and thereby overcomes it. By saying this, the writing of *The World Viewed* is itself candidly acknowledging, and thereby overcoming, its doubt that it is capable of such candor.

A sense of withdrawing candor is manifest in Cavell's remark, in its "saying." These words are confessing, after all, that all his remarks up to this point in *The World Viewed*, however candid they appear, are setting the stage for the present dramatic announcement. What appears in the writing to be candor is now admitted to be a pose, in other words. But this pose is at the same time revealed to be a serious response—a candid response—to a sense of withdrawing candor.

The "questions and concepts" Cavell has been "led to admit" in the course of the writing of *The World Viewed*, his words are saying, are what set the stage for the present moment. That is, it is the writing of *The World Viewed* itself that leads Cavell to the position he now occupies, the position—it is a position outside the language of his writing—that he now acknowledges as his. In that sense, the writing of *The World Viewed* claims to fulfil the human wish to have one's words simply happen to one. The words of *The World Viewed* simply happen to Cavell. This is because he has allowed his writing to be led by his words, to be led to his words, to be led "along blocked paths and hysterical turnings to hang on to a thread that leads from a lost center to a world lost."

With its arrival at the idea that in order to assure the world's presence "the camera must now, in candor, acknowledge not its being present in the world but its being outside its world," the mood of *The World Viewed* darkens. Starting with the formulation that follows—"The world's presence to me is no longer assured by my mechanical absence from it, for the world no longer naturally holds a coherent world *from* which I am absent"—Cavell's prose takes upon itself the serious burden of assuring the world's presence by acknowledging *his* outsideness (130–33).

For Cavell to acknowledge his outsideness to the world on film is for him to acknowledge his connection with us, because that is a condition we share. But for him to acknowledge his outsideness to the language of *The World Viewed* is for him to declare his separateness from us, because only he is capable of performing—or failing to perform—that acknowledgment. Only Cavell is capable of achieving—or failing to achieve—the autonomy of *The World Viewed*, capable of enabling—or failing to enable—the writing of *The World Viewed* to arrive at its necessary conclusion. Only we are capable of acknowledging this acknowledgment, or withholding our acknowledgment.

The mood darkens as the writing of *The World Viewed* acknowledges that its beauty and significance, its promise of "the pain and balm in the truth of the only world: that it exists, and I in it," are born of loss. As the writing of *The World Viewed* acknowledges the necessity—if it is to assure the world's presence—of coming to an end, as Cavell acknowledges the necessity of closing the book on his natural relation to movies, perhaps one might expect what follows to be tinged by melancholy. But Cavell's next line—"I feel the screen has darkened, as if in fury at its lost power to enclose its world"—unexpectedly bespeaks a heightened anxiety—what we might well call "a mood of numb and helpless rage"—as if at the nightmarish possibility that the world on film has been irretrievably lost, that the loss of film's world of possibility is the loss of the world itself, that the writing of *The World Viewed* is powerless to assure the world's presence, or to assure Cavell's existence in the world, that its failure is absolute, its writing madness.

Almost to the last words of the chapter, this dark mood is sustained, as can be conveyed by simply listing a few of the terms that make their appearance: "shock," "blinded," "freezing in their tracks," "maddened," "vengeance," "blot out," "stupefy," "debased," "skinned for show," "fraudulent," "nauseated mockings," "hateful," "betrayal." The mood is broken only by the chapter's penultimate sentence, in which Cavell reminds himself, and us, that it is still possible for film to keep its promise, which he here gives its most eloquent characterization: "To let the world and its children achieve their candidness" (131). Striking a note that will continue to reverberate through Chapter 18, the final sentence contains a stern warning: The hardest acknowledgments "of the camera's outsideness to its world and my absence from it" are still to come.

Chapter 18: "Assertions in Techniques"

Invoking the philosophical principle that "nothing is a 'possibility of a medium' unless its use gives it significance," the penultimate chapter of

The World Viewed begins by announcing that in it Cavell is collecting, "not quite at random," some uses of the devices or techniques that it has become fashionable to use in ways that betray film's promise to allow the world to exhibit itself (133). The thrust of Chapter 18 is that these devices also *can* be used to keep faith with film's promise. In running through the examples that follow, he shows how particular uses of each device discover—or fail to discover—obvious, or not so obvious, significances of that device. Cavell uses these examples to illustrate some of the general principles about art and language, explicitly articulated in *Must We Mean What We Say?*, that underwrite *The World Viewed*. He also uses those general principles to illuminate particular aesthetic possibilities specific to film.

Reading Chapter 18, we might note, one is likely to be reminded, not for the first time, that *The World Viewed* was written over a quarter of a century ago. One might well feel prompted, reading this chapter, to wonder what examples from recent films one might cite to illustrate those principles, what particular aesthetic possibilities recent films discover, or fail to discover. Yet again, the most fruitful way to read *The World Viewed* is to allow its words to prompt one's own thinking, and to follow one's own thoughts with the attention necessary to follow Cavell's.

Slow-Motion

"It may not have needed Leni Riefenstahl to discover the sheer objective beauty in drifting a diver through thin air," Cavell writes, "but her combination of that with a series of cuts syncopated on the rising arc of many dives, against the sun, took inspiration." He goes on, "The general message is clear enough in everything from the high-jumping children in *The World of Henry Orient* and *Popi* to the floating women in television commercials honoring feminine hygiene . . . : for a fast touch of lyricism, throw in a slow-motion shot of a body in free fall" (133).

The meaning of the English word "cat" may be arbitrary or conventional (in other languages, other words more or less mean what "cat" means in English). Given our human form of life, however, it is not arbitrary or conventional that, say, shots of divers free-falling in slow-motion are beautiful. For us, there *is* a "sheer objective beauty" in bodies projected on a screen falling in slow-motion through the air. The discovery that there is a lyrical beauty in such shots is a discovery of a significance of the device of slow-motion, a discovery of a possibility of the medium of film, and a discovery of something about being human.

A "more surprising significance," as Cavell puts it, can be found in

221

Rouben Mamoulian's *Love Me Tonight*, where a shot of horses in slow motion is read as silent, and in the slow-motion duel death in Kurosawa's *Seven Samurai*, where the slow motion confers on the shot not only a lyrical beauty but also a sense of silence that enhances our impression of a "mortal thrust followed by the long drop into endlessness" (134).

The end of *Bonnie and Clyde* "persists in an elegy of bullets long after the pair is dead" (134). By again conveying silence as well as lyrical beauty, the slow-motion invests this passage with the elegiac mood to which Cavell alludes. The device also conveys the feeling, to which he alludes as well, that the shower of bullets persists *long after* death comes to Bonnie and Clyde. The slow-motion enhances our sense that the unseen gunmen are determined to keep firing until they have extinguished every spark of life in these bodies. It also enhances our sense that they are determined not to stop until they have done all they can to keep these bodies from appearing dead. (The force of the bullets imposes on their bodies a foreign animation, grotesque yet strangely beautiful, granting Bonnie and Clyde the illusion of life.)

By slaughtering the flesh-and-blood Bonnie and Clyde even as it transforms them into timeless legends, society is "making sure of itself" (134). "Art is not so satisfied," he adds, intimating that by this ending the film is confessing artistic failure, not expressing satisfaction in its achievement. "The camera is at once confessing its invasion of their existences and its impotence to preserve them, and our pasts in them; it is at once taking vengeance on them for their absence and accompanying them across the line of death."

The film's ending locates the camera on both sides at once of "the line of death," as one both with its subjects and with their unseen killers. The camera fails to achieve a position of its own. *Bonnie and Clyde* confesses its failure to overcome, or transcend, "film's growing doubt of its ability to allow the world to exhibit itself," as Chapter 17 puts it.

The Freeze Finish

The ending of *Bonnie and Clyde* is thus akin to the ending of *Butch Cassidy and the Sundance Kid*, in which the final freeze frame of the two figures "instantly translates them to immortality" (134). In general, the "uncontrollable tic of the freeze finish mimics two old ending *topoi* from movies," Cavell observes.

> The comic epilogue after the mystery is solved or the conflict is over, which lets society breathe a sigh of relief, reassured of its innocence, is now invoked by freezing a face at a point of grimace, a comic "take"—as if the film couldn't

Slow-motion duel death (*Seven Samurai*).

afford to let the subject do his own acting. The outside pull-away up from the house or neighborhood in which the drama has ended, letting the world return, is now replaced by stopping the departing subjects in their tracks—partly returning the figures and their world to their privacy, but unable really to let them go, since otherwise you wouldn't be convinced they had ever appeared. (134–35)

Once again, Cavell finds film's growing doubt of its ability to allow the world to exhibit itself.

Flash Insets

In *Hiroshima, mon amour*, what Cavell calls "flash insets" signify "the presence of the past, the pastness of the past." Specifically, they represent moments in the consciousness of a woman

whose life has become an effort to keep past and present from suffocating one another, and to keep her present and the world's present from betraying one another. It is essential that we feel it is *her* consciousness breaking in upon itself, *her* past. . . . Many people in Nevers had seen the young German soldier lying dead on the bridge . . . , but only she bears in a wall of her memory the impression of the curve his fingers made as his body clotted in the roadbed. And only for her is that place flashed to light by the resting body of her new enemy-lover. (135)

In Resnais's film, the significance of the flash insets depends on our accepting them as revelations of this woman's consciousness of a past that is hers and no one else's. What Cavell derides as the imitative use of this device in *The Pawnbroker* "does not accept this burden of significance but expects the device to provide its own." "What the pawnbroker is shown to remember of his experience in the concentration camp is what anybody looking through a grisly picture book of the camp might imagine people remember. So the flash device deprives this bereft man even of his own memories" (135).

The flash insets in *The Pawnbroker* do not allow this man's consciousness to reveal itself; they impose on him a picture of a past not specifically his. Hence Cavell offers this as an example of a use of the device that betrays film's promise to allow the world to reveal itself. To achieve selfhood, we must acknowledge others; when a response is called for, we must respond, however we shrink from it. To "appeal to a favorite speechless horror" to cover a failure to respond is to fail to acknowledge others, and also to fail to acknowledge something about ourselves that we cannot simply fail to know—that we are capable of responding. (For Cavell, again, the quest for selfhood is a *moral* imperative.)

Freeze Frames

Cavell contrasts the use of freeze frames in *Darling* and Truffaut's *Jules and Jim*. In *Darling*, "they show what the world sees of a darling, and the convenience and perversity in having, and having the chance, to pick what the world will see" (127). In *Jules and Jim*, "they show what Jules and Jim see together in the woman of their world." In *Darling*, the device seems to be "integrated in the movie as a whole, which is after all about the shallowness and the depth of appearances; what better motivation for using the technique of a succession of stilled frames than to show them as products of a fashion photographer's hopeful catchings?" In *Jules and Jim*, the device does not seem integrated in the movie as a whole; "however good that idea of Jeanne Moreau stopped against the wall, the thing is used out of the blue." And yet, in Cavell's judgment, *Darling* is a clever film, while *Jules and Jim* is a masterpiece.

224

What Jules and Jim together see in the woman of their world (Jeanne Moreau) (*Jules and Jim*).

The first lesson Cavell draws from this is that we should not take a list of rhetorical devices "for more or less than it is worth" (137). The second is that how a particular device is motivated in a film "is no simpler a question than how a number is motivated in an opera or a musical comedy, or what relations are to be found between the music and the text it sets." Cavell goes on to compare the literal justification of the freeze frame device in *Darling* to justifying Fred Astaire's dancing "by its being a dance in the world depicted (as when he's doing an act in a theater or nightclub, or dancing in a dance studio)."

> But Astaire is also capable of transforming objects and locales at hand—an office with its desk tops and papers, on skates in Central Park, driving golf balls—into a setting for his dance, letting his wish provide the occasion, as in the brave it will. Here the resourcefulness in using his setting is integral to the resourcefulness of the routine as a whole, making the world dance to his music. (137–38)

What is quintessentially Cavellian in this passage is its *praise* of the hero brave and resourceful enough to let his wish provide the occasion for making the world dance to his music. In a footnote, Cavell observes that it is a feature common to Astaire's films that in his first ballroom duet there is a moment at which "the woman turns from him in an effort to leave the scene of their mutual desire, and he throws a magnetic Svengali gesture at her retreating figure, upon which she halts and backs back

225

into the dance" (137 n). We read this, Cavell suggests, as "her accepting the desire she had already admitted when she accepted the invitation to dance." His invitation is not a claim of dominance, but a request motivated by his acceptance of this woman as she is, and his acceptance of his feeling for her. The routine is created from "his wish to attract [her] interest by showing himself, in his sweetness and resourcefulness and faithfulness, worthy of her feeling." Astaire is resourceful enough to make the objects around him—with their "fixed and inner lives"—dance to his music. But this woman is no object; he cannot make her dance, cannot make her his partner, unless she *wishes* to dance with him. (As Cavell writes in Chapter 12, "They were not foolish virgins who yielded to Cary Grant and Fred Astaire.") The freeze frame device in *Jules and Jim* is comparable to *such* Astaire dance routines, Cavell implies.

In *Jules and Jim*, "the image private to the two men appears as if materialized by their desire, which freezes her at the height of laughter, from which she then descends" (138). It confirms "her identity with the figure they first saw in her—the statue they had gone in search of come to life (an identity established by the smile as well as by the motionlessness)." It also confirms that "she is their creation, their greatest work as artists, the one work on which they could stake their lives."

For Jules and Jim, the freeze frame image proves that they are artists, that they have staked their lives on their creation ("Apart from the wish for selfhood [hence the always simultaneous granting of otherness as well], I do not understand the value of art"). The image is also to be—if their lives measure up to their creation—"their proof as men" (138). (That they stand in need of such proof reflects the depth of the film's involvement in the skeptical problematic.) Cavell suggests that their proof fails. He immediately qualifies this, though, by remarking that perhaps we fail to recognize its success.

The question by which Jules and Jim measure themselves, Cavell writes, is "to what degree the human frame can house the unaligned fidelities which human nature requires" (138). They do not *willingly* let "comradeship and desire and art and politics destroy the place of each in each." They thus go far enough "to test the world by the test of themselves." He adds, "It is this last point that determines whether the film holds one's conviction," whether it goes far enough in reconciling its own fidelities to test the world by the test of itself.

> In a world in which it is common to rest assured that a given problem is either neurotic or existential, psychological or political, few works or acts are sufficiently autonomous to testify that the relation between self

226

and community (because they are composed of one another) is an undying dialectic, that you cannot know beforehand whether a given contradiction requires a revolution of self or an adaptation of community. (138)

Cavell's implication is that *Jules and Jim* is one of the rare works in our world that are autonomous enough—brave enough, resourceful enough— to testify that "the relation between self and community (because they are composed of one another) is an undying dialectic." When Cavell suggests that *Jules and Jim* "testifies" this, he means that the work *asserts* this principle, that it is a central theme of the film. He also means that the film's existence as a work of art, its achievement of "sufficient autonomy," offers evidence for the truth of this principle. And in praising *Jules and Jim* for being autonomous enough to testify to this principle, *The World Viewed* testifies to it, too. ("The relation between self and community is an undying dialectic" is another way of putting Cavell's maxim that selfhood requires "the always simultaneous granting of otherness as well.")

As the freeze frame image declares, the woman *is* the statue come to life, the totem of the community the three commit themselves to creating and preserving, a community dedicated to happiness in love married with freedom in work. The freeze frame image also declares that the woman is alive and separate. (If she were not an autonomous human being, if there were not three free to stand on the same ground, there could be no community among them.) "When the men's loyalties exclude her," Cavell observes, "she excludes herself, and draws them after."

> Her first leap into water comes early, when the men are enjoying Baudelaire's dirty remark on the topic of women in church—as though, being men, there can be no religious differences between them. Her second leap comes at the end, when the men join again, this time on the topic of Nazis burning books— as though, being adults partial to books, there can be no political differences between them. Her final solution is to take Jim for that ride off the earth and to say again to Jules, "Watch!" (139)

With grim irony, Cavell calls the woman's death-dealing gesture "her final solution." But of what problem? Clearly, he understands her to be addressing the kind of problem the preceding paragraph invokes ("it is common to rest assured that a given problem is either neurotic or existential, psychological or political"). The woman means her final gesture to be such—the film means it to be such (for the woman is this film's "presiding genius")—that it is not possible for Jules, or us, to "rest assured." We must watch, and take a stand. "Is it her vanity working, a neurotic inability to permit a loyalty that is not directed by her? Or is it still her loyalty to the three of them, an obedience to a shared knowledge that, in a world gone to

227

war they have taken loyalties to the extremest edge open to them, and that this is the last time in which they can end together, salvaging most?" (139).

We have to decide about this woman's final gesture. Cavell's decision is to interpret it as an example of the rare kind of act that is autonomous enough to testify that the relation between self and community is an undying dialectic. In his interpretation, the woman is responding to her knowledge that the survival of their community is at stake. "When the three had met, they had agreed upon a try . . . for happiness in love married with freedom in work. If one is faithful to such an enterprise, failure is as honorable as success. But the woman sees . . . not that the men have failed but that they have broken faith with the original vows of their community" (139).

Jim breaks faith with the vows of their community not because he fails to become a serious intellectual ("It is no failure as a human being not to be a serious intellectual," Cavell reassures us), but because he lets himself be "defeated by the book-burning before he has acted against it, with whatever rage and talent and position he commands. There is every reason to expect failure, but that is different from opting for it. So his conversation with Jules on the subject is a substitute for leading his life, and for accepting the terms of his friendship. It makes a sentiment of horror" (140).

And Jules does not simply fail to write a serious novel; he *opts* for failure by thinking of writing a novel about insects "as though that would be . . . just as good; or as if, were it to be serious, it would be easier to write. This cheating of his ambition suggests that his forgoing of his wife is not the natural exclusion there is in separateness . . . but has instead become a denial of his responsibility with her" (141).

The sense that both men have broken faith with their vows is precisely rendered by Truffaut's use of the device of inserting newsreel footage into the body of the film, Cavell argues in one of *The World Viewed*'s most searing passages. (In this passage, we might note, there is a major flare-up of the fire imagery that runs through the book: the "hidden fire" of the Dandy; the "scorching fantasy" that seals the man's mind in *Vertigo*; the "burning coils" that cause the mind to tear itself apart trying to pull free.)

> [The] newsreels used earlier in the film . . . had set the scene in Paris at a time in which the little community was in Paris; and the long newsreel passage, halving the film as the First World War halved the characters' lives, sets the battles of that war at a time in which the virtuous young men were in those battles at opposite sides—when, moreover, the meaning and fear of those battles is the knowledge that the friend . . . may be there . . . as he advances

against fire, firing. Truffaut uses the nostalgia of the old photographs . . . and the heart-breaking beauty and terror of the soldiers rising like flowers from their fields, to open us to the knowledge that these mortals whose lives we have been shown and will be shown were there, in the only world we inhabit. It is, to my knowledge, the most elegant, direct and sustained use of the familiar device of newsreel clips in movies, a possibility of the medium which declares that the world of movies is an extension of the world of news. The clip of the book-burning reinforces this meaning by showing us an event taking place at a time the men are *not* there. It therewith serves to rebuke their absence, or to state that the world has passed them by. The land of their community, in Alsace, neither quite France nor quite Germany, is already overrun. (140–41)

The land of their community is already overrun, the integrity of the community already destroyed. So the woman plunges Jim, and herself, to their deaths in the watery depths where no fire can reach them. But first she cries "Watch!" to Jules. "Not: watch my destructiveness," Cavell writes, "but: see that your ability to watch and wait, which was your strength, has become your destructiveness, our destruction. I will do as you ask; that much of our bargain we have always kept" (141). The woman's final gesture keeps the community alive, rekindles the faith, as it was her faith that it would.

"Upon cremation the bones of love remain," the passage goes on, sustaining the fire imagery.

As Jules and the child walk away hand in hand, the last words tell us that Jules is "relieved." By what? Of what? Not of fidelity, but of making room for incompatible faiths, faiths called incompatible by the world, by the self's limits in the room of its world, by men of little faith, by men. With the child, Jules knows he can keep faith; and the woman knows this, she could always count on it. . . . It is not all of faith, but it is faithful; and since all is reflected in each, it is enough to keep the idea alive. At any rate, that is the faith. (141)

Having completed this comparison of the use of freeze frames in *Darling* and *Jules and Jim*, Cavell inserts a typographical break. This provides an occasion for him to reflect on his motive in making this comparison. His point is not that "in one the device has a simple meaning and in the other a complex one," nor that one motivates it crudely and the other subtly. Integrating a device is not the artistic issue, because "integration can itself be a device" (141). Integration is no substitute for integrity. "Only the integrity of a given work can make out the significance of a given possibility. If the device is integral to what makes a work convincing, it has full significance; without the conviction it has any and none" (142).

In *Darling*, the freeze frames, presented as "products of a fashion photographer's hopeful catchings," have neither more nor less significance

229

than actual fashion photographs that reduce their subjects to mannequins rather than allowing them to reveal themselves. To be sure, the freeze frames are integrated in the film as a whole (as are fashion photographs in slick magazine spreads). However, *Darling* lacks the integrity needed to make out the significance of a given possibility. Its use of the device is integral not to what makes the work convincing but to the lack of integrity that makes it unconvincing.

■ ■

For the moment resuming his listing of the possible significance of various technical possibilities, Cavell notes that it is a necessity of movies, a condition of the material basis of film, "that the thread of film itself be drawn across light" (142). Then is this an *aesthetic* possibility of film? Again, in Cavell's understanding a given possibility is shown to be an aesthetic possibility of film only if art is made by means of it, if "some films we care about undertake to mean something by it." This is the case at the end of *Eclipse*, for example, when the motionlessness within each shot

> acknowledges the continuous current of film necessary to hold one view in view. . . . Whether you read those closing sonorities as a real eclipse or as the eclipse of the human . . . the passage reminds us that half the world is always eclipsed by the world itself. So it recalls . . . that night is still there for cover or for recovery or for entertainment, and for turning one's thoughts to stars. (142)

It is another necessity of film that the camera can be anywhere but has to be somewhere. *Grand Illusion* makes art by means of this condition. Renoir's film ends with "the two figures bobbing through a field of snow, away from us. Somewhere under that one white is . . . a fiction that men call a border. It is not on earth or in heaven, but whether you are known to have crossed it is a matter of life and death" (143).

Grand Illusion is about borders, Cavell suggests, "about the lines of life and death between German and Frenchman, between rich and poor, between rich man and aristocrat, between officer and soldier, between home and absence, between Gentile and Jew" (143–44); (and, we might add, between the one existing world, which we inhabit, and the world on film, which is complete without us in it). Specifically, *Grand Illusion* is about the illusion that borders are real and the grand illusion that they are not. "That last view carries this weight exactly because Renoir's camera does not take advantage of its possibility to move all the way up to the

230

figures, but asserts its power to remain, accepting some position as its last, its own."

Frank Borzage's *The Mortal Storm*, too, concludes in the snow at the German-Swiss border. But there the camera

> cannot resist a last close look at James Stewart's and Margaret Sullavan's faces, as she lies where she was hit and he refuses to go on without her; what until then has been a history of friendships and family love and young passion broken and cauterized in the fire storm of Nazism turns into a private tragedy of a failed escape attempt, the privacy heightened by the melodramatic irony of the last words, given to a member of the German ski patrol as Stewart continues the ski run with the dead woman in his arms—something like, giving the signal to cease fire, "They're in Switzerland. They're free." (144)

In the successful escape with which *Grand Illusion* ends, there is a meta-physical irony: "That such an action should constitute an escape and that there should have to be such things in our world are facts from which there is nothing like an escape" (144). In forgoing a last close look at these men who are free only to return to war, "the reticence of Renoir's camera is more than beautiful tact," Cavell asserts, in a passage that penetrates to the heart of his thinking about such matters: "It is the refusal to assert what no one is in a position to assert for us: where it is that one man's life ends and another's begins. Or the refusal to manufacture a response . . . which covers our complicity in the metaphysics of exclusions we have willed for our world, which in turn covers the ontological facts of our separateness and commonality, which we will not will" (144).

Like *Jules and Jim*, in other words, *Grand Illusion* is sufficiently au-tonomous to testify that the relation between self and community (because they are composed of one another) is an undying dialectic. Like Cordelia in *King Lear*, Renoir refuses to use the camera to manufacture a false response. This refusal is not a failure to respond, it is a true response; it is not a failure to assert a position, it is an assertion of a position Renoir honors, a position he chooses to occupy.

Renoir uses the camera to assert a position that keeps faith with film's nature and with human nature, with "the ontological facts of our separate-ness and commonality." It refuses to "cover"—to mask—the "exclusions," the "borders," the lines in our world that we cannot freely cross. And it refuses to cover our complicity in creating and preserving those lines, which are real only because we will them for our world. We will them for our world, in Cavell's view, as a cover for our inability to respond to the ontological facts of our separateness and commonality, our inability to acknowledge our humanity. Because these "exclusions" are covers for

231

our denials of the real conditions of our existence, for our failures to know what we cannot simply fail to know about ourselves and our world, Cavell refers to them as constituting a *metaphysics* of exclusion (the Cavellian equivalent of Derrida's "metaphysics of presence").

At this point, Cavell stops listing the possible significance of given technical possibilities of film. His purpose in collecting such a list, he reminds us, was to distinguish between conditions of the physical basis of a medium, which make the use of a particular device possible, and the discovery of aesthetic significance for the device, the achievement of art by means of it. But this distinction is problematic in modernism, when the physical basis itself becomes the subject of acknowledgment, when such acknowledgment becomes the achievement of art.

"A good reason not to go on with listing the possible significance of given technical possibilities," then, "is that it suggests a foolish idea of 'technique': that its mastery is something other than the endless acquisition of an art" (145). The formula "a great technician, but no soul," for example, does not recognize that a soulless "great technician" does not have "too much technique, but too little; he can do only what his technique dictates, not what his art demands." Equally foolish is the idea that technique is a matter of attending to details, "because the moral of art, as of a life, is that you do not know in advance what may arise as a significant detail. . . . The purest statement of the moral (apart from the *Art of the Fugue*) is Chopin's *Etudes*, in which atoms of technique are shown to contain their own skies, and in which it is declared that there is no preparation for art which is not already art" (145–46).

The inescapable element of automatism in the making of film images, the fact that they allow persons and things in the world to reveal themselves, seems to promise—but does not really do so—that "the magic of its results can be had by anyone who rubs its lamp," that film requires no technique that must endlessly be mastered, no art that must endlessly be acquired (145). The moral of Chapter 18 is that the "moral of art, as of a life," is the moral of movies, as well—that "you do not know in advance what may arise as a significant detail."

VIII

■■■■

CHAPTER 19:

"THE ACKNOWLEDGMENT OF SILENCE"

NATURALNESS HAS BEEN withdrawing—nature itself has been withdrawing—from film. But "nature's absence," as Cavell puts it in Chapter 15, "is only the history of our turnings from it." If nature has been turning away from film, film has been turning away from nature, indeed, from its own nature.

Increasingly, Chapter 16 argues, film itself has come to take over the task of exhibition, denying its nature; "film's growing doubt of its ability to allow the world to exhibit itself" has led film to a "new theatricalizing of its images."

We now have a new sense of film, Chapter 17 in turn suggests, a sense that the camera must now, in candor, acknowledge not its being present in the world but its being outside its world.

Chapter 18 argues that the "new rush of technical assertions . . . are, insofar as they are serious, responses to [this] sense of withdrawing candor." It lists some uses of these devices to determine the limits, the conditions of film's existence, they discover.

Recapitulating this survey in Chapter 19, *The World Viewed*'s final chapter, Cavell finds that he has emphasized silence, isolation in fantasy, and the mysteries of human motion and separateness. "This new emergence of the ideas of silence and fantasy and motion and separateness takes us back, or forward, to beginnings"—to film's origins, to *The World Viewed*'s own obscure promptings.

233

> For it isn't as if, long after our acceptance of the talkie, we know why the loss of silence was traumatic for so many who cared about film. What was given up in giving up the silence of the voice? Why suppose there will be some simple answer to that question, that there was some single spell broken by the sound of the human voice? For the voice has spells of its own. I think this issue now underlies all the explorations in film to which I have alluded. (147)

In *Must We Mean What We Say?*, Cavell made clear his understanding that ordinary language philosophy is about whatever ordinary language is about—"the necessities common to us all, those necessities we cannot, being human, fail to know. Except that nothing is more human than to deny them." In exploring the "silence of the voice," movies are exploring the limits of ordinary language, which is what modern philosophy, as Cavell understands and practices it, is exploring as well. No one appreciates more fully than Cavell, whose work is committed to raising the procedures of ordinary language philosophy to an explicit self-consciousness, the diversity of roles speaking plays in our human form of life. Why should silence be expected to play fewer roles than speaking? If talkies gave up the silence of the voice, that silence, in the so-called silent cinema, was an endless source of aesthetic possibilities.

The title of the final chapter of *The World Viewed*, "The Acknowledgment of Silence," is yet another formulation with almost punning double meaning: silence is to be acknowledged, but silence is also the form the acknowledgment is to take. And, we might note, Cavell understands the silence of the voice not only to be a feature of movies, a feature movies seemed to lose when they became talkies, but a feature of moviegoing, too. The conversation of companions was internal to the natural relation to movies whose loss prompts the writing of *The World Viewed*. There is a silence internal to that relation, too—a silence Cavell is breaking by undertaking this writing. (There is also a silence that the writing of *The World Viewed* aspires to achieve by trusting its words to lead to its necessary conclusion.)

> The technology of sound recording soon overcame the actor's stiff bondage to the microphone, and the camera was free to stray again. But the technology did not free it from a deeper source of bondage in the idea of synchronization itself. On the contrary, the possibility of following an actor anywhere with both eye and ear seemed to make their bonding necessary. No doubt that source has to do with the absolute satisfaction of a craving for realism, for the absolute reproduction of the world—as if we might yet be present at its beginning. But there is a further reality that film pursues, the further, continuous reality in which the words we need are *not* synchronized with the occasions of their need or in which their occasions flee them. (147–48)

Cavell is not referring here to "the various ways dialogue can stand at an angle to the life that produces it," nor to occasions in which words that could have been said for some reason remained unsaid ("times in which the occasion is past when you can say what you did not think to say," or "when the occasion for speech is blocked by inappropriateness or fear, or the vessels of speech are pitched by grief or joy"). What he has in mind are such examples as

> the pulsing air of incommunicability which may nudge the edge of any experience and placement: the curve of fingers that day, a mouth, the sudden rise of the body's frame as it is caught by the color and scent of flowers, laughing all afternoon mostly about nothing, the friend gone but somewhere now which starts from here—spools of history that have unwound only to me now, occasions which will not reach words for me now, and if not now, never. (148)

These examples seem obscure, to say the least. That is Cavell's point. These words are being used to invoke private moments one cannot know without having experienced them. For these are occasions—like the memorable movie occasions Cavell cites in Chapter 1—whose passing is marked by an absence of words.

It is not that we lack the words needed to convey our experience of such moments. When we lack words, we can invent them. In the kinds of occasions Cavell has in mind, when words are not reached now and if not now never, words are not lacking but "out of reach"—not the ineffable but the unsayable. "Time's answer to the ineffable," he provocatively puts it, registering the idea that the barrier separating words from the unsayable—like the barrier separating the one existing world from the world on film—is not space but time (148).

"I am not asking for more stream-of-consciousness," Cavell insists. "Stream-of-consciousness does not show the absence of words as the time of action unwinds; it floats the time of action in order to give space for the words." What he is asking for is "the ground of consciousness, upon which I cannot but move." This is the "further reality that film pursues"—what Cavell calls the "reality of the unsayable" (148).

In characterizing the reality of the unsayable as the "ground of consciousness," Cavell means "ground" as opposed to "figure." It is only against the unsayable as a background that the figures of consciousness are able to stand out, to be apparent to us. He also means "ground" in the sense of "grounding," as opposed to "floating," for example—if stream of consciousness floats the time of action, the unsayable is the solid ground we must have beneath our feet if our need for horizons, for uprightness and frontedness, is to be satisfied, if we are to walk in the gait that is natural for human beings on earth. Thus this passage echoes Chapter 15's characterization of the modernist paintings Michael Fried calls "objects of presentness," which exist "as abstracts of intimacy, declaring our common capacity and need for presentness, for clear separateness and singleness and connection, for horizons and uprightness and frontedness, for the simultaneity of a world, for openness and resolution. They represent existence without assertion; authority without authorization; truth without claim, which you can walk in. It is out of such a vision that Thoreau in *Walden* . . . speaks of nature as silent" (118).

Chapter 15's invocation of *Walden* adumbrates the deep connection that emerges in Chapter 19 between the unsayable and the mysteries of human movement and separateness that underlie serious uses of devices like slow motion, freeze frames, and flash insets. It also helps us to recognize that, when in *The World Viewed*'s final chapter Cavell characterizes the unsayable as the ground of consciousness, part of what he means is that it is the unmoving ground we human beings need beneath us if we are to find our feet, to walk, to move from place to place, from thought to thought, to express ourselves in any medium.

By calling the unsayable "the ground of consciousness upon which I cannot but move," Cavell may seem simply to be asserting that he would be unable to move were he not standing upon *terra firma* such as this. But what his words literally say is that standing upon this unmoving ground he cannot *but* move, that is, he cannot stand still.

This is a characterization of human consciousness in general: It is not possible for human beings to stop thinking. For human beings who find ourselves standing upon the unmoving ground of consciousness that is the unsayable—Cavell speaks of the unsayable as a "continuous reality," keeping in play the distinction between montage and continuity that runs through the chapter—movement, change, thought, expression, is not only possible but necessary. Always to be moving, always to be moved, always to be subject to montage, we might say, is the fate of human consciousness, a condition of our existence as human. And as Cavell's use of "I" here suggests, this formulation also refers specifically to his own consciousness, the thinking exemplified by the writing of *The World Viewed*. The continuous reality of the unsayable is the ground upon which *this* thinking, *this* writing, moves from "place" to "place."

The reality of the unsayable is what Cavell now finds in "film's new release from the synchronization of speech with the speaker, or rather in its presenting of the speaker in forms in which there can be no speech," as in the serious uses of cinematic devices enumerated in Chapter 18. "The possibilities of moving pictures speak of a comprehensibility of the body under conditions which destroy the comprehensibility of speech," Cavell asserts. "It is the talkie itself that is now exploring the silence of movies" (149).

Cavell does not have in mind things movies have begun to say that traditionally had remained unsaid by them, or topics they have begun to address for the first time. He has in mind, rather, ways movies have begun exploring the possibilities and limits of the movie itself—of film's way of enabling the world to express itself, its way of "speaking the being of the world" directly (as every art, in Cavell's view, wishes in its own way to do). He has in mind attempts movies are making to determine wherein, for film, the unsayable is to be located; to survey the boundary between the unsayable and the merely unsaid; to discover what, for film, silence *is*.

"A silent movie has never been made," Cavell reminds us in one of the chapter's most eloquent passages.

> We called some silent after others acquired speech; but that was to register the satisfaction of the world's reproduction, as if the movie had until then been thwarted from that satisfaction, as if the actors and their world had been inaudible. But they were no more inaudible than the characters in radio were invisible. . . . No person or object we could be shown could be the ones called into existence by those sounds. . . . No word we could hear could be the word spoken by that figure of silence. (149)

Before they became talkies, movies were not silent; they projected "a world of silence." So-called silent movies had their own ways of "speaking the being of the world" directly. A world exhibited to sight expresses itself without what Cavell calls the "clumsiness of speech, the dumbness and duplicities and concealments of assertion, the bafflement of soul and body by their inarticulateness and their terror of articulateness." Hence it is a world of "immediate intelligibility" (as radio's world of sound is a world of "immediate conviction").

> We are told that most silent-film stars had to be replaced because his or her voice disappointed our expectations, but that a few satisfied us and crossed the boundary intact. No; no one did; all were replaced, some by themselves. We were universally disappointed. The new creations of synchronized sight and sound were merely powerful enough to distract us from the disappointment, and they deserved to. Now the disappointment is waking again. With talkies we got back the clumsiness of speech, the dumbness and duplicities and concealments of assertion, the bafflement of soul and body by their inarticulateness and by their terror of articulateness. Technical improvements will not overcome these ontological facts; they only magnify them. These ontological facts are tasks of art, as of existence. The advent of sound broke the

237

spell of immediate intelligibility—a realistic renunciation, given the growing obscurity of the world. Then the task is to discover the poetry in speech. It will not be the poetry of poetry. It seemed at first as if it ought to have been, as if when the filmed world expressed itself in speech it would have the same absolute intelligibility as its exhibition to sight. But every art wants the expression of the world, to speak the being of it directly, and none can simply hand its own powers to the others. . . . The best film dialogue has so far been the witty and the hard-nosed. . . . They work . . . because they provide natural occasions on which silence is broken, and in which words do not go beyond their moment of saying; hence occasions on which silence naturally asserts itself. For the world is silent to us; the silence is merely forever broken. (149–50)

The arts of poetry and music incorporate the world's silence and "speak the world's being" directly in ways that the world itself, unmediated by art, cannot. In talkies, the filmed world expresses itself in speech. But film speech, like ordinary speech, does not have the immediate intelligibility, the lucidity, of the world of silence exhibited in so-called silent films. Then how can talkies be capable of conveying the reality of the unsayable? How can sound film be a medium of art at all?

Talkies are capable of conveying the reality of the unsayable by showing experience that is beyond the reach of words. In order to find new ways of showing this, Cavell argues, movies have begun exploring the possibilities of presenting speakers in forms in which there can be no speech. However, "there is another half to the idea of conveying the unsayable by showing experience beyond the reach of words," he adds.

> It is by freeing the motion of the body for its own lucidity. The body's lucidity is not dependent upon slowing and flashing and freezing it and juxtaposing it to itself over cuts and superimpositions. It was always part of the grain of film that, however studied the lines and set the business, the movement of the actors was essentially improvised—as in those everyday actions in which we walk through a new room or lift a cup in an unfamiliar locale or cross a street or greet a friend or look in a store window or accept an offered cigarette or add a thought to a conversation. . . . Our resources are given, but their application to each new crossroads is an improvisation of meaning, out of the present. (152–53)

Film speech cannot incorporate the world's silence the way a poem can. In and out of the movie house, the poetry of speech—the capacity of ordinary language to convey the reality of the unsayable—emerges, rather, from "the fact that just that creature, in just those surroundings, is saying just that, just now" (153). In Chapter 17, in the course of staking out the analogy summed up by his formula "The camera is outside its subject as I am outside my language," Cavell remarks, "When my limitation to myself feels like a limitation of myself, it seems that I am always leaving something unsaid; as it were, the saying." But the "saying itself"—one's saying of these particular words now, for one's own private reasons—is not something one is leaving unsaid; it is something unsayable—unreachable by words. In movies, the synchronization of speech and speaker assures that the "saying itself" is not left out of the picture. In movies, the unsayable is always real; experience is always beyond the reach of words. It is part of the "natural vision of film," as Cavell puts it, that actions move "within a dark and shifting circle of intention and consequence, that their limits are our own, that the individual significance of an act (like that of a word) arises in its being this one rather than every other that might have been said or done here and now, that their fate (like the fate of our words) is to be taken out of our control" (153).

It is part of the natural vision of film that movies appear automatically to satisfy "the explicit wish of human action since Kierkegaard and Nietzsche summed up Protestantism and Stanislavsky brought theater into line" to "act without performing, to allow action all and only the significance of its specific traces, the wound embracing the arrow and no self-consciousness to blunt or disperse that knowledge" (153). Thus, Cavell points out, movies automatically give Brecht "an unanticipated version of his wish for the epic in theater and the alienated in acting"— not the dissociation of actor and character "but their total coalescence, allowing a dissociation or freeing of action from speech." Movies automatically satisfy Brecht's wish for "the turning of the spectator into somebody who just looks on (i.e., the absence of the 'involvement' of the spectator in the events on a stage, but without 'forcing him to make decisions')" (153–54).

As this last point suggests, however, movies do not automatically satisfy Brecht's wish for detached lucidity directly issuing in effective action for change. After all, movies have not effected the radical changes in the consciousness of individuals and society Brecht espoused. Yet Brecht's art, too, failed to effect radical change. In Cavell's understanding, it is a fact that "art alone is not going to achieve the change of consciousness which its own reception also requires." Accepting this fact, Cavell devastatingly points out that it ought to be part of epic theater "to contain the confrontation of its own continuous failing—every night our knowing the truth of our condition and every day dawning just the same—in order to make this failing neither palatable nor bitter, but to make it something we can live with faithfully, in consciousness, and with readiness for the significant detail when it really is ours to act upon" (154).

When Cavell adds that movies also automatically give Brecht "the vision that everything in the world other than nature is a human construction, humanly open to change," his point is that Brechtian theater, too, can change, can come to acknowledge, rather than deny, the moral the conclusion of Chapter 18 sums up with the formulation "You do not know in advance what may arise as a significant detail."

There is no telling in advance the impact a movie is going to have, the place it will come to occupy in our lives. "The impact of movies is too massive, too out of proportion with the individual worth of ordinary movies, to speak politely of involvement. We involve the movies in us," Cavell writes. "They become further fragments of what happens to me, further cards in the shuffle of my memory," he goes on, reprising a theme that figures prominently in the Preface (154). (In this formulation, the word "montage" could be substituted for "shuffle." We might note, however, that the opening line of the Preface, "Memories of movies are strand over strand with memories of my life," uses a different metaphor, one which shifts the emphasis from montage to continuity. When one picks a card from a shuffled deck, the card one chances to pick determines one's fortune. Viewed from the perspective achieved by the Preface, however, the fabric of Cavell's life appears as whole cloth to him, no matter the particular strands out of which it happens to be woven.)

The movies we involve in our lives, Cavell suggests, are among the cards that at any moment we might draw, determining our fortunes. They are also "like childhood memories whose treasure no one else appreciates, whose content is nothing compared with their unspeakable importance for me." And they are like memories of traumatic childhood experiences one wishes, rather, to forget.

> St. Augustine stole a pear; lots of children have. Rousseau got a spanking with his pants down; lots of little boys have. Why seems it so particular with them? Everybody has his stolen pear, and his casual, permanent seductions; if they are to know their lives, those are to be known. Parents are forever being surprised at their children's memories. Some find it amusing or quirky of them to remember such details; some boast, on that evidence, of their child's intelligence. The parents do not know what is important to the child, and their amusement and boasting mean that they are not going to try to learn. (154)

When Cavell poses the question "Why seems it so particular with them?," his wording echoes the question Hamlet's mother asks when she cannot fathom the way her son is grieving over his dead father. (The final paragraph of the chapter explicitly invokes *Hamlet*.) Enraged by his mother's blindness and lack of feeling, Hamlet replies that his grief does not merely *seem* "so particular to him," it *is* so—it is his and no one else's. Lots of children have stolen pears, lots of little boys have gotten spankings, but these events, as St. Augustine and Rousseau wrote about them, not only *seem* but *are* "so particular to them." Had they not "spoken" about these events, we could not have known their importance.

"Everybody has his stolen pear, and his casual, permanent seductions," as Cavell puts it. If we are to know our lives, if we are to know ourselves, we must know the events that are so particular with us that they are of "unspeakable importance" to us. If we do not speak of these things, others cannot know their importance. Even when we do speak of them, their importance remains "unspeakable," beyond the reach of words. To know ourselves, we must acknowledge the reality of the unsayable (the ground of consciousness upon which we cannot but move) in our own experience.

"The movie's power to reach this level"—film's capacity to become unspeakably important to us, like childhood memories we wish to treasure, or to forget—"must have to do with the gigantism of its figures, making me small again," Cavell remarks, adding that "it must also have to do with the world it screens being literally of my world" (154).

During the performance of a play, Cavell argues in "The Avoidance of Love," the audience occupies the same time but not the same space as the figures on stage. "I have been told," he writes in *The World Viewed*, "that [this] is obviously false: In a theater we obviously are in the same room as the actors, whereas at a movie we obviously are not" (155).

This objection wrongly assumes, first, that by crossing the footlights we would enter the space of the characters as well as the actors, when all we would accomplish would be to interrupt the performance. "The sacredness of the stage still holds," Cavell asserts. "Not any longer because certain figures are authorized to be there," but because characters in a play have a past and future we cannot have been part of; like gods, they exist in a space that differs metaphysically from ours (155).

Second, the objection wrongly assumes that we cannot enter the world of a movie because breaking through the screen, say, would not accomplish this. Cavell reminds us, however, that in a movie house, as in Plato's Cave, reality is *behind* us. ("[Reality] will become visible," he adds, "when you have made yourself visible to it, presented yourself" [155].)

When we view a movie, the stars are *there*, in our world. To get to them, though, we would have to go where they are. As things stand, we cannot go there *now*, but their space is not metaphysically different from the space we occupy; it is the same human space that ours is. During the performance of a play, we are forbidden "to cross the line between

241

actor and incarnation, between action and passion, between profane and sacred realms." In a movie house, there is no line we are forbidden to cross. As Cavell provocatively puts it, "the barrier to the stars is time" (155). (In Cavell's understanding, time is also the barrier that separates our experience from words when words are out of reach.)

The world on film is all profane, all "outside"; there is no realm from which the stars, or we, are barred. "They and we could have been anywhere, may be anywhere next," Cavell writes. "The discontinuities in the environment of a film are discontinuities not of space but of places" (155–56). Remaining fixed in space, we somehow get from place to place, but do not discontinuously go from one place to the other. For us, the discontinuities are those of attention: One after another, bits of the world are presented to our attention, and we must somehow put them together into *those* lives, as we put together our own lives. That at any given moment we find ourselves in a given place on earth, or on earth at all, is contingent. But it is necessary, not contingent, that at any given moment we find ourselves in *some* place. Placement is a necessity of our human form of life. And the absolute reality and placement of people in movies is a necessity of their appearing on film at all.

> I think everyone knows odd moments in which it seems uncanny that one should find oneself just here now, that one's life should have come to this verge of time and place, that one's history should have unwound to this room, this road, this promontory. The uncanny is normal experience of film. Escape, rescue, the metamorphosis of a life by a chance encounter or juxtaposition— these conditions of contingency and placement underpin all the genres of film, from the Keaton and Chaplin figures who know nothing of the abyss they skirt, to the men who know too much. (156)

In movies, the absolute reality and placement of people are conditions of their appearance. Thus film escapes Aristotelian limits according to which the possible has to be made plausible.

> It was a great achievement of realistic theater when Ibsen created an event, a suicide, in itself so improbable and in the character so right that he could rely on his play to rebuke the curtain line—'But people just don't do things like that!'—with the force of fact. That is the ordinary condition of the audience of film. Things like that don't happen in the world we go our rounds in— your father does not turn out to be a foreign spy, one's life does not depend upon finding a lady with a strange hat whom no investigation or headline can unearth, one man does not hold another by his sleeve from the top ledge of the Statue of Liberty, people do not . . . turn into werewolves and vampires . . . But there they are. (156–57)

"There is nothing people do not do, no place they may not find themselves in," Cavell sums up the implications of the fact that the absolute reality

242

and placement of people in movies are conditions of their appearance. People in movies escape the Aristotelian limits that constrain characters in plays. People in movies are *free*. It is noteworthy, moreover, that the formulation "There is nothing people do not do, no place they may not find themselves" does not distinguish the condition of people in movies from the condition of people outside movies—from our own condition, for example. The formulation applies to us, to the reality of our freedom, as surely as to the "human somethings" in movies.

When Cavell next asserts, "That is the knowledge which makes acceptable film's absolute control of our attention," his formulation serves to remind us that movies do, in fact, exert absolute control of our attention—at any given moment, the movie singles out the bit of the world we are to attend to (157).

Deploring film's control of our attention and attributing it specifically to montage, Bazin championed techniques (the long take, deep focus) which he believed would minimize film's constraints on our freedom. Cavell accepts it as a fact about film that its control of our attention is absolute. In a footnote, he contrasts film with painting, which allows attention absolute freedom ("nothing will happen that is not before your eyes"), and with music, which asserts absolute control of our attention, as film does, but justifies this control by continuously rewarding our attention (157 n). By contrast, what makes film's absolute control of our attention acceptable is *knowledge*—the knowledge that "There is nothing people do not do, no place they may not find themselves."

When Cavell asserts that this knowledge "makes acceptable film's absolute control of our attention," he means that it is because we know we are free that we find film's control of our attention acceptable. He also means that when we accept film's absolute control of our attention, when we allow our freedom to be constrained in this way, we are rewarded with this knowledge of our freedom. Movies bring home the knowledge, or self-knowledge, that "we exist in the condition of myth," as Cavell puts it, that "we do not require the gods to show that our lives illustrate a story which escapes us; and it requires no major recognition or reversal to bring its meaning home" (157).

■ ■

At this point in *The World Viewed*, there is a blank space on the printed page, a typographical silence, as it were, that separates the body of "The

243

Acknowledgment of Silence"—and the body of the book of which it is the final chapter—from the haunting four-paragraph coda that is the book's conclusion. It may well seem uncanny that we should find ourselves just now at this point, that the writing of *The World Viewed* should have unwound to this silence.

"Let me recall how we got to this point."—These are the words with which the final chapter of *The World Viewed* opens. There, "this point" means the "point" that the conclusion of Chapter 18 asserts, or reasserts, that "a 'possibility' of a medium can be made known only by successful works that define its media," that in modernism "a medium is explored by discovering possibilities that declare its necessary conditions, its limits." "This point" also means the "place," unlocatable in advance of writing *The World Viewed*, to which this writing has arrived as Chapter 19 opens, a point from which the writing can see its way clear to complete its exploration of the possibilities of the new medium of philosophy it has discovered, to go on to the ending it finds necessary, to declare its own limits, to achieve, and acknowledge, its own silence.

As the title "The Acknowledgment of Silence" suggests, the final chapter of *The World Viewed* is about film's capacity to acknowledge the world's silence and about the capacity of film's silence to acknowledge reality beyond the reach of words. It is also about the capacity of *this* writing to acknowledge silence, and about the capacity of silence—what the writing of *The World Viewed* consigns to silence—to acknowledge the reality of the unsayable, to speak the being of the world directly.

The coda begins with the line, "The knowledge of the unsayable is the study of what Wittgenstein means by physiognomy" (157). Wittgenstein's extended sketches of the kind of study he envisions, which begin with an investigation of the concept of "seeing as," occur in Part II of *Philosophical Investigations*, where he "gives various examples in which some drawn figures (like some words, in some places) can be taken variously." One of his examples is our old friend the duck-rabbit. Another is a triangle that can be seen as fallen over. Others are drawings of faces and descriptions of postures "in which, as Wittgenstein puts it, different aspects of them can dawn, and in dawning strike us" (158).

For a philosopher thinking about the subject of film, Wittgenstein's discussion of "seeing as" has "what looks like a ready-made application," as Cavell observes (158). The application he has in mind is the so-called Kuleshov experiment, in which an actor's face was shown to alter its aspect when intercut with a bowl of borscht, a dead woman, and a little girl with a teddy bear.

244

"Bazin," Cavell writes, "in a series of fine passages on the topic, turns this fact against what its admirers have taken it to show, *viz.*, the omnipotence of montage in film's narrative." Rather, "Bazin takes the demonstrated power of montage to show its weakness, because the inherent ambiguity or mystery of the human face is denied in presenting a context which forces one definite interpretation upon us" (158).

But in a sketch of a Wittgensteinian study, Cavell probes the issue more deeply. Linking up with Chapter 2's investigation of what makes photographs different from other kinds of things, this passage brings home again the singularity, and the mysteriousness, of photographs.

> [S]hown (a photograph of) a human face, I might, as in the case of the duck-rabbit, be struck right off with one of its possible aspects. This is unlike the case of the triangle, in which to read it as "fallen over" I have to imagine something in connection with it, surround it with a fiction. But like the triangle and unlike the duck-rabbit, I *can* surround the face with a fiction in order to alter its aspects. And unlike the triangle and the duck-rabbit . . . , I must surround the face with a reality—as though the seeing of a reality is the imagining of it; and [the face] may itself either dictate or absorb the reality with which I must surround it, or fascinate me exactly because it calls incompatible realities to itself which vie for my imagination. (158)

If we are shown a photograph of a person's face, we are seeing the face of a real human being, someone who was in some real place, surrounded by some particular reality, when the photograph was taken. What that place happens to be, what we imagine it to be, is utterly contingent; we can always imagine that person in some other place, surrounded by a different reality. But we cannot imagine the person in no place, surrounded by no reality at all ("We must surround the face with a reality, as though the seeing of a reality is the imagining of it"). Absolute reality and placement, which are conditions of the existence of people or things in the world, are conditions of their appearance in photographs. Because "the endless contingency of the individual human being's placement in the world," as Cavell puts it in "More of *The World Viewed*," cannot be separated from what is mysterious about human existence, the inherent ambiguity, or mystery, of the human face is not denied when, through montage, a shot of a face is presented in a context that surrounds it with a *particular* reality (181).

Nor is the inherent ambiguity, or mystery, of the human face on view in a given shot denied by the fact of recurrence of an actor in his type. The visible incarnation of character into star, and of star into successive characters, limits a performer's "range of expression, the physiognomical aspects which may dawn (one film working in montage to another), but it also threatens the limit" (158–59). Again, what a human being is capable of becoming on film is not determinable *a priori*; film does not fix in advance the range of the human.

Having seen Bogart in several films, his physiognomy and gestures may seem so familiar that we feel we know the limit of what a man of his type is capable of expressing on screen. But it is possible for a new film—*The Treasure of the Sierra Madre* or *The African Queen*, for example—to place him in an unanticipated environment in which his familiar mannerisms take on an unanticipated significance or power, or in which he finds himself moved to perform unanticipated gestures to express ideas or feelings true to his type but never before revealed by him on screen.

Indeed, it can be internal to a type that he threaten his own limit, Cavell observes. This does not require the explicitness of *Dr. Jekyll and Mr. Hyde*. "The threat is present when Harpo inevitably finds his harp. Then the usual frenzy of his information and gluttony and satyromania are becalmed in the angelic sounds with which this man of whistles and honks and noiseless roars and sobs can also express himself, the camera doting on the innerness of that face" (159).

This surfacing of the idea that within our knowledge of a face there is a region of unknownness, that "innerness" is something familiar human faces on film are capable of expressing, along with the idea that the camera tends to "dote" on familiar faces expressing innerness, leads Cavell to contemplate what he calls the "special use of unknown faces for their sheer impression upon us (as familiarly in Dreyer and Fellini)" (159). What Cavell has in mind, in particular, are situations in which directors require faces with the capacity "both to invite and to refuse the imposition of imagination" (159), faces "which do not merely happen to be unknown but whose point, whose essence, is that they are unknown," as he puts it in "More of *The World Viewed*." Not just any unknown face will have this quality. "It must be one which, on the screen, conveys unknownness; and this first of all means that it conveys privacy—an individual soul's aliveness or deadness to itself," hence its aliveness or deadness to others (*WV*, 182).

In Dreyer's *The Passion of Joan of Arc*, for example, Maria Falconetti's face conveys unknownness by conveying a "sheer impression" that she is a woman who is alive to herself, as she is alive to others. (As so often in *The World Viewed*, a woman, not a man, serves as an exemplary figure of humanity.)

By contrast, the faces of the bishops who interrogate and condemn Joan (with the notable exception of the bishop played by Antonin Artaud)

The camera doting on the innerness of Harpo's face (*A Night at the Opera*).

convey the "sheer impression" that these are men who have no inner life, or none they are willing to express. Like the men in the film melodramas and operas Cavell studies in *Contesting Tears* and *A Pitch of Philosophy*, men who claim the authority to judge a woman, a claim the woman rightfully rejects, these bishops "want and want not to hear the woman's voice; to know and not to know what and that she desires" (*PP*, 132). On screen, the denial of human potentiality expressed in the deadness of these men's faces is no less mysterious than the embrace of freedom that the woman's face, in its aliveness, expresses.

"The inflection of meaning available to a type is the background against which the inflexibility of a face commands its power of mystery," Cavell writes (159). The limit of the expressiveness of a performer's face on film, when viewed against the background of the range of expression available to the performer's type, enables the inherent ambiguity, or mystery, of the face to stand out, enables its unknownness to command its power of mystery. And Cavell follows this formulation with another

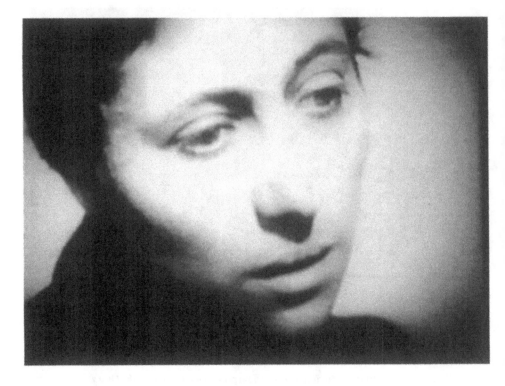

Maria Falconetti (*The Passion of Joan of Arc*).

whose wording parallels it, the parallel sentence structure underscoring the mysterious analogy upon which the transition hinges. "Film's promise of the world's exhibition is the background against which it registers absolute isolation" (159).

On film, there is no place a person cannot be. What it means for a person, what it means to a person, to be in a given place at a given moment of a given film is a function of what Wittgenstein calls "physiognomy"—a function of the range of expression available to a person of this type, the aspects this face is capable of registering, the aspects that can possibly "dawn" in such a face. Whatever the character this person happens to be incarnating in a particular film, whatever the place that character happens to find himself, whatever his response to finding himself in this place, there is something in his physiognomy—his type—that remains inflexible, fixed. The inflexibility of a particular human face—the limit of the expressiveness

248

Antonin Artaud; bishops with no inner life (*The Passion of Joan of Arc*).

available to its type—is the "unmoving ground" that makes this face capable of being expressive, incapable of not being expressive.

Film's "rooms and cells and pinions hold out the world itself," Cavell's next sentence asserts (159). There is no "place" that cannot be exhibited on film. And yet, whatever bit of the world is exhibited at any given moment, something remains inflexible, fixed, in the physiognomy of the world on film. What is this "unmoving ground" that makes film capable of exhibiting the world, makes film incapable of not exhibiting the world? It is the very fact that film's "rooms and cells and pinions hold out the world itself." Whatever bit of the world is being exhibited at any given moment, it is the world itself, the world as a whole, that film "holds out." Holding the world out to us, holding the world out from us, holding us out of the world, film registers our isolation from the world framed by the movie screen.

Film's "fullest image of absolute isolation is in Dreyer's *Joan of Arc*," Cavell goes on, "when Falconetti at the stake looks up to see a flight of birds wheel over her with the sun in their wings. They, there, are free. They are waiting, in their freedom, to accompany her soul. She knows it. But first there is this body to be gone through utterly" (159).

In this sequence from *The Passion of Joan of Arc*, Dreyer uses montage to surround Falconetti's face with a *particular* reality. Yet this does not deny her face its inherent ambiguity, or mystery. Indeed, if no film sequence more fully registers absolute isolation, as Cavell asserts, it is equally true that no sequence more fully registers the power of mystery that the human face on film, when it reveals an individual soul's aliveness to itself, is capable of commanding.

Even as flames consume her body, the image of these wheeling birds, the sun in their wings, "waiting, in their freedom, to accompany her soul," asserts absolute control over Joan's attention, seals the denial of her freedom, and seals her isolation, as well. (No one else in Joan's world sees these birds. All others are riveted—in horror or in fascination or in righteous vengeance—to the spectacle of this woman's body burning at the stake.) And yet, this image also holds out the promise of freedom, and of the end of her isolation. Once this body is utterly consumed, she will be free, and no longer alone: that is Joan's faith.

This invocation of Joan burning on the stake is the culminating instance of the fire imagery that runs through *The World Viewed*. When Cavell characterizes the birds Joan sees as flames are consuming her body as *wheeling* over her, we might also note, this surprising—but quite accurate—word links the book's fire imagery with the trope of the wheel

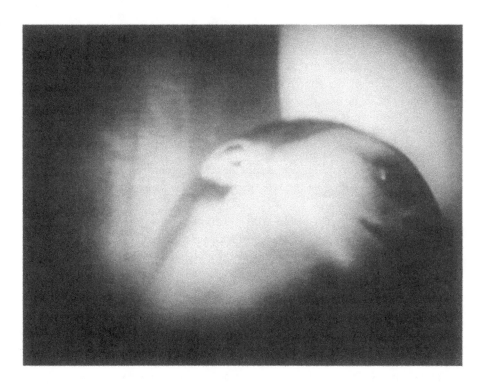

Falconetti at the stake; the flight of birds she sees (*The Passion of Joan of Arc*).

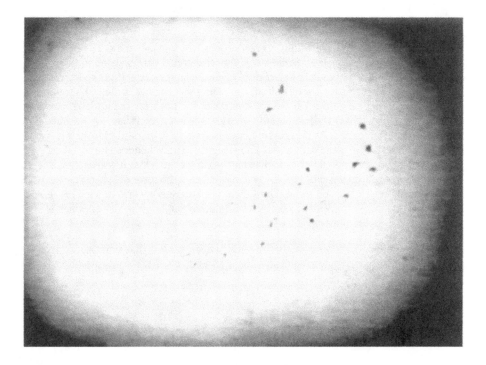

or circle, which plays such a crucial role in *King Lear*, as "The Avoidance of Love" interprets it (*MWMWWS*, 340). In "The Avoidance of Love," Cavell takes Lear's climactic line "I am bound upon a wheel of fire" as an expression of the character's recognition that "his life is whole, like a wheel which turns," that our actions move "within a dark and shifting circle of intention and consequence" (as Cavell puts it earlier in Chapter 19 of *The World Viewed*), that "their limits are our own, that the individual significance of an act (like that of a word) arises in its being this one rather than every other that might have been said or done here and now, that their fate (like the fate of our words) is to be taken out of our control" (153).

"To satisfy the wish for the world's exhibition, we must be willing to let the world as such appear," the penultimate paragraph of *The World Viewed* begins. "According to Heidegger, this means that we must be willing for anxiety, to which alone the world as world, into which we are thrown, can manifest itself; and it is through that willingness that the possibility of one's own existence begins or ends" (159). Without this willingness, we cannot really exist, we can only haunt the world. For this wish to be satisfied, however, we must "be willing to allow the self to exhibit itself without the self's intervention," as Cavell puts it (159). We must be willing to allow ourselves to exhibit ourselves *completely*, to open ourselves *completely* to being known (by others, by ourselves), to make ourselves *completely* intelligible.

"The wish for total intelligibility is a terrible one," Cavell writes with grave eloquence.

> It means that we are willing to reveal ourselves through the self's betrayal of itself. The woman in *Hiroshima* is almost there: "I betrayed you tonight," she says in a monologue to her dead lover, looking at herself in the mirror, confessing her new lover. [Indeed, confessing that she has confessed her old love to her new lover.] It does not mitigate the need for acknowledgment that her old lover is dead, because what she has betrayed is her love for him, which is not dead. As things stand, love is always the betrayal of love, if it is honest. It is why the path of self-knowledge is so ugly, hence so rarely taken, whatever its reputed beauties. The knowledge of the self as it is always takes place in the betrayal of the self as it was. That is the form of self-revelation until the self is wholly won. Until then, until there is a world in which each can be won, our loyalty to ourselves is in doubt, and our loyalty to others is in partialness. (159–60)

Early in our reading of the Preface, we suggested that what prompts its opening paragraph is the entirety of the book whose completion it announces, but that this would not become apparent until we reached the book's ending. Now that we have arrived at this place, we can recognize that the Preface not only announces that the writing of the body of the book has been concluded, it adumbrates the book's conclusion. It sustains the serenely elegiac mood, in the face of all but unendurable loss, that characterizes the writing of *The World Viewed* as it nears its conclusion. And it manifests the philosophical perspective whose achievement *is* the book's conclusion, its conclusive achievement.

In the haunting opening sentence of the Preface ("Memories of movies are strand over strand with memories of my life"), we can now recognize, Cavell is speaking to us from the spiritual "place" to which the writing of *The World Viewed* transports him, the position he chooses to occupy, and to honor. This position grants him a philosophical perspective on his experience of movies, on the "natural relation" to movies he had enjoyed for a quarter of a century, on the loss of that relation, and on the writing that transported him to this "place," writing that is also an act of self-betrayal. (In the fabric of *The World Viewed*, made from the words he has found he could trust to render his experience intelligible, as in the fabric of his experience itself, memories of movies are strand over strand with memories of his life.)

In the Preface, Cavell suggests that it is the business of *The World Viewed* as a whole to find a sufficient answer to the questions "What broke my natural relation to movies?" and "What was that relation, that its loss seemed to demand repairing, or commemorating, by taking thought?" To a reader beginning the book, what prompts this suggestion cannot but be obscure, as we suggested. Now that we have followed the book's thinking to the verge of its conclusion, we can recognize that *The World Viewed is* the answer Cavell takes to be sufficient to these questions. What breaks Cavell's natural relation to movies cannot be separated from the writing of *The World Viewed*, which concludes by this self-revelation, this declaration of self-knowledge.

In composing his metaphysical memoir of the period in which he enjoyed a "natural relation" to movies, in achieving this philosophical perspective on his life of regular moviegoing and the companionship it incorporated, Cavell commemorates the passing of that life, the death of the moviegoer who lived it. *The World Viewed* commemorates a world of movies and moviegoing that has passed into Cavell's memory. It commemorates, as well, the moviegoer its author no longer is, the companions with whom he no longer shares his experiences. In this writing, Cavell mourns the loss of that world, the death of that self. In the final paragraph of *The World Viewed*, he at once closes the book on his "natural relation" to movies and raises its writing to its highest plane. The book concludes with its fullest acknowledgment that the beauty and significance of its writing, its promise of "the pain and balm in the truth of the only world: that it exists, and I in it," are born of loss.

"A world complete without me which is present to me is the world of my immortality," the paragraph begins (160). During the period he enjoyed a "natural relation" to movies, the world on film, to Cavell, was a "world complete without me which is present to me." Hence to him the world on film was "the world of my immortality." In the world on film, he could not die, because it was a world into which he had never been born. And in viewing the world on film, he was not alone; he was with companions who were as free from mortal cares, in the world on film, as he was. Both the freedom and the companionship the image of the wheeling birds promises to Joan, even as flames consume her body, were given to Cavell, as if his body had already been utterly gone through.

That the world complete without one which is present to one is the world of one's immortality "is an importance of film—and a danger," the paragraph goes on. When Cavell specifies the danger—"It takes my life as my haunting of the world, either because I left it unloved (the Flying Dutchman) or because I left unfinished business (Hamlet)"—one might suppose he is thinking simply of the fact that one is not thrown into the world on film, as Joan is, or as we are thrown into the "real" world in which our existence begins and ends (160).

Viewing the world on film from the outside, we haunt that world rather than staking our own existence within it. But what would be the danger in that? No harm could come from our haunting the world on film if it were not for the massive way we involve movies in our lives. The danger in his taking the world on film to be the world of his immortality, Cavell's words literally say, is that it takes *his own life* to be a haunting of the world.

If we accept the world on film as complete without us, and if we accept the world on film *as* the world, the world as a whole, it follows that we also accept that there *is* no world apart from the world on film. This means we accept that the world which is complete without us, the world we merely haunt, is *the* world, the one existing world in which we live, the world in which movies are strand over strand with our lives. It means we accept that our lives *are* our haunting of the world. This means that, like the Flying Dutchman or the Ghost in *Hamlet*, we must forgo all hope

254

of marrying our fantasies to the world, all hope of reaching this world and achieving selfhood. "So there is reason," Cavell concludes, "for me to want the camera to deny the coherence of the world, its coherence as past: to deny that the world is complete without me" (160). In acknowledging his wish for film to deny its own nature, he is yet again calling upon us to acknowledge that what is true for him, in this case, is true for us, too.

If *The World Viewed* is a work of mourning, it is also a work of self-revelation. Its path, rarely taken, is the path of self-knowledge. This means it is a work of confession, as well. When Cavell sums up the painful moral of *Hiroshima, mon amour* with the beautiful but chilling words "As things stand, love is always the betrayal of love, if it is honest," he is confessing something about the writing which accords these words their privileged place. *The World Viewed* is an expression of Cavell's love for film, a love that is as alive, to him as it ever was. But in confessing his love, he is betraying his love. For until our world becomes a community in which each human being can win his or her self, "the knowledge of the self as it is always takes place in the betrayal of the self as it was."

Cavell has reason to want the camera to deny that the world is complete without him, to deny that the world on film is the world as a whole, "to deny the coherence of the world on film, its coherence as past." He has reason to want nature to turn away from film, for film to turn away from its own nature, for his "natural relation" to movies to end. On the verge of ending, the writing of *The World Viewed* confesses its motive for wanting the world of movies and moviegoing, the world whose passing it commemorates, to be past. And Cavell confesses his own motive for wanting his moviegoer self, whose passing he mourns, to be dead.

There remains one last piece of testimony that the author of *The World Viewed* must in candor offer. Without taking back what has just been confessed, the book's final words enable a new physiognomical aspect to dawn. "But there is equal reason to want it affirmed that the world is coherent without me," Cavell writes. "That is essential to what I want of immortality: nature's survival of me. It will mean that the present judgment upon me is not yet the last" (160).

During the period of his life in which going to the movies was a normal part of his week, Cavell enjoyed a "natural relation" to movies. This relation is now lost. Gone. What broke this "natural relation," *The World Viewed* confesses, cannot be separated from the fact that its author wanted—wants—this world of movies and moviegoing to be past. This does not mean he wants movies, or his experience of movies, simply to be over and done with. It is the central thrust of *The World Viewed* that

255

what movies have from the beginning promised, their way of speaking the being of the world directly, is as much as ever to be wanted. And that it is still possible for film's promise—letting the world and its children achieve their candidness—to be kept.

If the fact that our "natural relation" to movies is gone cannot be separated from our wanting it to be gone, the fact that film is still capable of keeping faith with its nature cannot be separated from our still wanting film to keep its promise, to affirm that the world is still capable of being coherent without us. That is essential, Cavell says, "to what I want of immortality: nature's survival of me."

We want nature to survive *us*, to survive our turnings away from nature, our turnings away from our own nature (from what is inflexible, fixed, in human physiognomy, the unmoving ground upon which we cannot but move). If nature has survived all our violence and betrayals, this means that human nature, too, has survived. It means it is not yet too late for us to keep faith with our nature, to declare ourselves, to reach this world and achieve selfhood. For Cavell this means, as he puts it in the hopeful final line of *The World Viewed*, that "the present judgment upon me is not yet the last."

Knowing Cavell's disappointment at the public response to *Must We Mean What We Say?*, it is tempting to suppose that, when he wrote this strangely apocalyptic line, Cavell was anticipating the world's all but total rejection of *The World Viewed*, as if he were fantasizing that because nature will survive him, because the world will go on after he is gone, there will be future judgments upon him, and future judgments, as well, upon those who have passed the present judgment upon him, and that in the end, at that point past imagination at which happiness and truth coalesce, justice will be done (and be seen to be done).

Surely, however, when Cavell invokes what he calls the "present judgment upon me," he is (also?) referring specifically to the judgment he has just brought upon himself by confessing that he wanted his moviegoer self to die, that he wanted the world of his "natural relation" to movies to be broken, that he is in that way implicated in, responsible for, film's turning away from nature, from its own nature. How is Cavell to be judged for that? Who is to judge him? For he calls upon us to acknowledge that we, too, want the world of our "natural relation" to movies to be broken, that we, too, are responsible.

If justice is to be done (and seen to be done), the judgment passed upon Cavell must be passed upon us, and upon the whole world. If film is still capable of holding a coherent world, if nature has survived our turning away from it, it means that the present judgment—the judgment Cavell has brought upon himself, the judgment he has brought upon the world, the judgment the world has brought upon itself—is not yet the last judgment. The Last Judgment, the end of the world, is not yet at hand.

When Joan looks up and sees the birds wheeling above her, the sun in their wings, she knows that, in Cavell's words, "They, there are free. They are waiting, in their freedom, to accompany her soul." If these birds were not free, if they were waiting not because they want to be her companions but because they are her servants, their presence would confirm the present judgment upon Joan, the judgment she brought upon herself—that she is a witch—when she recanted her false confession. But these birds are not the unnatural familiars of a witch; in their freedom, they are part of nature, as she is. What Joan knows, in knowing that these birds are free and that they will survive her, is that nature will survive her. Terrible flames are utterly consuming her body, but in her image of these wheeling birds, the sun in their wings, is the knowledge that she, too, is free.

Joan knows that these birds are free, Cavell asserts; she knows that they are waiting, in their freedom, to accompany her soul; she knows it is her nature to be free. But how can he know these things? How can he know what Joan knows, the reality, so particular to her, with which she surrounds what she sees at this moment in which words are out of reach? In claiming to know what this woman knows at this moment, Cavell is not "identifying" with her in the sense of imagining that she and he are one, not appropriating her experience, claiming the right to speak for her in his own voice. After all, he would hardly call this the "fullest image of absolute isolation" if he believed that it denied this woman's innerness, her privacy, her separateness from him. This woman's experience is hers, not his; she is who she is, as he is who he is. Her silence, as it expresses itself on film, speaks the being of the world directly.

We might say that Cavell claims to know what Joan knows on the basis of knowing the particular reality he would surround this image with if he were in her situation. And yet, how Cavell can know what he would know if he were in Joan's situation is no less a mystery than how he can know what she knows. How can he know such a thing about himself unless he knows that he *is* in her situation, that her life illustrates his own? But how can the author of *The World Viewed*, as he is composing the final words of his book, so much as imagine this?

Dreyer's idea, Cavell observes in "More of *The World Viewed*" about the filmmaker's late masterpiece, *Gertrud*, is that "the condition of privacy, of unknownness, of being viewed—the human condition—is itself the condition of martyrdom, the openness to interrogation and rejection" (*WV,* 205–6). If we exist in the condition of myth, if our lives illustrate a story whose meaning escapes us, if any life may illustrate any story, if any change may bring its meaning home, why should it not be possible for Cavell to find that Joan's life illustrates his own?

St. Augustine stole a pear; lots of children have. Rousseau, like lots of little boys, got a spanking with his pants down. For years, going to the movies was a normal part of Cavell's week, as it was for millions of Americans. And for Cavell, as for most regular moviegoers, the natural relation to movies has been broken. Why seems this so particular to him?

The breaking of the natural relation to movies is so particular to Cavell, *The World Viewed* makes clear, because among all of us who have involved movies massively in our lives, among all of us who have lost our "natural relation" to movies, he is the one prompted by that loss to think philosophically about what movies are and what makes them important. Cavell is the one prompted to step forward to write this book, to take upon himself the burden of its writing, to accept the necessity of the loss it mourns, to confess his own implication, to make himself intelligible, to open himself, like Joan, to interrogation and rejection. He is the one capable of enabling the writing of *The World Viewed* to achieve the silence that is its necessary conclusion. Now that the body of the book has been utterly gone through, he is the one who must set this writing free, must now fall silent to acknowledge that he is outside these words as he is outside the world on film.

As we have said, for Cavell to acknowledge his outsideness to the world on film is for him to acknowledge his commonality with us, because that is a condition we share. For him to acknowledge his outsideness to the words of *The World Viewed* is for him to declare his separateness from us, because only he is capable of performing that acknowledgment, as only we are capable of acknowledging it. That he is outside the words of *The World Viewed* means that these words are autonomous, complete without him, free to acknowledge the reality of the unsayable. That is Cavell's faith.

In its obscurity and in its fervor, *The World Viewed* registers an isolation in Cavell's temperament, an isolation the writing itself brings to a head, the way the writing of *Walden* brings Thoreau's isolation to a head. The author of *Walden* builds his house in the woods so that he may abandon it in the hope of finding his way, changed, to a changed world. But *Walden* does not end by placing its author in the world again, does not chart his way, or way back. When he abandons his house, he departs from all settled habitation, all conformity of meaning, in order to walk a path of philosophy, a path of self-knowledge, which is an uncharted path. And he hopes that we, too, will find such a path for ourselves.

In the writing of *The World Viewed*, Cavell walks a path of philosophy, too, hoping that philosophy might enable him to be free, and in good company, in a world that is fit for human beings to inhabit. In this writing, the self is not yet wholly won. But in it he finds a way to speak truthfully and in his own voice—to speak within philosophy, which means to speak as an ordinary human being, to speak in a way he can expect others to comprehend—of what he loved and loves, of who he was and is. Therein lies the sense of liberation *The World Viewed* is capable of providing. For this writing is capable of bringing home to us—capable of reminding us that film is capable of bringing home to us—the wonder of our lives. The wonder is that our aliveness to ourselves has survived, hence our capacity for hope, and that we still wish for our own further chances.

■ ■

The World Viewed opens with the words, "Memories of movies are strand over strand with memories of my life." And writing about movies has been strand over strand with Cavell's philosophical writing from his first book about film, published between *Must We Mean What We Say?* and *The Senses of Walden*; to *Pursuits of Happiness*, companion piece to *The Claim of Reason*; to *Contesting Tears*, his latest book about film.

That *The World Viewed* derives philosophically from *Must We Mean What We Say?* has been a recurring theme in the foregoing pages. For that reason, we have added an Appendix in which we collect, and ponder, some of the remarks about Cavell's understanding and practice of philosophy that are to be found in *Must We Mean What We Say?*.

The World Viewed, woven strand over strand from his memories of movies and memories of his life, is an exacting study of words, and silences, that speak the self. This project is developed in *Pursuits of Happiness*, a study of words and selves that are acknowledged, and in *Contesting Tears*, a study of words and selves that fail to be acknowledged. In a forthcoming volume collecting Cavell's unpublished and uncollected writings on film, we shall trace his thinking about film subsequent to *The World Viewed*, all of it marked by this book's initial articulation of film's philosophical importance.

In placing his writings about film in the context of the development of Cavell's philosophical project as a whole, that volume will also further explore his understanding and practice of philosophy in relation to the history of film study. Viewed from the philosophical perspective Cavell's writing exemplifies, we find, as the foregoing pages are meant to attest, paths of discovery not to our minds sufficiently explored by film study generally. The theories that have so far dominated film study both embrace skepticism and claim to defeat it. They seem to wish to assure us both that we have nothing to lose by accepting that knowledge is impossible, and that they alone provide systems of thought that can accord film study something like the authority of a science. *The World Viewed* seeks to deny us both assurances. The possibility and necessity of skepticism are driving forces of *The Claim of Reason* (published in 1979 and only recently receiving systematic attention), and our discussion of these complex matters will be guided in part by the tasks and controversies in and around that text.

Turning in on itself, *The World Viewed* turns us to ourselves, or asks us to "check our experience," as Cavell, in an Emersonian mood, puts the idea in *Pursuits of Happiness*. Calling upon us to take seriously our experience of film, to find our own words for our experience, to speak our selves with conviction and enthusiasm, *The World Viewed* also reminds us that apart from the acknowledgment of others we cannot reach this world and achieve selfhood. The language in which we express our thoughts and feelings, and acknowledge the thoughts and feelings of others, is not a private language; it is our common language. The language of the self *is* the language of others, *The World Viewed* teaches. In calling upon us to give voice to our own experience, it reminds us of the urgency, the pleasure, the fear, of making ourselves intelligible, and thus opening us to the possibility of conversation, but also to the possibility of rejection. Assuming that the language of the self has been discredited, some will condemn Cavell's aspiration as romantic. Then is the despair of selfhood less romantic? We seem nowadays incessantly to be told that we live in an age that has moved beyond modernism. But are we to accept it as given that we have been released from our condition as modern human beings, that we no longer experience art's saving importance, that we no longer wish to master the self's fate, or no longer believe in anything answering to that mastery?

Cavell's Philosophical Procedures and
Must We Mean What We Say?

What makes film a subject that calls for philosophy, what makes film a necessary subject for philosophy, are questions at the heart of *The World Viewed*. It is a leading claim of Cavell's book that serious thinking about film requires the perspective of self-reflection only philosophy is capable of providing. In entering this claim, *The World Viewed* keeps faith with the understanding and practice of philosophy originally staked out in *Must We Mean What We Say?* It is not possible to read Cavell's first book without being aware that it is making claims about philosophy, claiming to be philosophy. The view of philosophy articulated in *Must We Mean What We Say?* underlies, and underwrites, *The World Viewed*, too. Yet virtually everything the former has to say about philosophy literally goes without saying in the latter.

In the pages of *The World Viewed*, film and philosophy are happily married, but the kinds of remarks about philosophy everywhere to be found in *Must We Mean What We Say?* are all but completely absent. *The World Viewed* does begin by suggesting its writing is "philosophically motivated," that it undertakes "to account philosophically for the motive in writing it" (*WV*, xix). But what it means for an account to be philosophical, what Cavell understands philosophy to be, is a matter *The World Viewed* consigns to silence. (Silence is also a central subject of the book.)

We therefore thought that some readers would find it useful if we complemented the reading of *The World Viewed* that has been our main

261

business in the present volume by collecting and pondering some of the remarks about philosophy found in *Must We Mean What We Say?*

Philosophical Appeals to Ordinary Language

In "An Audience for Philosophy," the Foreword (and last-completed essay) of *Must We Mean What We Say?*, Cavell predicts that it will be said that two of its essays ("Ending the Waiting Game" and "The Avoidance of Love: A Reading of *King Lear*")

> are literary criticism, or at best applications of philosophy, while the remainder are (at least closer to being) straight philosophy. I wish to deny this, but to deny it I would have to use the notions of philosophy and of literature and of criticism, and the denial would be empty so far as those notions are themselves unexamined and so far as the impulse to assert such distinctions, which in certain moods I share, remains unaccounted for. (*MWMWWS*, xvii-xviii)

Cavell's claim is that "Ending the Waiting Game" and "The Avoidance of Love" exemplify a mode of criticism that *is* philosophy. However, to enter this claim in a philosophically exemplary way, he finds it necessary to "examine" the concepts ("philosophy," "literature," "criticism") that must be used in order to enter the claim at all. In examining these concepts, *Must We Mean What We Say?* employs a mode of investigation pioneered by Ludwig Wittgenstein and J. L. Austin (Cavell's own professor of philosophy) and often associated with the term "ordinary language philosophy."

This mode of philosophical investigation treats as data, and attempts to account for, our impulses to employ particular concepts in one way rather than another, to say one thing rather than another, in specific circumstances. Cavell's claim is that what makes the essays in *Must We Mean What We Say?* philosophy, at least in part, is their commitment to examining concepts by employing investigations of this kind. As is suggested by the fact that he enters such a claim in the Foreword of the book, the essays that comprise *Must We Mean What We Say?* not only embrace the procedures of ordinary language philosophy, they also investigate, philosophically, the very procedures they embrace. The essays that follow treat the medium of ordinary language philosophy, which is their own medium, as a significant subject for philosophy.

During the period Cavell was writing *Must We Mean What We Say?*, the Anglo-American philosophy world was torn by debates between followers of Wittgenstein and Austin, many based at Oxford, who argued that the procedures of ordinary language philosophy allowed for the immediate repudiation of traditional philosophy, and philosophers who repudiated ordinary language philosophy as trivial, or who attempted to make its procedures more systematic or scientific. The earliest written essays of *Must We Mean What We Say?* at times convey the impression that Cavell is siding with the Oxford philosophers in these debates. As becomes increasingly evident, however, Cavell never really assumes that there exists a school of philosophers, in or out of Oxford, who share his commitment to investigating, as well as employing, philosophical appeals to what we ordinarily say and mean. Extending the medium of ordinary language philosophy to an explicit self-consciousness is Cavell's own philosophical project in *Must We Mean What We Say?* He never assumes he shares this project with those of his contemporaries who practice ordinary language philosophy. And although *Must We Mean What We Say?* repeatedly acknowledges indebtedness to Wittgenstein and Austin, Cavell never simply identifies his philosophical aspirations with theirs. When in *Must We Mean What We Say?* Cavell takes on the task of characterizing the philosophical implications of Austin's procedures, for example, he is acknowledging his debt to his teacher, but is at the same time breaking with him. For Austin himself, Cavell notes with regret, never characterizes his own procedures with the same rigor he applies to the philosophical topics he does address. Cavell embraces Austin's procedures, but extends them to the limit of their applicability by bringing them to an explicit self-consciousness as Austin himself never did.

As Cavell reminds us, philosophers since Socrates have taken it to be an activity signaling philosophy to lead us "from confusion to clarity by means of defining concepts" (*MWMWWS*, 166). But it is Cavell's original idea to take this activity of defining concepts to reveal the kind of subject philosophy is. In *Must We Mean What We Say?* there is no methodological difference between a philosophical investigation of such concepts as "art," "metaphor," or "criticism" and a philosophical investigation of the concept "philosophy." "Philosophy is one of its own normal topics," Cavell writes, adding that this fact is "defining for the subject" (*MWMWWS*, 168). In his view, indeed, that which makes "Philosophy is one of its own normal topics" a *philosophical* remark is its use within an activity of investigating concepts in a way that is defining for philosophy.

To investigate concepts in the way Wittgenstein and Austin pioneered is to proceed from "the fact *that* a thing is said; that it is (or can be) said (in certain circumstances) is as significant as what it says; its being said then and there is as determinative of what it says as the meanings of its individual words are." The point is not "to provide some new sense to be attached to a word, with the purpose of better classifying information or outfitting a new theory," but "to clarify what the word does mean, as we use it in our lives" (*MWMWWS*, 167).

This philosophical activity makes us aware of the ways the meaning of a concept changes, and the ways the subject of which it is the concept changes, with changes of the context in which a word is used. It also makes us aware of differences among our own concepts of which we had not previously been aware. Thus it makes us aware of the diversity of what Wittgenstein calls "language games," the things we use words to do, the roles words play in our lives. (There is no one thing that every word does, as is implied, for example, by calling all words "signifiers.")

The positive purpose of this activity is to make us look at what we say, to bring our forms of language to consciousness, to bring us to a consciousness of the words we have, hence the lives that in fact are ours, lives we could not have without the words we have. As Cavell puts it, "The philosophy of ordinary language is not about language, anyway not in any sense in which it is not also about the world" (*MWMWWS*, 95). It is about whatever ordinary language is about.

When an ordinary language philosopher distinguishes between what we can and cannot say or mean in particular circumstances, the thrust is not "to provide labels for differences previously, somehow, noticed," but "to compare and (as it were) to elicit differences" (*MWMWWS*, 103), to make us conscious of differences of which we had not been conscious, to render them perspicuous (to use one of Wittgenstein's favorite words). The goal is *clarity*, and it is achieved, Cavell evocatively puts it, by "mapping the fields of consciousness lit by the occasions of a word, not through analyzing it or replacing a given word by others." The philosopher's purpose in comparing and contrasting our uses of words "resembles the art critic's purpose in comparing and distinguishing works of art," Cavell writes, articulating and exemplifying his point. "Namely, that in this crosslight the capacities and salience of an individual object in question are brought to attention and focus." In making critical claims about art works, at some point we are prepared to say "Don't you see, don't you hear, don't you dig? The best critic will know the best points. Because if you do not see something, without explanation, then there is nothing further to discuss. . . . At some point, the critic will have to say: This is what I see" (*MWMWWS*, 93).

By registering differences that elucidate the diverse roles particular words play in our lives—the logic underlying the ways we use these concepts, what Wittgenstein calls their "grammar"—an ordinary language philosopher makes claims whose own grammar is closer to that of aesthetic judgments than to ordinary empirical judgments. "Those of us who keep finding ourselves wanting to call such differences 'logical,'" Cavell observes, are "responding to a sense of necessity we feel in them, together with a sense that necessity is, partly, a matter of the ways a judgment is supported, the ways in which conviction in it is produced" (*MWMWWS*, 93).

When making a claim as to what we ordinarily say and mean, such a philosopher turns to the reader, as an art critic does, not to convince without proof but to get the reader to prove something, test something against himself or herself. The philosopher is saying: " 'Look and find out whether you can see what I see, wish to say what I wish to say' " (*MWMWWS*, 94). Even when others are convinced, though, the philosopher's judgments, like the art critic's, remain essentially subjective, in Kant's sense. Thus the problem for the philosopher, as for the critic (or the artist, for that matter), is not to discount but to *include* his or her subjectivity, "not to overcome it in agreement, but to master it in exemplary ways." To be sure, such a philosopher often seems to answer or beg the question "by posing it in plural form: 'We say . . .' ; 'We want to say . . .'" ; 'We can imagine . . .' . . . . But this plural is still first person: it does not, to use Kant's word, 'postulate' that 'we,' you and I and he, say and want and imagine and suffer together. . . . All . . . this kind of philosopher can do is to express, as fully as he can, his world, and attract our undivided attention to our own" (*MWMWWS*, 96).

In "Austin at Criticism," Cavell spells out differences between philosophical appeals to ordinary language and empirical investigations of language. When one makes a *philosophical* appeal to what we ordinarily say or mean, it seems

> (1) that one can as appropriately or truly be said to be looking at the world as looking at language; (2) that one is seeking necessary truths "about" the world (or "about" language) and therefore cannot be satisfied with anything I, at least, would recognize as a description of how people in fact talk—one might say one is seeking one kind of explanation of *why* people speak as they do; and even (3) that one is not finally interested *at all* in how "other" people talk, but in determining where and why one wishes, or hesitates, to use a particular expression oneself. (*MWMWWS*, 99)

Coming to know what we say through such a procedure "is like recognizing our present commitments and their implications" (*MWMWWS*, 57). Cavell adds, "The question 'How do we know what we say (intended to say, wish to say)?' is one aspect of the general question 'What is the nature of self-knowledge?' More important than any of Freud's or Wittgenstein's particular conclusions is their discovery that knowing oneself is something for which there are methods," something that can be taught (though not in obvious ways) and practiced (*MWMWWS*, 67).

Cavell is well aware that most commentators take Wittgenstein's *Philosophical Investigations* to deny that we can know ourselves. But as Cavell reads the book, its intention is to elucidate what self-knowledge is. In investigating what self-knowledge is, Cavell argues, Wittgenstein embraces the principle that "we can find out what kind of object anything (grammatically) is by investigating expressions which show the kind of thing said about it" (*MWMWWS*, 78). Wittgenstein also embraces the principle that appeals to what we ordinarily say and mean are useless as data unless they are "met in independence of any particular philosophical position or theory" (*MWMWWS*, 238). Cavell, too, embraces these principles.

Acknowledgment

Philosophical appeals to what we ordinarily say and mean are appeals to facts—about language, about the world, about ourselves—so obvious we cannot simply fail to know them. It can be difficult to know such facts. The nature of this difficulty is a question that crops up throughout *Must We Mean What We Say?* For example, having given seemingly obvious answers to questions about *King Lear* that had vexed generations of Shakespeare critics, Cavell asks how it is possible that no one had previously arrived at these answers. All it takes is attending to the words of the play, to the specific words spoken by these specific characters in these specific circumstances. Why have critics found this so difficult?

New Critics attended to the words of plays, but not to the voices that say those words, and through them to the "straits of mind in which only those words said in that order will suffice" (*MWMWWS*, 269). But how could any serious critic ever have denied that "we care about the utterly specific words of a play because certain men and women are having to give voice to them?"

One reason New Critics shunned direct contact with characters, Cavell suggests in "The Avoidance of Love," is that they pictured the words of a play as "a (more or less hidden) structure of which the individual words are parts." They had been "made to believe or assume," on the basis of some theory, "that characters are not people, that what can be known about people cannot be known about characters." To put the words of Shakespeare's plays back into the characters who give voice to them, it is necessary to break the grip of prejudicial theories. That can be difficult.

But if it were not possible with characters, as it is with people, to know them by the words they voice and by their silences, it would make no sense to think of the words characters speak as theirs, to think of these characters as giving voice to them, or finding their voices in them. When King Lear speaks his words, it is difficult for us to attend to him, but it is no less difficult for Lear to attend to Cordelia rather than to the scapegoat he makes of her. If it were not a fact about human existence that it can be difficult to attend "with utter specificity to the person now before you, or yourself," Lear's tragedy would not be, for human beings, so much as a *possibility* (*MWMWWS*, 269).

In "Ending the Waiting Game," too, Cavell reflects on this difficulty. He notes that the words the characters speak in Samuel Beckett's *Endgame* seem to us "willfully to thwart comprehension" (*MWMWWS*, 119). (Cordelia's words seem this way to Lear.) In *Endgame*, what keeps the meaning of these words hidden is precisely the fact that they are so utterly bare, so literal, so obvious. (This is also true of Cordelia's words.) We miss their meaning because we assume they must be intended to mean something more, other, than what they literally say. To discover the meaning of these words is to discover that "it is *we* who had been willfully uncomprehending, misleading ourselves in demanding further, or other, meaning where the meaning was nearest."

In typical cases of knowing, a failure to know is a piece of ignorance that can be cured by additional information. When what we fail to know is so obvious we cannot simply fail to know it, our failure to know is a denial or avoidance of knowledge, a refusal to know. It is a refusal to know *what* we are keeping ourselves from knowing. It is a refusal to know *that* we are keeping ourselves from knowing. It is a refusal to know something we cannot simply fail to know about the world, and a refusal to know something we cannot simply fail to know about ourselves. Knowing things we can fail to know only by refusing to know them reveals what Cavell calls "a special concept of knowledge, or region of the concept of knowledge," one which is not a function of certainty but of acknowledgment (*MWMWWS*, 258). Knowing oneself is a paradigm of such knowledge.

"Acknowledgment" is a word that recurs throughout *Must We Mean What We Say?* Those who fault Cavell for not defining it are doubly inattentive. First, they assume that he uses the word as a technical term. But, insofar as Cavell is a philosopher who proceeds from ordinary language, what he means by the word "acknowledgment" is simply what the word means. Second, they assume that he fails to define the word, when in fact he is engaged in defining it in the way he takes to be defining for philosophy: by investigating its grammar, the logic underlying our ways of using the word. "Acknowledgment" is one of a number of concepts Cavell at once uses and investigates in *Must We Mean What We Say?*, as he does, for example, when he writes, "Acknowledgment goes beyond knowledge. (Goes beyond not, so to speak, in the order of knowledge, but in its requirement that I *do* something or reveal something on the basis of that knowledge)" (*MWMWWS*, 257).

In investigating the kind of knowledge of which self-knowledge is a paradigm, Cavell employs philosophical procedures that enable one to achieve self-knowledge. Hence it is misleading to picture him as having first accepted or adopted a method and then accepted its results; it is not possible to accept or adopt this method apart from its results. Without knowing oneself, one cannot know what self-knowledge is.

The motive of philosophical appeals to ordinary language, like that of lyric poetry or confession, is absolute veracity. That is why Wittgenstein's *Philosophical Investigations* contains what serious confession must, the

> full acknowledgment of temptations . . . and a willingness to correct them and give them up. . . . In confessing, you do not explain or justify, but describe how it is with you. And confession, unlike dogma, is not to be believed but tested and accepted or rejected. Nor is there occasion for accusation, except of yourself, and by implication those who find themselves in you. There is exhortation . . . not to belief, but to self-scrutiny. And that is why there is virtually nothing in the *Investigations* which we should ordinarily call reasoning. (*MWMWWS*, 71)

Philosophical Investigations is not personal the way an autobiography is. What Wittgenstein confesses, acknowledges to be true for him, he claims to be true for others as well. In appealing to what we ordinarily say and mean, he relies upon himself as a source of data. He also acknowledges that others have equal standing as sources of the relevant data. Without such an acknowledgment, it is impossible to make claims of the kind that are everywhere to be found in *Philosophical Investigations*. For they are claims that

> no one knows better than you whether and when a thing is said, and . . . that you know no better than others what you claim to know. With respect to the data of philosophy our positions are the same. This is scarcely a discovery of ordinary language philosophy; it is the latest confirmation of what the oracle said to Socrates. The virtue of proceeding from ordinary language is that it makes (or ought to make) this message inescapably present to us. (*MWMWWS*, 239–40)

On what grounds can ordinary language philosophers claim that in speaking for themselves they are speaking for others, that they are speaking for philosophy? On what grounds can we accept or reject such claims? "When, in what follows, I feel pressed by the question of my right to speak for philosophy," Cavell writes in "An Audience for Philosophy," "I sometimes suggest that I am merely speaking for *myself*." At other times, he suggests that philosophy is not *his* at all, that its results are worthless if not true for everyone. "Are these suggestions both right, or are they evasions? They express an ambivalence about the relevance or importance of philosophy—one might say, about its possession—which is also one of philosophy's characteristic features" (*MWMWWS*, xxvi).

Cavell has no guarantee that his words—even *these*—"are those of and for" others, nor even that "any particular arrival of his words"—even *this*—"ought to be accepted by others." Yet in *Must We Mean What We Say?* he does step forward to speak for philosophy. In speaking for philosophy, Cavell means his words to have the weight an ordinary person would give them. And he speaks as an ordinary person, "so that if he is wrong in his claims he must allow himself to be convinced" in the ways anyone thinking "will be, or will not be" (*MWMWWS*, xxvi).

In making a claim as to what we ordinarily say and mean, Cavell does not expect much opposition, however. He believes that if he articulates it fully, if he follows out the complete tuition for his intuition (to put it in Emersonian terms), he will be speaking for all, will have found necessities common to all. "Philosophy has always hoped for that; so, perhaps, has science. But philosophy concerns those necessities we cannot, being human, fail to know. Except that nothing is more human than to deny them" (*MWMWWS*, 96).

Some philosophers have taken appeals to ordinary language to provide "some sort of immediate repudiation of that continuous strain or motive within traditional philosophy which is roughly characterizable as skepticism" (*MWMWWS*, 238). Even Austin sometimes takes his procedures to repudiate skepticism by finding that the skeptic's words contradict what we ordinarily say, hence that the skeptic cannot really mean those words. In Cavell's view, however, the skeptic *knowingly* repudiates what we ordinarily say. Not only do philosophical appeals to what we ordinarily say and mean not immediately refute the skeptic, they put the critic of skepticism at the skeptic's mercy. They grant the skeptic equal authority in evaluating the data on which the criticism is based.

"Understanding from inside a view you are undertaking to criticize is sound enough practice whatever the issue," Cavell writes, "but in the philosophy which proceeds from ordinary language, understanding from inside is methodologically fundamental" (*MWMWWS*, 239). In the arguments between philosophy and skepticism that have dominated Western philosophy since Descartes, each side has attempted to refute the other, not recognizing that this is pointless because the cause and topic of their quarrel, as Cavell evocatively puts it, "is the self getting in its own way" (*MWMWWS*, 85). As he views it, philosophy's task is not to refute skepticism, but "to convince the skeptic—that is, the skeptic in yourself—that you know what he takes his words to say." To mount a formidable criticism of skepticism, a philosopher needs data and descriptions and diagnoses "so clear and common that apart from them neither agreement nor disagreement would be possible."

Cavell's interest in appealing to ordinary language does not lie in preserving our beliefs against philosophical heresies such as skepticism. It lies in discovering what we do in fact believe, and what our beliefs come to in our lives. "This is not the same as providing evidence for them"; it is "a matter of making them evident" (*MWMWWS*, 241). Again, the goal is not for opposed positions to be reconciled, but for the halves of the mind to go back together.

Since the connection between using a word and meaning what it says is not inevitable or automatic, we may be inclined to call it a convention. And yet it is not a convention we would know how to forgo. "It is not a matter of convenience or ritual unless having language is a convenience or unless thinking and speaking are rituals" (*MWMWWS*, 221). For Cavell, as for Wittgenstein as Cavell reads him, philosophy "comes to grief not in denying what we all know to be true, but in its effort to escape those human forms of life which alone provide the coherence of our expression" (*MWMWWS*, 62).

In Cavell's view, most commentaries make *Philosophical Investigations* much too conventionalist, as if when Wittgenstein says that "human beings 'agree in the language they use' he imagines that we have between us some kind of contract, or an implicitly or explicitly agreed-upon set of rules (which someone else may imagine we lack)" (*TNYUA*, 41). Cavell's view, by contrast, is that the "mutual absorption of the natural and social is a consequence of Wittgenstein's envisioning of what we may as well call the human form of life." In being asked to accept, or suffer, the human form of life as given for ourselves, "we are not asked to accept, let us say, private property, but separateness." Because we are human, "*this* (range or scale of) command, for work, for pleasure, for endurance, for will, for teaching, for suffering," is given for us, as it is given that "the precise range or scale is not knowable *a priori*." For Cavell, as for Wittgenstein as Cavell reads him, "the limitations of knowledge are no longer barriers to a more perfect apprehension, but conditions . . . of anything we should call knowledge" (*TNYUA*, 44).

One might suppose that emphasizing the role of the natural in *Philosophical Investigations*, as Cavell does, would reinforce the impression, shared by many commentators, that Wittgenstein's book is politically or socially conservative. But Cavell's interpretation aligns Wittgenstein, rather, to his own vision of humanity as standing in need of "something like transformation—some radical change, but as it were from the inside, not *by* anything; some say by another birth" (*TNYUA*, 44). The task of philosophy is to acknowledge the limitations of knowledge that are the conditions of human knowledge, conditions of any language, any culture, any form of life, we would call "human." For this task to be accomplished would be for the human form of life to bring itself to an explicit self-consciousness. And that would be a *radical* change.

Wittgenstein's method for acknowledging the conditions of the human form of life is to bring words back from what he calls their "metaphysical" to their everyday uses. The procedures of ordinary language philosophy are capable of this, Cavell argues, because they show us that "we did not know what we were saying, what we were doing to ourselves" (*MWMWWS*, 62). By extending Wittgenstein's procedures to an explicit self-consciousness, Cavell aspires to transform ordinary language philosophy into a radical mode of philosophical criticism.

Philosophical Criticism

"Philosophy is only just learning, for all its history of self-criticism and self-consciousness, to become conscious of itself in a new way," Cavell writes. The mode of criticism his writing aspires to exemplify is a mode of self-criticism, a mode of criticism whose subject and object is philosophy itself (*MWMWWS*, 110).

In Cavell's understanding, a certain sense of the question "Why this?" is essential to all criticism, whether the "object" be poetry or philosophy. That sense is one in which we are, or seem to be, asking about the artist's intention in the work. If philosophy "can be thought of as the world of a particular culture brought to consciousness of itself," as Cavell suggests, then the new mode of philosophical criticism he envisions "can be thought of as the world of a particular work brought to consciousness of itself," that is, brought to consciousness of the intentions motivating it (*MWMWWS*, 313).

As Cavell is well aware, it has become commonplace to repudiate the relevance of intention, not on the ground that "what an artist meant cannot alter what he has or has not accomplished," but on the basis of a prejudicial theory "according to which the artist's intention is something in his mind while the work of art is something out of his mind, and so the closest connection there could be between them is one of causation." He tellingly adds, "I am far less sure that any such philosophical theory is correct than I am that when I experience a work of art I feel that I am *meant* to notice one thing and not another, that the placement of a note or rhyme or line has a *purpose*, and that certain works are perfectly realized, or contrived, or meretricious" (*MWMWWS*, 182).

The passage goes on:

> It is common for a critic to ask . . . *why* the thing is as it is, and . . . to put this question . . . in the form "Why does Shakespeare follow the murder of Duncan with a scene which begins with the sound of knocking?" The philosopher may, because of his theory, explain that such questions are misleadingly phrased, and that they really refer to the object itself. . . . But who is misled, and about what? An alternative procedure, and I think sounder, would be to accept the critic's question as perfectly appropriate—as, so to speak, a philosophical datum—and then to look for a philosophical explanation which can accommodate that fact. (*MWMWWS*, 182)

For the criticism that is philosophy as for all criticism, it is sound procedure "to enter all criticisms which seem right, but to treat them . . . as temptations or feelings; in a word, as data, not as answers" (*MWMWWS*, 110). This procedure is sound, Cavell argues, because "it begins and ends in the right place, with the description of a human existence." In this vein, he gives his most eloquent characterization of what is at stake in philosophical appeals to ordinary language: "The issue is one of placing the words and experiences with which philosophers have always begun in alignment with human beings in particular circumstances who can be imagined to be having those experiences and saying and meaning those words. This is all that 'ordinary' in the phrase 'ordinary language philosophy' means, or ought to mean" (*MWMWWS*, 270).

Philosophy and the Modern

Philosophers are human beings in the world. Philosophy is performed by particular people for particular reasons in particular circumstances. As we have observed, however, Cavell embraces the principle that it is only when philosophers use their words in independence of any particular philosophical theory that the ways words are used within philosophy are usable as data for philosophical appeals to what we ordinarily say and mean. Within philosophy, ordinary language must be *achieved*, in other words. And it is achieved only when philosophers say what they mean, not

272

what some theory gives them to say. It is achieved only when philosophers find their way within philosophy to speak as ordinary human beings, to align the activities of philosophy with their lives in the world, to align their words with those human circumstances and experiences philosophy enables them to voice.

Even when philosophers use words in ways that fail to achieve alignment with ordinary language, their activities are ripe subjects for philosophical investigations that proceed by appealing to facts so obvious we cannot simply fail to know them. In "An Audience for Philosophy," Cavell points to several facts about contemporary philosophical practice that he takes to be defining for philosophy.

One such fact is that "[t]he isolated analytical article is the common form of philosophical expression now, in the English-speaking world of philosophy" (*MWMWWS*, xx). Some philosophers have interpreted this fact "as symptomatic of philosophy's withdrawal from its cultural responsibilities"; others have interpreted it as "philosophy's finally . . . assimilating itself to the form in which original scientific results are made known." Neither interpretation takes this fact to reveal something about philosophy, as Cavell does by suggesting that it reveals that philosophy has become difficult in a new way. It is the difficulty

> modern philosophy shares with the modern arts . . . , a difficulty broached, or reflected, in the nineteenth-century's radical breaking of traditions within the several arts; a moment epitomized in Marx's remark that " . . . the criticism of religion is in the main complete . . ." and that " . . . the task of history, once the world beyond the truth has disappeared, is to establish the truth of this world. . . ." This is the beginning of what I have called the modern, characterizing it as a moment in which history and its conventions can no longer be taken for granted; the time in which music and painting and poetry . . . have to define themselves against their pasts; the beginning of the moment in which each of the arts becomes its own subject, as if its immediate artistic task is to establish its own existence. (*MWMWWS*, xxii)

The essential feature of the modern, as Cavell understands it, lies in the fact that the relation between the present practice of an enterprise and the history of that enterprise has become problematic. Modernism, then, is not an effort to break with a tradition, but to keep faith with that tradition in a situation in which keeping faith requires nothing less than a radical break. In a modernist situation, the difficulty is that of "maintaining one's belief in one's own enterprise," of "making one's present effort become part of the present history of the enterprise" (*MWMWWS*, xxii).

Throughout *Must We Mean What We Say?* Cavell at once asserts and investigates a distinction between the traditional and the modern in philosophy. As he insists in "An Audience for Philosophy," he is not claiming that "all contemporary philosophy which is good is modern." But "the various discussions about the modern I am led to in the course of these essays," he suggests, "are the best I can offer in explanation of the way I have written, or the way I would wish to write" (*MWMWWS*, xix). By these words, Cavell is characterizing the essays that follow *as* modern. He is declaring, or confessing, that *Must We Mean What We Say?* is written from within a modernist situation.

In philosophy, Cavell reminds us, innovation has traditionally gone together with "a specifically cast repudiation of most of the history of the subject" (*MWMWWS*, xix). In a modernist situation, however, the repudiation of the past has a transformed significance, "as though containing the consciousness that history will not go away except through our perfect acknowledgment of it (in particular, our acknowledgment that it is not past), and that one's own practice and ambition can be identified only against the continuous experience of the past." Within this formulation, "the past" does not refer simply to the historical past; in a modernist situation, "the past" also refers to "one's own past, to what is past, or what has passed, within oneself." Thus "one could say that in a modernist situation 'past' loses its temporal accent and means anything 'not present.' Meaning what one says becomes a matter of making one's sense present to oneself" (*MWMWWS*, xix).

What Cavell takes himself to have learned from Wittgenstein's and Austin's appeals to ordinary language is a method precisely for "making one's sense present to oneself," for meaning what one says within philosophy. Cavell's philosophical procedures in *Must We Mean What We Say?*, which bring the medium of ordinary language philosophy to an explicit self-consciousness, enable him to align his words with the modernist situation in which he finds himself. Rather than being struck dumb, he discovers a new perspective, a point of departure, a medium for saying what he has it at heart to say. He discovers a route to becoming a genuine author in Kierkegaard's sense, an author who has a position of his own, who can "give to the age what the age needs, not what it demands," as opposed to the fraudulent author, who will " 'make use of the sickness of our age' by satisfying its demands; the genuine author 'needs to communicate himself,' whereas the false author is simply in need (of praise, of being in demand, of being told whether he means anything or not); the genuine is a physician who provides remedies, the false is . . . sick . . . and contagious" (*MWMWWS*, 177).

What Cavell finds exemplary in *Fear and Trembling*—exemplary for his age, and ours, as well as Kierkegaard's—is "not its indirectness (which, so far as this is secured by the Pseudonym, is a more or less external device) nor its rather pat theory about why Abraham must be silent," but, rather, its

> continuous awareness of the pain, and the danger, of that silence—of the fear of the false word, and the deep wish that the right word be found for doing what one must: what, to my mind, Kierkegaard's portrait of Abraham shows is not the inevitability of his silence, but the completeness of his wish for directness, his refusal of anything less. Exemplary, because in our age, which not only does not know what it needs, but which no longer even demands anything, but takes what it gets, and so perhaps deserves it; where every indirectness is dime-a-dozen, and any weirdness can be assembled and imitated on demand—the thing we must look for, in each case, is the man who, contrary to appearance, and in spite of all, speaks. (*MWMWWS*, 179)

Insofar as the possibility of fraudulence is characteristic of the modern, the issue of sincerity is *forced*. We can "no longer be sure that any artist is sincere—we haven't convention or technique or appeal to go on any longer: *anyone* could fake it." And by "depriving the artist and his audience of every measure except absolute attention to one's experience and absolute honesty in expressing it," modern art can be said to "lay bare the condition of art altogether" (*MWMWWS*, 211).

Each "genuine article" of modern art *Must We Mean What We Say?* cites—the music of Arnold Schoenberg and Anton Webern, the sculpture of Anthony Caro, the painting of Morris Louis, the theater of Bertolt Brecht and Samuel Beckett—"really does challenge the art of which it is the inheritor and voice," Cavell argues. "Each is, in a word, not merely modern, but modernist." Each is trying to discover the limits or essence of its own procedures, to discover what its art finally depends on, what counts, or will count, as a musical composition, or a sculpture, or a painting, or a work of theater. We do not have *a priori* criteria for defining an art; we must discover such criteria, discover them in the art itself. And "to discover this we need to discover what objects we *accept* as instances of that art, and why we so accept them. To accept something as an instance of a particular art is to accept it as an instance of art, "as something carrying the intentions and consequences of art" (*MWMWWS*, 219).

"To say that the modern 'lays bare,'" Cavell writes, "may suggest that there was something concealed in traditional art which hadn't, for some reason, been noticed, or that what the modern throws over—tonality, perspective, narration, the absent fourth wall, etc.—was something inessential to music, painting, poetry, and theater in earlier periods." Cavell rejects these suggestions.

> For it is not that now we finally know the true condition of art; it is only that someone who does not question that condition has nothing, or not the essential thing, to go on in addressing the art of our period. And far from implying that we now know, for example, that music does not require tonality, nor painting figuration nor theater an audience of spectators, etc., exactly what I want to have accomplished is to make all such notions problematic, to force us to ask, for example, what the art was which as a matter of fact did require, or exploit, tonality, perspective, etc. Why did it? What made such things media of art? . . . What is a medium of art? (*MWMWWS*, 220)

In finding words that give voice to what he has it at heart to say, the task of the modern philosopher, like the task of the modern artist, is to find something it is possible for him or her to be sincere and serious in, something he or she can mean. And in modern philosophy, being an audience is no less difficult than being a performer. Both are difficult in the same way, the way knowing oneself is difficult. To be an audience for modern philosophy, one must test the philosopher's words against one's own experience, must ask oneself with absolute veracity whether these are words one could honestly say and mean in this context. To be an audience for philosophy, one must perform philosophy. And to perform philosophy, one must discover an audience for philosophy within oneself. In Cavell's understanding, these have always been conditions of philosophy; the modernist situation only makes these conditions evident. Knowing who speaks for all is no easier than speaking for all. It is no easier than knowing who speaks for oneself. And that "is no easier than knowing oneself" (*MWMWWS*, xxvi-xxvii).

What is the importance of philosophy? In the closing of "An Audience for Philosophy," Cavell speaks eloquently to this issue. "The question of philosophy's audience"—the question of who or what the audience for philosophy is; the question that must come from the audience for a performance of philosophy to begin—"is born with philosophy itself."

> When Socrates learned that the Oracle had said no man is wiser than Socrates, he interpreted this to mean . . . that he knew that he did not know. . . . What I take Socrates to have seen is that, about the questions which were causing him wonder and hope and confusion and pain, he knew that he did not know what no man can know, and that any man could learn what he wanted to learn. No man is in any better position for knowing it than any other man—unless *wanting* to know is a special position. And this discovery about himself is the same as the discovery of philosophy, when it is the effort to find answers, and permit questions, which nobody knows the way to nor the answer to any better

than you yourself. Then what makes it relevant to know, worth knowing? But relevance and worth may not be the point. The effort is irrelevant and worthless until it becomes necessary for you to know such things. There is the audience of philosophy; but there also, while it lasts, is its performance. (*MWMWWS*, xxix)

NOTES

1. For appreciative and illuminating critical responses to Cavell's work, see, for example, Joseph H. Smith and William Kerrigan, eds., *Images in Our Souls: Cavell, Psychoanalysis, and Cinema* (Baltimore: Johns Hopkins University Press, 1987); Richard Fleming and Michael Payne, eds., *The Senses of Stanley Cavell* (Lewisburg: Bucknell University Press, 1989); Michael Fischer, *Stanley Cavell and Literary Skepticism* (Chicago: University of Chicago Press, 1989); Ted Cohen, Paul Guyer, and Hilary Putnam, eds., *Pursuits of Reason* (Denton: University of North Texas Press, 1993); Stephen Mulhall, *Stanley Cavell: Philosophy's Recounting of the Ordinary* (Oxford: Clarendon Press, 1994); Stephen Mulhall, ed., *The Cavell Reader* (Cambridge, Mass.: Blackwell Publishers, Ltd., 1996); Timothy Gould, *Hearing Things: Voice and Method in the Writing of Stanley Cavell* (Chicago: University of Chicago Press, 1998); and Paul J. Gudel, *Modernism and Skepticism: Terms of Criticism in Clement Greenberg, Michael Fried and Stanley Cavell*, as yet unpublished.

2. Timothy Gould's recent book, *Hearing Things: Voice and Method in the Writing of Stanley Cavell*, is an extended and intellectually rigorous analysis of the kind of reading that is internal to Cavell's work, as well as a host of other matters of great pertinence to our own undertaking. We do not always see eye to eye with Gould (See, for example, William Rothman, "Some Thoughts on Hitchcock's Authorship," in Richard Allen and S. Ishi Gonzales, eds., *Alfred Hitchcock Centenary Essays* [London: British Film Institute, 1999; 37–42]). But our countless lively and penetrating conversations with Tim Gould have strengthened our friendship with him, and his friendship has meant the world to us.

3. Rosalind Krauss, "Dark Glasses and Bifocals, a Book Review," *Artforum* (May 1974): 59–62.

4. Ibid., 59.

5. This issue is the explicit subject of "What Becomes of Things on Film?" *Philosophy and Literature* 2.2 (fall 1978): 249–57. Reprinted in a collection of Cavell

essays, *Themes Out of School: Effects and Causes* (San Francisco: North Point Press, 1984, reprinted, Chicago: University of Chicago Press, 1988).

6. Among Michael Fried's early writings, Cavell cites "Art and Objecthood," *Artforum* (June 1967), reprinted in Gregory Battcock, ed., *Minimal Art* (New York: E. P. Dutton, 1968), 16–47; "Manet's Sources," *Artforum* (March 1969): 28–79; "Shape as Form," *Artforum* (November 1966), reprinted in Henry Geldzahler's catalogue, *New York Painting and Sculpture: 1940–1970* (New York: E. P. Dutton, 1969); and *Three American Painters* (Cambridge: Fogg Art Museum, Harvard University, 1965). Paul J. Gudel's as yet unpublished *Modernism and Skepticism: Terms of Criticism in Clement Greenberg, Michael Fried and Stanley Cavell*, an extraordinarily lucid account of the complex relationships among these three quite different writers, provides an extremely useful overview of Fried's work. Gudel's account makes clear that despite the fact that they are generally, and for good reason, lumped together, there are very important differences between Fried and Cavell, on the one hand, and Greenberg, on the other. For example, Greenberg is reluctant to acknowledge openly that the function of paintings is to be looked at, which is a fact about painting that both Fried and Cavell face directly. (In Gudel's view, these matters are complicated by the fact that there often seem to be two Greenbergs, one concerned to acknowledge what the other is concerned to repress. We might add that in this way there never seem to be two Frieds, nor two Cavells.)

7. Noel Carroll, *Philosophical Problems of Classical Film Theory* (Princeton: Princeton University Press, 1988), 98.

8. Ibid., 100.

9. Ibid., 102.

10. Cavell's relation to Derrida is a large subject, as large a subject as the historical split between the Anglo-American and Continental branches of the Western philosophical tradition.

In "Nothing Goes Without Saying," a reading of Marx Brothers scripts and films, Cavell closes with an anecdote about a conversation he had with an unnamed French philosopher (Derrida, it so happens). (Stanley Cavell, "Nothing Goes Without Saying," *London Review of Books* 16.1, 6 January 1994, 3–5.) In the course of the conversation it emerged that Derrida's friends had been "urging him to read Emerson and Thoreau," but that this "seemed to both [Cavell and Derrida] unlikely." Musing about this implicit dismissal of American thought, Cavell writes: "No one would, or could easily, without insult, urge an American intellectual to read Montaigne or Descartes or Rousseau or Hegel. . . . Culture is—is it not?—European culture." "Nothing Goes Without Saying" reflects on what Cavell calls "that tangle of American culture" that encompasses both Emerson and the Marx Brothers (one can almost imagine Groucho, Chico, and Harpo incorporating Emerson into their act as their long-lost brother Waldo), and on the French resistance to taking American culture seriously (5). (Cavell is not saying that no French thinkers have ever taken American culture seriously, only pointing out that the present French thinkers who are important to Americans have not. As this reminds us, resistance to taking American culture seriously is deeply woven into American intellectual life, too.)

In addition to "Nothing Goes Without Saying," several extended discussions on Derrida's writing (challenging Derrida's readings of Austin, for example) appear in Cavell's most recent writing: *Philosophical Passages: Wittgenstein, Emerson, Austin, Derrida* (Cambridge, MA: Blackwell, 1995) and *A Pitch of Philosophy: Autobiographical*

Exercises (Cambridge, MA: Harvard University Press, 1994). Cavell's "Naughty Orators: The Negation of Voice in *Gaslight*," in Sanford Budick and Wolfgang Iser, eds., *Languages of the Unsayable: The Play of Negativity in Literature and Literary Theory* (New York: Columbia University Press, 1989), republished as a chapter of Cavell's *Contesting Tears* (Chicago: University of Chicago Press, 1996), a study of the genre Cavell calls "the melodrama of the unknown woman," contains a sustained discussion of Derrida's work, with a focus on the procedures and anxieties of learning, of teaching and being taught, hence of inheriting and refusing to inherit a tradition, a language, a culture, a form of human life.

11. Douglas Lackey, "Reflections on Cavell's Ontology of Film," *Journal of Aesthetics and Art Criticism* 32 (1973): 271.

12. Ibid., 273.

13. Cavell's response acknowledges the thoughtful spirit in which Sesonske advances his criticisms. "I have not made any of these remarks in the belief that I have thereby refuted Cavell," Sesonske writes. "For I am quite sure that he was aware of all these things at the time he wrote his book. I point them out rather as shoals threatening the course of our understanding of *The World Viewed*, and in the hope that he will indicate how the true course of his thought runs around them." (Alexander Sesonske, Review of *The World Viewed*, *Georgia Review* 28 [1974]: 561.)

14. Joel Snyder, "What Happens by Itself in Photography?," in Ted Cohen, Paul Guyer, and Hilary Putnam, eds., *Pursuits of Reason* (Lubbock: Texas Tech University Press, 1993), 361–74.

15. Sesonske, review of *The World Viewed*, 565.

16. See Cavell's remarkable (and remarkably neglected) essay on television, "The Fact of Television," *Daedalus* (fall 1982): 75–96 (reprinted in *Themes Out of School*). See also his "The Advent of Videos," *Artspace* (May-June 1988): 67–69.

17. In a recent essay, Paisley Livingston takes issue with this passage:

> Cavell's reference to a rather singular "human something" is evocative, but hardly provides us with a satisfactory analysis or even a "plain description" of the phenomenon. Presumably Cavell would not have us say that we are present at anything we happen to look at, in actuality or in a depiction. Is the astronomer present at the moon, and is someone who views Poussin's painting present at the rape of the Sabine women? Cavell's strange idea of *presence at* requires explanation and can hardly provide a ready clarification of the puzzles of the cinematic experience. (Paisley Livingston, "Characterization and Fictional Truth in the Cinema," in David Bordwell and Noel Carroll, eds., *Post-Theory: Reconstructing Film Studies* [Madison: The University of Wisconsin Press, 1996], 156)

Needless to say, Cavell is not claiming that the term "human something" provides us with a "satisfactory analysis" of the phenomenon, or even a "plain description" of it. The "plain description" Cavell is talking about is his description of the "human something" projected on the movie screen as being "in our presence while we are not in his." (The Sabine women represented in Poussin's painting cannot be described this way; when we are looking at the painting, these women are not present, not in our presence.) When Cavell glosses this "plain description" by adding that we are "present *at*," but not "present *to*," the "human something" projected on the movie screen, he is registering an impulse to make such a distinction. He is not claiming, of course, that such a distinction provides "a ready clarification of the puzzles of the cinematic experience."

18. Erwin Panofsky, "Style and Medium in the Moving Pictures," in Daniel Talbot, ed., *Film* (New York: Simon and Schuster, 1959), 31.

19. Lackey, "Reflections," 272.

20. Ibid.

21. Panofsky, "Style and Medium," 235.

22. Ibid.

23. Sesonske, Review of *The World Viewed*, 566.

24. Panofsky, "Style and Medium," 233.

25. When Cavell was writing *The World Viewed*, and for many years afterward, no one in film study recognized the value of his intuition that Baudelaire's writings about art, and the emergence of the modern that was their context and subject, were worth pondering in connection with the origins of film. To the field, this section of *The World Viewed* seemed altogether eccentric, not to say completely off the wall. Recently, however, the field of film study has begun to pay attention, however belatedly, to Baudelaire and his historical moment, taking itself to be authorized in doing so by the writings of Walter Benjamin, which it has likewise belatedly begun to pay attention to. Two admirable volumes that testify to this welcome new development are Leo Charney and Vanessa R. Schwarts, eds., *Cinema and the Invention of Modern Life* (Berkeley, Los Angeles, and London: University of California Press, 1995) and Dudley Andrew, ed., *The Image in Dispute: Art and Cinema in the Age of Photography* (Austin: University of Texas Press, 1997).

26. In "What Becomes of Things on Film?" (in *Themes Out of School*), Cavell will locate the source of Buster Keaton's comedy in the discovery that objects on film have inner and fixed lives. Cavell links Keaton's discovery with the particular mode of perception or consciousness of the world Heidegger characterizes as "the worldhood of the world announcing itself." When an object does not conform to our expectations, when a train crashes, for example, the object reveals, by what Heidegger calls its "conspicuousness, obtrusiveness, and obstinacy," its separateness from us, its unknownness (Martin Heidegger, *Being and Time* [New York and Evanston: Harper & Row, 1962], 102). Keaton's discovery that objects on film have inner and fixed lives required that he discover the medium's capacities for revealing "human limitation, denying neither the abyss that at any time may open before our plans, nor the possibility, despite that possibility, of living honorably, with good if resigned spirits, and with eternal hope" (*TOS*, 175).

27. That Marlene Dietrich is in this sense the "presiding genius" of *Blonde Venus* is a leading thought in Charles Warren's extended reading of that film in his as yet unpublished collection of essays *Earth and Beyond: On Film*.

28. David Cook, for example, writes, in his influential and in many ways admirable textbook *A History of Narrative Film*, "[P]erhaps the final comment on Hollywood in the thirties should be . . . [that] with regard to the social, sexual and political dimensions of human experience, the American sound film throughout the thirties remained quite effectively 'silent'" (David A. Cook, *A History of Narrative Film* [New York: W. W. Norton, 1996], 283). One need look no further than Chapter 8 of *The World Viewed*, not to mention the entirety of *Pursuits of Happiness* and *Contesting Tears*, to learn that American movies of the Production Code era are *not* "effectively 'silent'" about "the social, sexual and political dimensions of human experience."

29. In fact, Jean Arthur does not set foot on the Senate floor, so there is no

opportunity for Capra to employ the explicitly Christian iconography Cavell imputes to the passage. In the Preface to the Enlarged Edition of *The World Viewed*, Cavell acknowledges his mistake, and reflects on what might have motivated him to misremember this moment (x).

30. See William Rothman, *Hitchcock—The Murderous Gaze* (Cambridge: Harvard University Press, 1981), 206, 359, 361.

31. In the Foreword he contributed to a recent anthology of critical essays on *Hail Mary*, Cavell accepts *Hail Mary* as taking precisely the turn he had missed in films like *La Chinoise*. (Maryel Locke and Charles Warren, eds., *Jean-Luc Godard's Hail Mary: Women and the Sacred in Film* [Carbondale: Southern Illinois University Press, 1993], xvii–xxi). Is it Cavell who had missed this turn in those films, then, or is it Godard who had missed it?

"If you were inclined to side with the earlier Godard's politics, so with his apparent enlisting of art in the service of politics," Cavell writes, "then you are apt to sense a falling off, or backing off, in the later work, and become disappointed or disaffected with its apparent avoidance or evasion of politics." Contrariwise, "if you were inclined against Godard's earlier politics," as Cavell was, "and perhaps sensed his hatred of hateful, exploitative society as a cover for his spiritual coldness and isolation," as Cavell did,

> then you are more apt to feel, and welcome, a redemptive move in the later work, a search for perspective on the individualities of his work that signals an affecting effort to take responsibility for it, for its irresponsibilities that are as necessitated artistically as they were politically. But in that case *Hail Mary* will have traveled the familiar route from a totalizing politics to a totalizing religion, and from an apparent quest for a transcendence of the self (if just from one circle or stance to the next) to a self-indulgent transcendentalizing (or philosophizing) of nature or retheologizing of science. (*Jean-Luc Godard's Hail Mary*, ix–xx)

Refusing simply to choose between these opposing views, Cavell considers the possibility that *Hail Mary* "is not an evasion of politics but a critique of it, of what Godard had at some time named politics," and that Godard's criticism in this film of his own irresponsibilities as an artist "is a continuation of a mode of criticism there in his work from the beginning." So, too, Cavell's criticism of his remarks about Godard in *The World Viewed*—of his own "stuffy admiration," as he now calls it—is a continuation of a mode of criticism there in his own work from the beginning.

32. Cavell is mistaken in both of these examples, as he observes in the Preface to the Enlarged Edition of *The World Viewed*. (x–xi)

INDEX

absence: as root topic for Antonioni and surrealism, 167; of conscience, 158; of feeling, 167; of God, 158; of nature, 191, 215, 233; of us from nature, 192; of us from world in photographs, 66; of us from world on film, 71–74, 91, 96, 215, 216, 219, 220; of world on film, 72, 91, 96, 215

acknowledgment: of the camera, 208, 210–14, 219, 234; concept of, 8, 186, 187, 188, 194, 203–6, 210, 218, 266–71; of conditions of painting, 186–89, 192, 194, 197, 232; of desire, 84, 177, 178; of feeling, 92–99; of film, 14–17, 19, 140, 141, 150, 156, 196, 204, 205, 206, 210–14; of humanity of women, 100, 101, 109, 122; of loss, 254; of a medium as one's own, 183, 184, 185, 186, 202, 218; of others, 23, 28, 65, 102, 113, 165, 203, 224, 260; of outsideness, 219; of reality of the unsayable, 241, 244, 258; of silence, 234, 244, 258; of subjectivity, 66, 77, 92

Adam's Rib (1949), 123, 124

aesthetic possibilities, 14, 79–81, 197, 221, 234

African Queen, The (1951), 246

Agee, James, 102

Alphaville (1965), 152, *152. See also* Godard, Jean-Luc

Althusser, Louis, 19

America: 120–26, 129–32, 149, 176, 191, 195, 280 n. 10; film study in, 16–20, 55, 259–60; philosophy in, 20, 22, 26, 27, 132, 262, 280 n. 10

American cinema, 13, 16, 17, 26, 40, 52, 79, 83, 104, 109, 110, 148, 149, 159

Andrew, Dudley, 282 n. 25

Antonioni, Michelangelo, 14, 70, 143, 167. See also *L'avventura; Red Desert*

Appaloosa, The (1966), 115

Arnold, Matthew, 42, 105, 106, 136, 275

Art of the Fugue (Bach), 232

Artaud, Antonin, 246, *249. See also Passion of Joan of Arc, The*

Arthur, Jean, 113, 282 n. 29

Astaire, Fred, 44, 149, 225, 226

Astor, Mary, 116, 132

audience: for Cavell's work, 10, 87; for documentary film, 20; for film, 15, 19, 30, 43, 47, 48, 52, 53, 72, 73, 83, 85, 87, 128, 144, 196, 209, 211, 242; for modernist art, 43, 49, 52; for philosophy, 276, 277; for pornographic film, 102, 157; for theater, 37, 46, 72, 73, 89, 90, 94, 161, 168, 241, 276

Austin, J. L., 18, 95, 188, 262, 263, 265, 269

auteur theory, 45, 46

authenticity, 15, 51, 105

authority, 17, 18, 20, 84, 163, 164, 195, 201, 236, 247, 259, 260, 269

autobiography, 25, 32, 35, 42, 46, 268

automatism(s): as feature of physical basis of film medium, 62, 63, 67, 92, 139, 174, 175, 178, 179, 181, 197, 232; as

automatism(s) (*continued*)
    forms, genres or techniques, 174, 175,
      184, 215; and modernist art, 185–87;
      of painting, 186; of philosophy, 185,
      218
avant-garde, 16, 51, 53, 91, 188
Awful Truth, The (1937), 108–10, 131, 205

Bacall, Lauren, 132
Bancroft, Anne, 144
Band Wagon, The (1953), 143
Bardot, Brigitte, 166
Barthes, Roland, 19
Baudelaire, Charles, 95–98, 102–4, 115,
    116, 124, 282 n. 25
Bazin, André, 13, 14, 23, 31, 39, 55, 57, 60,
    61, 63, 74, 78, 88–90, 139, 243, 245
Beatles, the 48
Beckett, Samuel, 275
Being and Time (Heidegger), 40
Bellamy, Ralph, 205
Belmondo, Jean-Paul, 134, *135*, 145, 170
Benjamin, Walter, 282 n. 25
Bergman, Ingmar, 14. See also *Smiles of a
    Summer Night*
Bergman, Ingrid, 132–34
Best Years of Our Lives, The (1946), 13
Bicycle Thief, The (1948), 13
Big Sleep, The (1946), 76
Birds, The (1963), 133. See also Hitchcock,
    Alfred
black and white (films), 150, 152, 159–61,
    166, 167
Blake, William, 66
Blonde Venus (1932), 104
Blood of a Poet, The (1930), 91
Blue Angel, The (1930), 76, 77
Bogart, Humphrey, 76, 78, 115–18, *118*,
    132, 134, 149, 200, 201, 246
Bonnie and Clyde (1967), 144, 222
Brakhage, Stan, 52
Brando, Marlon, 134, 149, 165
Breathless (1959), *135*, 145, 167, 169, 170.
    See also Godard, Jean-Luc
Brecht, Bertolt, 169, 239, 240, 275
Bresson, Robert, 14
Bullitt (1968), 143, 151
Butch Cassidy and the Sundance Kid (1969),
    222

Cabinet of Dr. Caligari, The (1919), 91,
    150, 152

Cagney, James, 82
Cahiers du cinéma, 14–16, 19, 20, 55
camera: acknowledgment of, 214–17, 219,
    233; active and passive aspects of,
    37, 57, 70, 222; gaze of, 26, 50, 86;
    implication of, 206–12; need of, to
    be in a place, 230, 231; relation of, to
    human innerness, 246–50; subjects'
    relation to, 76, 78, 82, 84, 85, 159, 179,
    199–202
Camille (1936), 75. See also Garbo, Greta
candidness: in acting, 189; of the camera,
    214, 216; film's promise of, 199, 200,
    220, 233, 256; and modernist painting,
    189, 193; and self-reference, 205; and
    speech, 208; in still photography, 159,
    193, 197, 198; withdrawal of (from
    film), 215, 216, 233; of *The World
    Viewed*, 219, 255
capitalism, 131, 172, 260
Capra, Frank, 124, 282–83 n. 29. See also
    It Happened One Night; *It's a Wonderful
    Life*; *Mr. Smith Goes to Washington*
Caro, Anthony, 275
Carroll, Madeleine, 132
Carroll, Noel, 60, 280 nn. 7–9
Casablanca (1942), 76
Cavell, Stanley: "The Advent of Videos,"
    281 n. 16; "An Audience for
    Philosophy," 262, 269, 273, 274, 276;
    "Austin at Criticism," 265; "The
    Avoidance of Love," 27, 38, 73, 90,
    132, 176, 241, 252, 262, 266; *The Claim
    of Reason*, 10, 27; *Conditions Handsome
    and Unhandsome*, 22, 106; *Contesting
    Tears: The Hollywood Melodrama of the
    Unknown Woman*, 10, 27, 106, 110,
    119, 121, 122, 247, 280 n. 10, 282 n.
    28; *Disowning Knowledge: In Six Plays of
    Shakespeare*, 24, 25, 109, 110; "Ending
    the Waiting Game," 38, 73, 262, 267
    "The Fact of Television," 281 n. 16;
    "Knowing and Acknowledging," 92,
    187; "More of *The World Viewed*," 23,
    30–32, 51, 52, 54, 65, 68, 69, 71–73,
    81, 83–85, 104, 177, 199, 201, 203,
    245, 246, 257; *Must We Mean What
    We Say?*, 10, 26, 27, 29–31, 36–38,
    44, 49, 71, 73, 90, 92, 131, 136, 151,
    169, 176, 186, 188, 197, 221, 234, 252,
    256, 259, 261–77; "Naughty Orators,"

280 n. 10; "Nothing Goes Without Saying," 280 n. 10; *Philosophical Passages: Wittgenstein, Emerson, Austin, Derrida,* 280 n. 10; *A Pitch of Philosophy: Autobiographical Exercises,* 247, 280 n. 10; "The Politics of Interpretation," 108; *Pursuits of Happiness: The Hollywood Comedy of Remarriage,* 10, 27, 100, 105, 106–10, 119, 121–23, 140, 145, 147, 149, 177, 282 n. 28; *Senses of Walden: An Exploration of Thoreau's Masterpiece,* 10, 23; *Themes Out of School,* 74, 77, 108; *This New Yet Unapproachable America,* 270, 271; "What Becomes of Things on Film?," 77, 100, 279 n. 5, 282 n. 26

Chabrol, Claude, 14

Chaplin, Charles, 85, 242; as the Tramp, 93. See also *City Lights*

Charney, Leo, 282 n. 25

Children's Hour, The (1962), 111, 113, 118

Cinémathèque Française, 14

cinematic: concept of, 128, 139

City Lights (1931), 44, 93. *See also* Chaplin, Charles

classical cinema, 17, 99

Clift, Montgomery, 134

Cohen, Marshall, 51

Cohen, Ted, 72, 279 n. 1

Colbert, Claudette, 147, 178

color, 128, 138, 140, 150–53, 157, 159, 160, 165–68, 172, 182, 235

comedy: classical, 145, 147; of remarriage, 100, 107–10, 123, 145, 167; of self-reference, 205, 206; romantic, 25, 29, 79, 81, 108, 119, 149, 159

comic types, 85, 86

community: myth of, 102, 104, 107; need to discover, 165, 195; search for, 83; relation between self and, 226, 227, 228, 231, 255

Conant, James, 20, 24, 26, 27

consciousness: of class, 162; of film, 17, 46; ground of, 235, 236, 241; need for radical change of, 131, 175, 239; stream of, 235; unconsciousness, 164, 186; unhinging of, consciousness from world, 64, 89

Contempt (1963), 51, 166, 170, 172, 204, 212. *See also* Godard, Jean-Luc

continuity, 44, 53, 128, 139, 149, 236, 240

convention(s): modernist questioning of, 273–75; of movies, 50; radical contingency of, 151, 156; of theater, 73, 74, 94, 168

conventional marriage, 106, 107, 110

conventionalist readings of *Philosophical Investigations,* 270, 271

conventionality, 114–16, 133

Cook, David, 282 n. 28

Cooper, Gary, 83

Corsican Brothers, The (1941), 107

Courbet, Gustave, 95

criticism: of culture, 42, 43, 49, 169, 170–73, 262–73; of film, 14, 17, 19, 36, 27, 109; procedures of, 119–20; relation of philosophy to, 52–54, 80, 170–73, 262–73; theoretical revolution in, 19–21

Crosby, Bing, 149

cycles, 78, 81, 127

Dada, Surrealism and Their Heritage (Rubin), 186

dadaism, 91

Damsel in Distress (1937), 149

dance and dancing, 83, 143, 149, 225, 226

Dandy, the, 96, 102, 114–17, 124, 126, 129, 134–36, 228

Darling (1965), 224, 225, 229, 230

Davis, Bette, 44, 141

Dean, James, 134, 165

Debussy, Claude, 128

Delacroix, Eugène, 95

democracy, 113, 191

DeNiro, Robert, 136

Derrida, Jacques, 64, 280 nn. 10, 11

Descartes, René, 194, 203, 270

Destry Rides Again (1939), 107, 115

Detective, The (1968), 143

Devine, Andy, 141

Dietrich, Marlene, 104, 109, 132, 282 n. 27

displacement, 67, 91, 92, 94, 177, 178

Doll's House, A (Ibsen), 106

Double Indemnity (1944), 108

Douglas, Kirk, 212, 213

Dr. Jekyll and Mr. Hyde (1941), 246

Dr. Strangelove (1964), 45. *See also* Kubrick, Stanley

drama: acknowledgment and, 165; black and white and, 159–61; color and, 168; history and, 163, 164; ideology and,

drama (*continued*)
166; types and, 82
dream(s), 18, 46, 109, 158, 177, 179, 180, 206, 265
Dreyer, Carl, 14, 70, 246, 250. See also *Gertrud; Passion of Joan of Arc, The*
duck/rabbit, 179, 180, 244

Eisenstein, Sergei, 13, 51, 139
Emerson, Ralph Waldo, 22, 25–27, 64, 109, 132, 140, 188, 270
exhibition: relation of art to, 65, 196; film's, of the world, 209, 214–16, 219–23, 233, 238, 248, 252; theatricality and, 197–201, 205
expressionism, 65

Fahrenheit 451 (1966), 151. See also Truffaut, François
Falconetti, Maria, 248, 250, 251. See also *Passion of Joan of Arc, The*
fantasy: color as unifying world of, 166–68; film's depiction of, 67; films as escapes into, 176–80; private world of, 30, 47, 48, 101, 102, 144, 146, 153–59, 162, 177; relation of reality to, 116, 150, 153–59, 182, 206, 214, 254
farce, 78, 79, 144, 162
Fear and Trembling (Kierkegaard), 275
Fellini, Federico, 14, 143, 246
feminism, 98, 99
Field, Sally, 136
Fields, W. C., 85, 206, 229, 264
Film Culture, 14–16
film study (academic field): emergence of, 9, 10, 16, 17; reception of *The World Viewed* by, 9, 10, 23, 24; relation of *The World Viewed* to, 18–20, 25, 26, 55, 61–63, 68–70, 78, 103, 104, 259, 260
Fischer, Michael, 279 n. 1
Flaherty, Robert, 70
flash inset(s), 204, 223, 224, 236
Fleming, Richard, 24, 279 n. 1
Flying Dutchman, The (Wagner), 254
Fonda, Henry, 44
Fonda, Jane, 136
Fonda, Peter, 115
Fontaine, Joan, 149
For Love of Ivy (1968), 137
Ford, John, 14, 15, 19, 122, 126. See also *Man Who Shot Liberty Valance, The; My Darling Clementine; Stagecoach; Young Mr. Lincoln*

freeze frame(s), 204, 222, 224–27, 229, 230, 236
Freud, Sigmund, 85, 155, 156
Fried, Michael, 49, 56, 185, 186, 236, 279 n. 1, 280 n. 6

Gable, Clark, 83, 177, 179
Garbo, Greta, 75, 104, 109, 132
genre(s): of film, 25, 78, 81, 124; as medium, 140, 182. See also comedy; horror; melodrama; Western
Gertrud (1964), 257. See also Dreyer, Carl
Godard, Jean-Luc, 14, 143, 152, 167–71, 173, 212, 283 n. 31. See also *Alphaville; Breathless; Chinoise, La; Contempt; Hail Mary; Vivre sa vie*
Gone with the Wind (1939), 150
Gould, Timothy, 279 nn. 1, 2
Graduate, The (1967), 111, 144–48, *149*
Grand Illusion (1937), 83, 230, 231. See also Renoir, Jean
Grant, Cary, 133, 134, 149, 226
Great Lie, The (1941), 108
"Greek Tragedy: Problems of Interpretation" (Vernant), 121
Greenberg, Clement, 23, 280 n. 6
Griffith, D. W., 68
Gudel, Paul J., 279 n. 1, 280 n. 6
Guess Who's Coming to Dinner (1967), 137
Guyer, Paul, 72, 279 n. 1

Hail Mary, 283 n. 31. See also Godard, Jean-Luc
Hamlet (Shakespeare), 240, 254
Hammett, Dashiell, 76
Hawks, Howard, 14, 15, 19, 122
Hays Office, 99, 124. See also Production Code
Hedren, Tippi, 133, 156
Hegel, Georg Wilhelm Friedrich, 42, 66, 175, 203
Heidegger, Martin, 21, 22, 24, 40, 66, 282 n. 26
Hepburn, Audrey, 132, 149
Hepburn, Katharine, 132, 205
High Noon (1952), 107
Hiroshima, mon amour (1959), 223, 255. See also Resnais, Alain
His Girl Friday (1940), 205

Hitchcock, Alfred, 14, 15, 37, 133, 151, 153, 155–57, 215, 216. See also *Birds, The; Lady Vanishes, The; Man Who Knew Too Much, The; Marnie; North By Northwest; Notorious; Psycho; Rear Window; Strangers on a Train; Vertigo*
Holiday Inn (1942), 149
Hombre (1967), 115
homosexuality, 111, 112
horror, 81, 224, 228, 250

identity: of America, 131; of art of film, 181; self-identity (of stars), 143; of Western hero, 120, 122; of woman in comedies of remarriage, 100
ideology: and dramatic explanation, 166; and film, 19, 20, 26, 104; Marxist, 154; modernism as discredited ideology, 49–50; patriarchal, 100, 104; photographs as ideological constructs, 60; reality as ideological construct, 55, 56
illusion, 83, 211, 222, 230, 231
In the Heat of the Night, 137, 143
individuality: of camera's subjects, 19; and the Dandy, 135; and isolation, 64; and modern society, 164, 165; and myth of youth, 134; and stars chosen for "look," 137, 138; and types, 82–85
Intermezzo (1939), 105, 107
Intolerance (1916), 68
intuition, 24–28
invisibility, 92–94, 98, 100
isolation: and autonomy, 113, 118, 184; of the Dandy, 129, 134, 135; and fantasy, 30; film and, 103, 248, 250, 257, 158; metaphysical, 90; and subjectivity, 64, 65, 184
It Happened One Night (1934), 145, 147, 149, 177–79. See also Capra, Frank
It's a Wonderful Life (1946), 13. See also Capra, Frank

Jannings, Emil, 76, 77
Joyful Wisdom, The (Nietzsche), 158
Jules and Jim (1961), 69, 224–27, *225*, 229, 231. See also Truffaut, François

Kant, Immanuel, 66, 130, 154, 160
Karina, Anna, 170, *171*. See also Godard, Jean-Luc; *Vivre sa vie*
Keane, Catherine O'Brien, *59*
Keaton, Buster, 85, 141, 206, 242, 282 n. 26

Kelly, Grace, 133
Kern, Jerome, 48
Kerrigan, William, 279 n. 1
Kierkegaard, Søren, 175, 188, 239
Kilmer, Joyce, 204
King Lear (Shakespeare), 27, 37, 73, 75, 231, 252, 262, 266, 267
Kramer, Stanley, 215
Krauss, Rosalind, 51, 52, 279 n. 3
Kubrick, Stanley, 212, 214. See also *Dr. Strangelove; Paths of Glory*
Kuleshov, Lev, Mozhukhin experiment, 244
Kurosawa, Akira, 13. See also *Seven Samurai*

La Chinoise (1967), 172, 173. See also Godard, Jean-Luc
La Terra Trema (1948), 13
Lacan, Jacques, 19, 20, 55
Lackey, Douglas, 65, 68, 76, 77, 281 nn. 11, 12, 19
Lady Chatterley's Lover (Lawrence), 114
Lady Eve, The (1941), 27, 108
Lady Vanishes, The (1938), 156. See also Hitchcock, Alfred
Langlois, Henri, 14
L'Atalante, (1934), 83, 84, 147, *148*. See also Vigo, Jean
L'avventura, (1960), 167, *168*. See also Antonioni, Michelangelo
Lawrence, D. H., 114
Les Misérables (Hugo), 46
Letter to d'Alembert (Rousseau), 39
Livingston, Paisley, 281 n. 17
Locke, Maryel, 283 n. 31
Lombard, Carole, 132
Louis, Morris, 189, 190, 192, 202, 275
Louise, Anita, 132
Love Me Tonight (1932), 222
Loy, Myrna, 44
Luther, Martin, 188

magic: of art, 187; film's "magical" solution to problem of reality, 65, 90–92, 175; photography's aura of, 57, 72, 102, 232
Mahler, Gustav, 128
Mallarmé, Stéphane, 204
Maltese Falcon, The (1941), 76, 115, 116
Man in the Gray Flannel Suit, The (1956), 105, 107
Man in the Iron Mask, The (1939), 107
Man Who Knew Too Much, The (1956), 151. See also Hitchcock, Alfred

Man Who Shot Liberty Valance, The (1962), 44, 107, 117, 119–22, 124, 126, 141. *See also* Ford, John

Manet, Edouarde, 63, 95

Mann, Thomas, 85

Marnie (1964), 133. *See also* Hitchcock, Alfred

Marquise of O . . . , The (1976), 157. *See also* Rohmer, Eric

marriage: in *L'Atalante*, 84; and comedies of remarriage, 105–10; modern, 147–49; and morals of movies, 120–23; and world of private fantasy, 177

Marx, Groucho, 44

Marx, Harpo, 246, 247

Marxism, 19, 42, 131, 154, 162, 164, 175

Mast, Gerald, 51

material basis of film, 81, 89, 139, 199, 230

McCrea, Joel, 112

McQueen, Steve, 134

Meditations (on First Philosophy), 24. *See also* Descartes, René

Mekas, Jonas, 16 4, 276

melodrama, 25, 78, 79, 164; of unknown woman, 64, 106

memory: and *Hiroshima, mon amour*, 224; and impact of movies, 240; and writing of *The World Viewed*, 10, 41, 46, 47, 253

metaphysics, 85, 175, 231, 232. *See also* presence

Metz, Christian, 19

Michelson, Annette, 51

Midsummer Night's Dream, A (Shakespeare), 110

Military Man, the, 96, 102, 104, 107, 114, 116, 136

Milton, John, 203

Minnelli, Vincente, 14

Mizoguchi, Kenji, 13

modernism: concept of, 53, 54, 181; film's avoidance of, 15, 29, 30, 49–51, 175, 196, 197

modernist painting, 16, 56, 64–66, 95, 175, 185–87, 191, 193, 197, 202

modernist situation, 71, 127, 128, 136, 138, 139, 183–85, 205, 216, 218, 232

modernity, 95, 96, 136, 202, 260, 273–76

Monroe, Marilyn, 44

montage, 13, 139, 236, 240, 243, 245, 250

moral perfectionism, 22, 105–7, 115

morals of movies, 104–7, 110, 111, 113, 115, 124, 125

Moreau, Jeanne, 224, *225*. *See also Jules and Jim*

Mortal Storm, The (1940), 231

Mr. Smith Goes to Washington (1939), 113, 117, 124. *See also* Capra, Frank

Mulhall, Stephen, 279 n. 1

Mulvey, Laura, 99

Muni, Paul, 83

music: audience for, 43, 46, 48; film and, 84, 225, 243; medium of, 181–83; modernism and, 15, 49, 128, 273, 275, 276

My Darling Clementine (1946), 115, 122, *125*. *See also* Ford, John

myth(s) 25, 89, 95, 120, 127, 129, 134, 136, 137, 176, 215; of community, 102, 104, 107; of modern marriage, 137, 145–49; of modern romance, 144, 147, 149; mythical in the typical, 85; of Ring of Gyges, 92; of youth, 145

natural relation to movies, 35, 47, 220, 234, 253, 258

nature: denials of, 133, 134, 156, 177, 215, 216, 233, 255–57; film's relation to, 55, 70, 89, 137, 203, 204, 215, 216, 233, 255–57; human, 124, 138, 156, 226; modernist painting's relation to, 189–95, 236; society's relation to, 107

Never Give a Sucker an Even Break (1941), 205, 206. *See also* Fields, W. C.

New American Cinema, 16, 52

New Criticism, 27, 266

New Wave, 204

Newman, Paul, 134

Nichols, Mike, 145. See also *Graduate, The*

Nietzsche, Friedrich, 22, 42, 158, 175, 188, 239

Night at the Opera, A (1935), 247. *See also* Marx, Groucho; Marx, Harpo

Noland, Kenneth, 192

North by Northwest (1959), 151. *See also* Hitchcock, Alfred

nostalgia, 141, 143, 198, 229

Notorious (1946), 133, 134. *See also* Hitchcock, Alfred

Novak, Kim, 133, 155. See also *Vertigo*

novels, 48, 53, 55, 56, 85, 89, 139, 203, 228

Now, Voyager (1942), 44, 105–7

O'Brien, Pat, 82

Olitski, Jules, 192
Olivier, Laurence, 44
Olympia (Manet), 170, *171*
ontology, 18, 29, 52, 60, 61, 65, 83, 87, 207, 261
ordinary language. *See* philosophy
Othello (Shakespeare), 74, 84
Ozu, Yasujiro, 13

Pagnol, Marcel, 83
Painter of Modern Life, The (Baudelaire), 95, 96, 103
painting: figure of woman in, 99, 100; film's relation to, 29, 71, 89, 90, 95, 99, 166, 181, 185, 186, 197–99, 243; material basis of, 139, 182–84; photography's relation to, 31, 55–57, 63, 64. *See also* modernist painting
Palance, Jack, 81
Panofsky, Erwin, 15, 55, 78–81, 88, 282 nn. 18, 21, 282 nn. 22, 24
paranoia, 39, 40
Passion of Joan of Arc, The (1928), 246, 248–51. *See also* Dreyer, Carl
past, the: modernist art's acknowledgment of, 135, 136, 138, 274
pastness: and *avant-garde* art, 53; of experiences of movies, 46, 47, 255; and temporality of film, 69, 71; of world on film, 140–43, 198, 200, 223, 224, 255
Paths of Glory (1957), 212, *213*
Pawnbroker, The (1965), 224
Payne, Michael, 279 n. 1
Perkins, Tony, 215
perversity: of Baudelaire, 95; of philosophy, 160; as topic in Hitchcock films, 155–57
Petulia (1968), 143, 151
Philadelphia Story, The (1940), 108, 109, 145, 205
Philosophical Investigations, 31, 179, 244, 266, 268, 270, 271, 273. *See also* Wittgenstein, Ludwig
Philosophical Problems of Classical Film Theory (Carroll), 60
philosophy: American transcendental, 22, 23, 25, 26, 27, 132; Anglo-American (analytical) tradition of, 21, 22, 40, 262, 280 n. 10; Continental tradition of, 21, 22, 40, 64, 280 n. 10; film as subject of, 36–38; modern, 49, 50, 64;

175, 234, 273, 276; ordinary language, 18, 30, 31, 38, 56, 151, 188, 234, 262–71, 274; philosophical perspective of self-reflection, 23, 24, 27, 60, 259; power of, 172; relation of criticism to, 52, 272, 272; relation of drama to, 160, 161, 163; relation of literary studies to, 20, 21
photogenesis, 100
photograph(s) and photography: art of, 201; automatism of, 67, 72, 73, 92, 139, 181; ontology of, 56–68, 87, 140, 150, 174, 245; relation of painting to, 31, 56, 63, 64, 66, 95; relation of theatricality to, 159, 198, 200
physiognomy, 82, 201, 244, 246, 248, 250, 256
Pitt, Brad, 136
Plato, 42, 92, 172
poetry: 42, 84, 181, 238; of Cavell's writing, 190; of film, 238–43; of speech, 238
point of view, 157, 212, 214
Pollock, Jackson, 80, 186, 189, 192
Popi (1969), 221
pornography, 79, 98–102, 114, 157, 167
Porter, Cole, 48
Postman Always Rings Twice, The (1946), 108
postmodernism, 136, 259
poststructuralism, 9, 19
Powell, William, 44
presence: of the camera, 209–15; of characters in theater, 74, 89; film's defeat of our, 72, 73, 197; metaphysics of, 64, 232; of screen performers, 76, 100; of self, 92
presentness: concept of, 64; film and, 71, 197–99; modernist painting and, 63, 64, 95, 166, 183–87, 189, 194, 195, 236; photography and, 66; selfhood and, 183–85; subjectivity and, 89, 90
Pretty Poison (1968), 143
Prisoner of Zenda, The (1937), 107
privacy: of fantasies, 47, 146, 153, 156, 157, 159, 176–78; of memories, 31; modern condition and, 92, 94; of movie viewing, 48, 92; pornography and, 101, 102; of responses to films, 40; unknownness and, 83; of the writing of *The World Viewed*, 41, 87, 88
Production Code, 100, 101, 107, 282 n. 28. *See also* Hays Office

projection(s): mode of existence of, 54, 69, 70, 92, 139, 197; projected world, 26, 55, 67–69, 72, 179, 241; representations contrasted with, 55, 56, 61, 198, 199
Protestant Reformation, 64
Psycho, 133, 156, 215. *See also* Hitchcock, Alfred
Putnam, Hilary, 72, 279 n. 1

Rains, Claude, 113
Ray, Nicholas, 14
realism, 55, 62, 67, 89, 95, 159, 234
reality: as ideological construct, 26; relation of drama to, 159, 160; relation of fantasy to, 150, 153–55, 178–80, 206; relation of film to, 13, 14, 54–56, 65–72, 76–78, 92, 203, 242–45; relation of painting to, 63, 185, 195; as subject for film, 29, 140, 174; theatricality and, 198, 200; of the unsayable, 235–38, 241
Rear Window (1954), 156. *See also* Hitchcock, Alfred
Red Desert (1964), 151. *See also* Antonioni, Michelangelo
Redford, Robert, 136
"Reflections on Cavell's Ontology of Film" (Lackey), 65
religion: film's emergence out of, 90, 91, 115; finding the right to speak in, 169, 188; in Hitchcock's films, 156; reason and, 161
remarriage comedy. *See* comedy: of remarriage
Renoir, Jean, 14, 70, 83, 231. See also *Grand Illusion; Rules of the Game, The*
representation(s): concept of, 191; modernist painting and, 191, 192, 198; movies as ideological representations, 26; nature and, 191, 195. *See also* projection(s)
Republic (Plato), 92
Resnais, Alain, 143. See also *Hiroshima, mon amour*
Richard the Third (Shakespeare), 44
Riefenstahl, Leni, 221
Rio Bravo (1959), 122
Rivette, Jacques, 14
Robeson, Paul, 74
Robin Hood (The Adventures of) (1938), 150
Rohmer, Eric, 14. See also *Marquise of*

O . . . , The
romanticism, 66, 165, 189–91, 202, 203
Rome: Open City (1945), 13
Rosemary's Baby (1968), 153, 157–59, 173
Rothman, Sarah Shagan, 59
Rothman, William, 36, 59, 283 n. 30
Rousseau, Jean-Jacques, 42, 48, 161, 164, 240, 241, 258
Rubin, William, 186
Rules of the Game, The (1939), 83. *See also* Renoir, Jean
Russell, Rosalind, 132

Sarris, Andrew, 16
Schoenberg, Arnold, 128, 275
Schwarts, Vanessa R., 282 n. 25
Schwartzenegger, Arnold, 136
science fiction,
Scott, Randolph, 83
screen: as barrier, 70–72, 74, 178; displacement and, 92, 94; as frame, 70; nature's withdrawal from, 215, 216, 220; world projected on, 26, 55, 67–69, 179, 241
Screen (journal), 19
sculpture, 43, 49, 57, 166, 275
semiology, 19, 55
Sesonske, Alexander, 69, 73, 83, 281 nn. 13, 15, 282 n. 23
Seven Samurai (1954), 222, 223. *See also* Kurosawa, Akira
sexuality: acceptance of, 105, 107, 116, 117; childhood, 156; and morals of movies, 104, 105; and seductiveness of philosophy, 172
Shakespeare, William, 24, 64, 73, 121, 266, 272
Shane (1953), 81, 107, 115, 118, 119
Sherlock Jr. (1924), 205, 206. *See also* Keaton, Buster
Ship of Fools (1963), 215, 216
Sigma (Louis), 189, 190
Signs and Meaning in the Cinema (Wollen), 19
silence: called for by art, 169; conferred by slow motion, 222; of Dreyer's Joan of Arc, 257; "language" of film and, 17, 30, 237; of nature, 195; of theater audience, 73, 90; of the world, 238; of *The World Viewed*, 243, 244, 258
silent cinema, 15, 150, 153, 234, 237, 238

skepticism: film as moving image of, 68; film study and, 53, 67; historical emergence of, 22, 24, 64; as human possibility, 135, 146; ordinary language philosophy and, 269, 270; philosophical responses to, 21; problematic of, 24, 25, 226
Smiles of a Summer Night (1955), 109, 110, 116, 167. *See also* Bergman, Ingmar
Smith, Joseph H., 279 n. 1
Snow, Michael, 52, 114, 230, 231
Snyder, Joel, 72, 281 n. 14
society: emergence of modern and, 161–66; film's impact on, 17; film's thinking about, 16, 26, 27, 83, 102, 104–7, 116–23, 134, 149; of women, 113
social roles, 82, 85
Socrates, 263, 268, 276
Spacek, Sissy, 136
St. Augustine, 161, 240, 241, 258
Stage Door (1937), 205
Stagecoach (1939), 115, 122, 123. *See also* Ford, John
star(s): barrier to, 241, 242; as persona(s), 26, 78; repeated incarnations of, 76, 143; as subject(s) of camera, 77, 78; as type(s), 81–83
Steichen, Edward, 200–202
Stella, Frank, 107, 119, 192
Stella Dallas (1937), 107, 119
stereotypes, 82, 144
Stewart, James, 117, 120
Stolen Life, A (1946), 107
Stone, Sharon, 136
Strangers on a Train (1951), 151. *See also* Hitchcock, Alfred
Streep, Meryl, 136
subjectivity: art as expression of, 184; film study and, 17; modern wish to overcome, 64–67, 72, 89, 90, 92, 94, 103; philosophy and, 265; stars and, 77
Sunset Boulevard (1950), 141–43
surrealism, 91, 167, 186
Swanson, Gloria, 141–43, *142*. *See also* *Sunset Boulevard*

technique(s): artistic, 232, 275; cinematic, 26, 174, 175, 196, 221, 243; philosophical, 159. *See also* flash inset(s); freeze frame(s); montage; point of view
television, 15, 74, 221

theater: acting in, 74, 75, 83, 90, 239–42; audience in, 72, 73, 94, 168, 239–42; clothes in, 97, 98; defeat of, 197, 198; emergence of the modern and, 161–63; enclosed and total world of, 37, 38; realism in, 89
theatricality: and acknowledgment, 187; film and, 29, 197–200, 216; as response to modern isolation, 65
These Three (1936), 57, 111, 113
Thoreau, Henry David, 22, 26, 42, 78, 108, 109, 132, 140, 149, 163, 188, 190, 191, 195, 236
To Have and Have Not (1944), 76, *118*
Tolstoy, Leo, 42, 43, 49
tragedy: as human possibility, 267; in *The Mortal Storm*, 231; role of theater audience and, 73, 94; of *Vertigo*, 137; of Vietnam War, 131; Westerns and, 121
Travolta, John, 136
Treasure of the Sierra Madre, The, 246
Truffaut, François, 14, 229. See also *Fahrenheit 451*; *Jules and Jim*
tuition, 25, 26, 28, 269
type(s): centrality to traditional movie genres, 25, 81, 127, 137, 144, 159, 174, 175; comic, 85, 86; European films and, 83, 84; individuality and, 82; limits to knowledge of, 245–50; modern (in Baudelaire), 95–97, 176; stars as, 76, 78, 81; theatricality and, 198, 199

Under Two Flags (1936), 107
Unfurled(s) (Louis), 189, 202
unknownness: of filmmakers, 15; of human faces, 246–48; invisibility and, 92, 94; as martyrdom in films of Dreyer, 257; of movies, 18; as subject of films of Renoir and Vigo, 83

vaudeville, 205
Vernant, Jean-Pierre, 121
Vertigo (1958), 37, 153–57, 228. *See also* Hitchcock, Alfred
Vertov, Dziga, 51
Vietnam, 129–31
Vigo, Jean, 70, 83. See also *L'Atalante*; *Zero for Conduct*
Village Voice, The, 16
Vitti, Monica, 167
Vivre sa vie, *171*. *See also* Godard, Jean-Luc

voice(s): Cavell's, 259; of characters in plays, 266, 267; modernist art and, 275; philosophy and, 273, 276; of the serious writer, 163; silence of, 234; of silent film stars, 237; speaking in one's own, 202 of women, 247, 257
voyeurism, 156, 157

Wagner, Richard, 42, 128
Walden (Thoreau), 10, 23, 108–10, 140, 163, 195, 236, 258
Warhol, Andy, 52
Warren, Charles, 282 n. 27, 283 n. 31
Wayne, John, 117, 122
Weaver, Sigourney, 136
Webern, Anton, 275
Welles, Orson, 14
West, Mae, 65, 104, 109, 118
Western(s), 19, 81, 119, 121–26, 151
Western hero, 115, 117–21, 123
"What Happens by Itself in Photography?" (Snyder), 72

What Is Art? (Tolstoy), 42, 51
What Is Cinema? (Bazin), 39
Whitman, Walt, 42
wide screen, 14
Wild One, The (1954), 134
Wittgenstein, Ludwig, 18, 21, 24, 25, 64, 66, 100, 188, 190, 244, 248, 262–64, 266, 268, 270, 271. See also *Philosophical Investigations*
Wizard of Oz, The (1939), 150
Woman of the Year (1942), 108, 109
Women in Love (Lawrence), 114
Wordsworth, William, 66
World of Henry Orient, The (1964), 221
World War I, 147
World War II, 13, 129, 130

Young Mr. Lincoln (1939), 19. *See also* Ford, John

Zero for Conduct (1933), 83. *See also* Vigo, Jean

Books in the Contemporary Film and Television Series

Cinema and History, by Marc Ferro, translated by Naomi Greene, 1988

Germany on Film: Theme and Content in the Cinema of the Federal Republic of Germany, by Hans Gunther Pflaum, translated by Richard C. Helt and Roland Richter, 1990

Canadian Dreams and American Control: The Political Economy of the Canadian Film Industry, by Manjunath Pendakur, 1990

Imitations of Life: A Reader on Film and Television Melodrama, edited by Marcia Landy, 1991

Bertolucci's 1900: A Narrative and Historical Analysis, by Robert Burgoyne, 1991

Hitchcock's Rereleased Films: From Rope *to* Vertigo, edited by Walter Raubicheck and Walter Srebnick, 1991

Star Texts: Image and Performance in Film and Television, edited by Jeremy G. Butler, 1991

Sex in the Head: Visions of Femininity and Film in D. H. Lawrence, by Linda Ruth Williams, 1993

Dreams of Chaos, Visions of Order: Understanding the American Avant-garde Cinema, by James Peterson, 1994

Full of Secrets: Critical Approaches to Twin Peaks, edited by David Lavery, 1994

The Radical Faces of Godard and Bertolucci, by Yosefa Loshitzky, 1995

The End: Narration and Closure in the Cinema, by Richard Neupert, 1995

German Cinema: Texts in Context, by Marc Silberman, 1995

Cinemas of the Black Diaspora: Diversity, Dependence, and Opposition, edited by Michael T. Martin, 1995

The Cinema of Wim Wenders: Image, Narrative, and the Postmodern Condition, edited by Roger Cook and Gerd Gemünden, 1997

New Latin American Cinema: Theory, Practices, and Transcontinental Articulations, Volume One, edited by Michael T. Martin, 1997

New Latin American Cinema: Studies of National Cinemas, Volume Two, edited by Michael T. Martin, 1997

Giving Up the Ghost: Spirits, Ghosts, and Angels in Mainstream Comedy Films, by Katherine A. Fowkes, 1998

Bertolucci's The Last Emperor: *Multiple Takes,* edited by Bruce H. Sklarew, Bonnie S. Kaufman, Ellen Handler, and Diane Borden, 1998

Alexander Kluge: The Last Modernist, by Peter C. Lutze, 1998

Tracking King Kong: A Hollywood Icon in World Culture, by Cynthia Erb, 1998

Documenting the Documentary: Close Readings of Documentary Film and Video, edited by Barry Keith Grant and Jeannette Sloniowski, 1998

Mythologies of Violence in Postmodern Media, edited by Christopher Sharrett, 1999

Feminist Hollywood: From Born in Flames *to* Blue Steel, by Christina Lane, 2000

Reading Cavell's The World Viewed: *A Philosophical Perspective on Film,* by William Rothman and Marian Keane, 2000

CPSIA information can be obtained
at www.ICGtesting.com
Printed in the USA
BVHW041221050219
539508BV00006B/36/P

9 780814 328965